TEXTBOOKS IN THE THIRD WORLD

GARLAND REFERENCE LIBRARY
OF SOCIAL SCIENCE
(VOL. 450)

Reference Books in International Education

Edward R. Beauchamp
General Editor

1. *Education in East and West Germany: A Bibliography*
   by Val D. Rust

2. *Education in the People's Republic of China, Past and Present: An Annotated Bibliography*
   by Franklin Parker and Betty June Parker

3. *Education in South Asia: A Select Annotated Bibliography*
   by Philip G. Altbach, Denzil Saldhana, and Jeanne Weiler

4. *Textbooks in the Third World: Policy, Content and Context*
   by Philip G. Altbach and Gail P. Kelly

TEXTBOOKS IN THE THIRD WORLD
Policy, Content and Context

Philip G. Altbach
Gail P. Kelly

GARLAND PUBLISHING, INC. • NEW YORK & LONDON
1988

Library of Congress Cataloging-in-Publication Data

Altbach, Philip G.
Textbooks in the Third World: policy, content, and context / Philip G. Altbach and Gail P. Kelly.
p. cm. — (Garland reference library of social science ; vol. 450)
Bibliography: p.
Includes index.
ISBN 0–8240–4294–8 (alk. paper)
1. Textbooks—Developing countries. 2. Education and state—Developing countries. I. Kelly, Gail Paradise. II. Title. III. Series: Garland reference library of social science ; v. 450.
LB3048.D44A45 1988
371.3'2'091724—dc19 88–21825
CIP

Printed on acid-free, 250-year-life paper
Manufactured in the United States of America

CONTENTS

SERIES EDITOR'S FOREWORD

This series of reference works and monographs in education in selected nations and regions is designed to provide a resource to scholars, students, and a variety of other professionals who need to understand the place of education in a particular society or region. While the format of the volumes is often similar, the authors have had the flexibility to adjust the common outline to reflect the uniqueness of their particular nation or region.

Contributors to this series are scholars who have devoted their professional lives to studying the nation or region about which they write. Without exception they have not only studied the educational system in question, but they have lived and travelled widely in the society in which it is embedded. In short, they are exceptionally knowledgeable about their subject.

In our increasingly interdependent world, it is now widely understood that it is a matter of survival that we understand better what makes other societies tick. As the late George Z.F. Bereday wrote: "First, education is a mirror held against the face of a people. Nations may put on blustering shows of strength to conceal public weakness, erect grand facades to conceal shabby backyards, and profess peace while secretly arming for conquest, but how they take care of their children tells unerringly who they are" (*Comparative Method in Education*, New York: Holt, Rinehart & Winston, 1964, page 5).

Perhaps equally important, however, is the valuable perspective that studying another education system provides us in understanding our own. To step outside of our commonly held assumptions about schools and learning, however briefly, and to look back at our system in contrast to another, places it in a very different light. To learn, for example, how the Soviet Union handles the education of a multilingual society; how the French provide for the funding of public education; or how the Japanese control admissions into their universities enables us to understand that there are alternatives to our familiar way of doing things. Not that we can often "borrow" from other societies; indeed, educational arrangements are inevitably a reflection of deeply rooted political, economic, and cultural factors that are unique to a society. But a conscious recognition that there are other ways of doing things can serve to open our minds and provoke our imaginations in ways that can result in new approaches that we would not have otherwise considered.

Since this series is designed to be a useful research tool, the editors and contributors welcome suggestions for future volumes as well as ways in which this series can be improved.

Edward R. Beauchamp
University of Hawaii

INTRODUCTION

In recent years, international agencies as well as national governments have become increasingly concerned with educational efficiency. In most Third World countries, the past three decades have been characterized by a massive extension of education at all levels. Primary and secondary school enrollments have more than doubled in Latin America, Asia, Africa and the Middle East; higher education has grown even more. This educational expansion has meant that most countries have spent lavishly on schooling. In the past, decade as the world economy has declined, Third World nations have become increasingly alarmed about the efficiency of their school systems and the responsiveness of the schools to national policy agendas. Emphasis in education was on the quantitative dimensions of schooling--in the 1980s the focus has been on the qualitative dimensions. In this context, what is taught and what is learned in school have become a matter of concern. Only a few years ago, attention was called to the fact that Third World nations have inadequate teaching materials and few trained teachers. Policymakers began to insist that textbooks be developed for the schools in the hope that by so doing, educational quality could be assured.

This volume focuses on textbooks in the Third World. In it we ask fundamental questions about textbook supply in the schools, national policies and their relation to textbook supply and content, the role of national and international agencies in textbook publication and control, and the influence of textbooks on classroom practice. Our concern is how textbooks are made available and used in classrooms, as well as the content of the textbooks. In the essays that follow, we ask whether and how textbook contents reflect national policies. Do texts reflect changes in policies, or do they remain oblivious to them? To what extent do the contents of school texts present values alien to the society?

This book is a pioneering effort. As such, it can only begin to touch a series of issues related to textbooks in Third World countries. It does not present a definitive work on textbook policy, production, content, and use. Rather, we hope that these essays will generate further research on textbooks--research which will in the long run contribute to the improvement of schooling.

This book focuses on textbooks, and textbooks alone. We are aware that the textbook is only one of many elements that enters classrooms. In some countries there are few (if any) texts and students learn by rote from the teacher. In other countries, teachers rely on the texts as the sum total of knowledge to be transmitted in the classroom. In still others, texts represent only a part of the total knowledge transmitted in schools. Despite this, our emphasis on textbooks in this volume says something about the nature of school curriculum and what passes for school knowledge in many parts of the world. Thus, to study the textbooks is to study knowledge that is supposed to be transmitted in classrooms. It provides us with some idea of what students are supposed to learn, not necessarily what they do learn.

This book has two parts: the first focuses on government and international agency policies regarding the provision of texts in Third World countries; the second concentrates on the content of textbooks in specific Third World countries and the relation of those contents to national policy goals. Joseph P. Farrell and Stephen P. Heyneman analyze the economic, social, and pedagogical issues involved in textbook development in the Third World. Their study provides a broad overview of textbook policies and the many problems of textbook provision to primary and secondary schools in the Third World. Philip G. Altbach and S. Gopinathan's essay complements the Farrell and Heyneman chapter--they consider the role of textbooks in higher education. This essay points out that textbooks have been completely ignored in debates about higher education. Gail P. Kelly's chapter in Part 1 focuses on the relation of state policy to textbooks and teacher cultures. This essay on textbooks in French Indochina and West Africa provides us with historical insight into Third World textbook development and points out that not all Third World countries emerged from colonialism without a publishing infrastructure. She argues that emphasis on the textbook traditionally was part of overall policies of teacher control. Where teacher control was not an issue as in West Africa, neither a publishing infrastrucutre nor textbooks were developed.

The final essay in Part 1 involves teacher use of texts. Krishna Kumar's study indicates the importance of textbooks in some Third World settings. He points out that in India colonialism provided reinforcement for the development of a textbook culture in the classroom. A teachers' culture arose which adhered strictly to the text. Kumar argues that decolonization of Indian schools involves not only a shift in the content of the texts, but also movement away from teachers' slavish adherence to the text as the sum total of knowledge to be transmitted in the classroom.

Part 2 of this book consists of content analyses of textbooks in individual Third World countries. Several essays in Part 2 are concerned with how textbooks inadvertently transmit values from former colonial powers to their former colonies. Karen L. Biraimah's chapter, for example, focuses on the sex role divisions of labor presented in Togolese secondary school textbooks. She points out that the texts present roles typical of France and Western European countries which are at variance with Togolese male and female roles in both the family and the workforce. She indicates that many of these texts were written and published in France for the African market.

Other essays in Part 2 focus on the relation between the messages conveyed in textbooks and national educational and social policies. Hena Mukherjee and Khairiah Ahmed ask whether Malaysian policies designed to bring about national integration have been embodied in textbooks which were developed as a result of new national policies emphasizing nation-building. Their analysis of secondary school texts indicates that the texts deal inadequately with ethnicity and religious difference they tend to ignore non-Malay cultures. The model of integration which Malaysian secondary texts follow deviates markedly from stated national education and political policies.

The disjuncture between national policies and school textbooks is underscored by Dennis Mbuyi's chapter in Part 2. Mbuyi analyzes the texts in Tanzanian and Kenyan primary schools. He finds in the case of Kenya that the texts, as in Malaysia, contradict state policies. However, he does find that in Tanzania there is less of a conflict between the contents of school texts and national policy. His study suggests that in revolutionary situations more attention is paid to the texts. This hypothesis is borne out by two of the other essays in Part 2--Julia Kwong's on China and M. Mobin Shorish's on Iran. Kwong focuses on textbooks in use during the Cultural Revolution. She finds that even the mathematics texts, which are seemingly impervious to politics, became politicized during that period of Chinese revolutionary history and generally followed the line of the Cultural Revolution. Chuka Eze Okonkwo discusses language issues in his analysis of English and Igbo textbooks in Nigeria. Shorish, in studying textbooks in an Islamic revolutionary setting in Iran, shows a similar pattern--school texts were made to further the goals of the Islamic revolution. These essays, taken as a whole, allow us to see that texts can be made to follow state policies, although in many Third World countries this is not the case.

This volume is part of the research program of the Comparative Education Center of the State University of New York. Philip G. Altbach and Gail P. Kelly are faculty associated with the Center. Altbach has conducted research on publishing and knowledge distribution in the Third World. Kelly has focused her research on education in French colonies in the 1920s and 1930s. Several of the authors were students in the comparative education program at SUNY/Buffalo. Karen L. Biraimah, Chuka Eze Okonkwo, S. Gopinthan, and Dennis Mbuyi received their doctorates from SUNY/Buffalo. In Biraimah's, Okonkwo's and Mbuyi's cases, the research reported here reflect work done for their doctoral dissertations. We are indebted to Pat Glinski and Nancy Myers of the Quantitative Analysis Laboratory, Faculty of Educational Studies, State University of New York at Buffalo for the design and composition of this volume.

Philip G. Altbach
Gail P. Kelly
Buffalo, New York
March, 1988

PART 1

The Policy Context

CHAPTER 1

TEXTBOOKS AND THE THIRD WORLD: AN OVERVIEW

Philip G. Altbach and Gail P. Kelly

Textbooks stand at the heart of the educational enterprise. Teachers rely on them to set the parameters of instruction and to impart basic educational content. Students' school work often begins (and in some schools ends) with the textbook. Texts constitute the base of school knowledge, particularly in Third World countries where there is a chronic shortage of qualified teachers. In many instances teachers adhere closely to texts, using them as the sole source of school knowledge, assigning students lessons contained in the text and testing students only on the knowledge contained in the texts. In much of the Third World, texts become far more important in the educational enterprise than in the industrialized world--in the United States, Canada, the Soviet Union, and Western Europe schools are well equipped with audio-visual aids, libraries and sometimes computers. In these countries, teachers have access to duplicating machines and can select classroom materials on their own from a wide variety of sources to supplement and, in some cases replace textbooks. Schools in industrialized nations not only have access to alternative materials, they also have many texts from which they can choose.

In Third World countries there are few instructional materials available at all. Indeed, the provision of texts is a major problem. In many schools children share texts; in some schools they have none to share and the teacher writes daily lessons from a text on the chalkboard. In cases where there are texts, teachers rarely have the luxury of picking and choosing among texts.

The world crisis in education, which Philip Coombs has so deftly described in his book, is not only a crisis in the escalating costs of education, it is also a crisis in education's effectiveness.[1] As schools have expanded in the Third World they have barely provided adequate classroom space, not to mention trained teachers. The emphasis on expansion has meant that curriculum development has often been neglected as well as the provision of instructional materials and textbooks. As many analysts have pointed out, the effectiveness of educational expansion in terms of learning outcomes has been undermined by the lack of teaching aids, textbooks in particular.[2] It is presumed, not without reason, that children will learn more and thus achieve better if they have texts to assist them with learning.

The scarcity of texts in Third World countries is not a new phenomenon. For the most part, Third World school systems arose as a result of Western imperialism. Britain, France, Spain, Portugal and, to a lesser extent, Germany and Japan developed schools in their respective colonies to meet administrative needs for a small number of literate clerks and mid-level executives.[3] In most instances little attention was paid to the development of textbooks. In the small school systems that developed in Africa, Asia, Latin America and the Middle East, texts imported from the metropole were often the only books available. In some educational systems, like that of French West Africa, European pedagogues wrote books and developed curricula that emphasized European views of Third World societies concerning singing, dancing, farming, and so forth. Missionaries, who were the mainstay of education in many Third World countries during colonial rule, saw the catechism and the Bible as the sole necessary school texts. At independence, but even before then, when the social demand for education escalated, the scarcity of texts and the dependency on Europe for the few at hand characterized individual school systems.[4]

The colonial legacy extends beyond both scarcity and dependency. There was, in most colonies, no infrastructure to produce texts cheaply for the schools. Many countries lacked the basics for textbook production--printing presses, publishing houses, even paper. In the post-independence years, the demand for education skyrocketed. For parents, education was perceived as the route to social mobility for their children and expected it to provide access to the modern urban economy. Most governments believed educational expansion would fuel economic development and solve the problems of a plural society. Despite financial difficulties, Third World governments developed schools, focusing on building schools and to a lesser extent on teacher preparation. Concern with textbooks did not arise until the 1970s and 1980s.

This essay focuses on current issues facing educational planners and policy makers in the development and provision of textbooks. We will first discuss textbook policies and the infrastructure of textbook production in the Third World, then we will turn our attention to textbook content and end with recommendations for policy alternatives in the development and use of texts.

Textbooks and Policy

Textbooks are, of course, a ubiquitous part of every educational system. They are an important part of every curricular and many structural reforms in education and are part of the process of educational planning, yet textbooks have only recently been considered a major and integral part of the educational system. They are in the background, and policy toward them is frequently haphazard and uncoordinated. Many countries have no specific textbook policy. With a tradition of using textbooks produced abroad or, in some cases, by private sector agencies (such as missionary organizations, profit-making publishers, etc.), planners often assumed that the books would automatically appear once schools were built, curricula developed, and the need made clear. Rapid expansion was the order of the day, and the nuances of educational policy were lost in the rush. Schools were built but there were inadequate supplies of teachers and books, and the details of the curriculum were frequently left undeveloped.

Formulating and implementing a textbook policy and the ways and means of obtaining relevant books is a daunting task. Most Third World educational systems started from scratch without adequate infrastructures. The creation of a textbook requires many complex elements--authors, publishers, editors, printers, curriculum experts and the like. With most of these elements missing, the development of a coherent policy proved difficult. The use of foreign books also proved an obstacle. Imported books were traditionally used and the links to the multinational publishers were strong. In some instances, foreign assistance programs made imported books available at little expense and it proved economically difficult to develop an indigenous industry in the face of this foreign competition. Government officials and educational planners needed to know what questions to ask and what approaches to pursue in order to develop a textbook infrastructure. Often, this sophistication was lacking. In short, the seemingly easy task of providing reading materials for a school system proved to be a difficult task. In many nations, there were significant conflicts over the content of the curriculum and hence of textbooks. Sometimes, there was confusion over which language to use. Approaches to historical events, ethnic or religious cleavages, and other matters were contested. The lack of a consensus made the creation of textbooks difficult. While there are economic costs involved in textbook development, it seems that the greater problems were related to political and curricular decisions, the availability of infrastructures, and the like.

Efforts to plan educational change are commonplace and virtually all such reforms necessarily involve textbooks, yet it is rare that textbooks are considered as an integral part of a reform plan. Significant policy shifts, such as moving to an indigenous language for the medium of instruction in the schools, have a correspondingly significant text component, and there is evidence that such language shifts have suffered because textbooks were not included as a basic element from the beginning of the planning process. In Malaysia, for example, textbooks were not fully prepared for the change from English to Bahasa Malaysia that took place at all levels of the educational system. Textbooks have subsequently been produced on a "crash" basis with considerable disruption. Problems are particularly severe at the post-secondary level, where textbooks are complex and often aimed at introducing new approaches to the subject.

Textbook Production

Textbooks are not produced in a vacuum. They are related not only to the educational system, but also to the publishing industry, to the fiscal realities of the nation, and to the broader "book consciousness" of society. The production of a textbook is a highly complex matter that depends on adequate coordination of a variety of organizations and interests. When educators or Ministry of Education officials think about textbooks, they frequently ignore the broader context of book development in the country.

The nature and scope of the publishing industry is crucial to the development of textbooks. Textbooks are affected by the publishing industry and in turn have a significant impact on the total book industry. For many Third World nations, textbooks are the largest and sometimes the overwhelming part of the publishing equation. Decisions have to be made with regard to how textbooks are to be produced and who is to produce them. These decisions are of great significance and affect the local publishing industry, the quality of production of the books, the length of time it takes to produce books, and other aspects.[5]

There are also international ramifications to textbook development. As noted, the multinational publishing firms dominated text publishing during the colonial period and in some countries remain powerful forces. These firms often control both the major sources of domestic production and the import of books. International copyright treaties favor the copyright holders, the Western publishers, and these treaties often work against the interests of Third World nations by making it difficult to obtain permission to translate books. Recent copyright reforms have improved the situation, but the basic configuration of international power remains unchanged.

In many instances, a private sector publishing enterprise can produce books more quickly and sometimes at a lower cost than a government agency. Private publishers have argued that textbooks provide a steady income and permit them to expand their publishing into general and scientific books, thus helping the society. In some cases, governments have set up semi-independent publishing houses to produce textbooks in order to avoid the bureaucracy of a government ministry while maintaining a degree of control over the publication process. These "parastatal" enterprises have been especially popular in Africa but have met with mixed success. Despite these initiatives, text publishing is in government hands in many Third World nations.

In some Third World nations, such as India, Egypt, and Mexico, there is a large and effective publishing industry that can assist in textbook publishing if called upon to do so. The industry can also survive without texts. Local markets are large enough to support an independent publishing apparatus. Smaller nations face a much more difficult situation. There is little if any indigenous publishing enterprise and the markets for books, even for textbooks beyond the primary school level, are frequently quite small. These countries often lack even the most basic publishing infrastructures. Their problems in developing an indigenous capacity for textbook publication are quite serious.

Regardless of the policy adopted for textbook production, the nature and scope of the local publishing industry will be affected. Publishing itself is a highly complex enterprise requiring coordination and much expertise. If a local publishing industry is active, then the technical problems of publishing and distributing textbooks will be considerably easier. The orientation, status, and broader market for textbooks are important parts of the book industry in any country and the relationship between texts and the publishing enterprise should be kept in mind.

There are many problems confronting Third World countries in the development of a textbook publishing infrastructure. Several of these relate to the supply of material so that books can be published. For example, the provision of paper for textbooks is often a complicated set of issues.[6] Some countries have to rely on imported supplies of paper, which makes locally produced textbooks extremely expensive. The world paper market is dominated by a few industrialized nations, namely Canada, Sweden, and the United States. The price of paper also fluctuates and this adds to the uncertainties of book publishing in those Third World countries that rely on imported papers. It also means that it is difficult for school systems to budget accurately for textbooks since the price of the texts fluctuate from year to year. Sometimes paper becomes unavailable and the printing of textbooks comes to a halt. Some countries have tried to overcome the problems presented by paper importation by developing their own manufacturing capacities. However, not all countries can do this because the development of a local paper manufacturing industry depends on a supply of wood--soft woods are not readily available in many Third World countries--and on large capital investments that many Third World countries do not have. A seemingly simply matter such as the provision of paper for printing textbooks becomes a complex and sometimes controversial issue involving decisions about the kind of paper to be used in particular textbooks, the available domestic supplies, the ability or willingness to import paper, and other questions.

Textbook writing takes special skills and there must be an appropriate pool of authors ready to write them. An author must have detailed knowledge of the process of schooling, of the nature of the curriculum, of the psychology of learning as well as the subject matter and the sequencing of books in the field. He or she must be able to write and express ideas clearly for students at the appropriate grade level. In the United States, textbook authors are given considerable help by curriculum experts, communications experts, and designers. In most Third World nations, few of these infrastructures are available and textbook authors tend to be on their own. It is often necessary to provide special incentives to textbook authors and to ensure that they have a sufficiently good knowledge of the field to write a book about it. Furthermore there is sometimes an added handicap of language, since textbooks must frequently be prepared in indigenous languages that many text authors do not speak well, particularly where the universities use a European language as the major means of instruction.

Textbook authors are a special group; individuals who have expertise in a number of areas relating to education. As stated before, this combination of skills is difficult to find in many industrialized nations and textbook publishers frequently use teams of experts to prepare texts. The considerable funds used to develop a textbook in the West are generally unavailable in the Third World and the necessary back-up expertise is also impossible to obtain. As a result, Third World textbook authors have tremendous responsibility and sometimes few resources.

Teachers and students are the ultimate users of textbooks, and the teaching staff is particularly dependent upon good books. However, textbook authorities frequently ignore teachers in the preparation of textbooks. There is, in the Third World, very little research that goes into textbook preparation. It seems clear that teachers should have a significant input into the creation and development of textbooks. Teachers can provide guidelines on innovative approaches to a topic, to specific student interest, to effective learning strategies, and to the effectiveness of older books. Teachers and teacher organizations and unions can be brought directly into the process of textbook creation in a way that is currently very rare. Students also might be of some help in textbook preparation. It may be useful to use students' help with regard to effective learning devices, topics which are of considerable interest to students, and the like. In short, those who use textbooks are part of the complex system and these groups can be much more effectively involved.

From its inception, textbook development is a complicated process that takes place in a context that includes educators as well as many outside groups. Commercial issues such as the balance of trade and the availability of foreign exchange enter into the picture. The indigenous book industry is of key importance. The availability of paper, of printing equipment, of binding facilities and the like also play a role. Textbooks are part of a system and must be seen as an integral part of that system.

Third World countries not only face significant problems when it comes to developing and printing textbooks, but the problem of textbook distribution is of equal significance. It has often been pointed out that general books seldom reach beyond the large urban areas, and thus most of the population has little access to them. Publishers have very limited capacity to distribute books to the majority of the population in the Third World. Textbooks are in a somewhat better position in terms of distribution since the market is fairly clearly defined and books can be sent directly to schools or other educational institutions. It is, however, a real challenge to ensure that books are produced and distributed to students on time. If books are unavailable, the curriculum is hampered and the program of the school cannot proceed. In Third World countries, textbooks are frequently delayed, resulting in negative consequences for the educational system. The seemingly simple act of distributing books to students is often quite difficult. In countries with poor transportation systems, it is hard to ensure that books will be delivered to schools on time. The logistics of sending many different titles to hundreds or perhaps thousands of schools for hundreds of thousands of students is daunting.

While Third World nations continue to experience difficulties in producing and publishing textbooks for the schools, even greater problems are encountered in producing textbooks having content relevant to a national context.

Textbook Content and School Practice

Most Third World countries have been so immersed in the problems of providing schooling to children on the primary level and, to a lesser extent, on the secondary level that they have paid little attention to curriculum development and even less to the content of school textbooks. For the most part, many Third World countries were barely able in the 1960s and 1970s to ensure that textbooks were available in the schools. Some countries, in part in order to provide textbooks, have continued teaching in Western languages such as English or French and have imported school books from the United States, Great Britain, France, and to a lesser extent from the Soviet Union. This has meant that it has been difficult to adjust the school curriculum either to student needs or to the requirements of national policies. The persistence of European languages in many Third World countries is in part a function of the lack of textbooks for all levels of education.

Use of foreign textbooks at times has been facilitated by international agencies and by foreign donor nations.[7] For example, in the 1960s and early 1970s the United States subsidized the export of American textbooks to many Third World countries. France and the Soviet Union have similar programs. These programs have helped Third World countries get texts, but they have also hindered curricular reforms except insofar as those reforms can occur while using texts made available from abroad. Reliance on foreign texts has meant that the content of school textbooks--and therefore a sizeable part of the curriculum--remains outside of the control of national policy makers, that the curriculum is irrelevant to local needs and is ineffective.

Studies of textbooks have indicated that books developed and printed in Europe and the United States tend to unwittingly transmit a series of messages about daily life, including sex role divisions of labor, the role of education in obtaining white collar employment, urban living, and general life styles, that encourage expectations that are often at odds with Third World realities and government policies. Togolese secondary textbooks, for example, portray women in roles which are completely alien to those that Togolese women are called upon to perform.[8] These texts, published in France for the African market, encourage women to become housewives and mothers and deny the very real economic contribution Togolese women make to the sustenance of the family and to national economic development.

Often textbooks published in the West inadvertently promote major social change. They portray only nuclear families in countries where extended families are the norm; they stress urban life and ignore farming; they encourage students to enter occupations unheard of in many Third World societies while ignoring many of the skilled trades critical to economic development.[9] They often unwittingly promote consumerism.

Many Third World countries have become increasingly aware of the problems inherent both politically and pedagogically in using texts published in the United States, France, and other western industrialized countries. Many countries, such as Nigeria, Kenya, India, and Tanzania, have sought to develop texts specifically for their nation's schools written in indigenous languages. Initially, some of these early attempts were little more than translations of foreign texts into African and Asian languages. The New Peak series, developed for the Kenyan schools in the 1960s, for example, were English texts translated into Swahili. The Swahili language version substituted pictures of Africans in urban settings for those in the original text. The original values and knowledge transmitted in the texts remained untouched.[10]

While many countries have developed their distinct textbook series for school use written in indigenous languages, the contents of many texts have a dubious relation to national policy goals. A number of recent studies have indicated that textbooks, while becoming more national in terms of pictures and references to local names and places, fail to teach values that would support government initiatives toward economic development or nation-building. In the plural societies of the Third World, most textbooks tend to avoid the obvious problems of tribalism and ethnicity. Instead, when they focus on nation-building, they do so by denying ethnic heritages. A recent study of Nigerian school texts, for example, found that texts in three states stressed ethnicity more than the nation, despite the government's attempt to stress nation-building in the aftermath of that nation's civil war.[11] In part, this was because as the textbook industry developed in Nigeria with regard to local languages for the schools, each state could choose to adopt elementary texts and lower level secondary texts freely. Thus, Igbo language texts dwell on the Igbos, Hausa language texts on the Hausa, and so forth. When the texts discussed nation-building, they tended to focus on only one ethnic group's contribution. Indigenization of publishing, without attention to content, has meant in this case that textbooks come to support particularistic versus national values.

Malaysia represents a different case in the opposite extreme. New texts issued in the national language tended to undermine state policy in promoting national integration. Government policy focused on integrating all ethnic groups into the society; the texts, on the other hand, focus on promoting a Malay identity as the basis for Malaysian nationalism and deny the plural realities of the society.[12]

Content analysis of school textbooks has not only indicated that texts produced indigenously can and often do run counter to national policy, it has also shown that textbooks can also subvert economic development plans. In Kenya, which is a predominantly rural society, elementary textbooks in both Swahili and English produced in the 1970s present rural life in disparaging terms and see no possibility of rural development.[13] They encourage urban migration, despite government policies that focus on rural development and seek to discourage the influx of people to the cities where there is high unemployment.

School textbooks need not always subvert government policies. There have been enough studies, some of which are reported in this volume, which indicate that with careful planning and a sizeable investment in textbook development, texts can promote national policies. This has been more often the case in revolutionary societies with clearly articulated value systems. Several studies of Chinese school texts have indicated how communist ideology has permeated textbook content.[14] Even variations in that ideology, as it has shifted over time, are reflected in the texts. Julia Kwong, for example, has shown how even seemingly "neutral" subjects such as mathematics were made to convey a set of ideologies favorable to the Maoist faction of the Communist Party when they were in power during the Cultural Revolution.[15] Not only have communist revolutionary societies taken care to see that their values are reflected in school texts, other revolutionary societies have done so as well. Tanzanian texts, for example, have focused on promoting values of African socialism espoused by President Julius Nyerere; similarly, primers produced in Iran after the Islamic revolution reflect the government's Shiite values as well as its anti-American and anti-Western biases.[16]

The research basis that is currently available makes it patently clear, in sum, that the content of textbooks is as big a policy concern as the production and distribution of textbooks. Nationalizing the production of texts is not a sufficient condition for having texts become relevant to the society or to national goals. Policy makers may find that unless they pay attention to the values promoted in the texts and their relation to national policy goals, texts may subtly subvert the very reasons the government has invested so heavily in schools.

While the policy implications of the research on textbook contents are apparent, we still know little about the relation between the knowledge textbooks contain and the knowledge students obtain in school. Little research exists on how teachers use texts, the effect of textbooks on classroom practice, and the relative importance of the textbook versus other instructional materials in forming student attitudes and in improving the cognitive outcomes of schooling. However, there is research that tells us that the availability of texts is directly related to student learning outcomes, which underscores the importance of textbook policies in school systems throughout the world.

Recommendations for Textbook Policies and Research Agendas

It is clear that textbooks are important in the development of national school systems and in improving the contribution of schooling to policy goals such as national unity and economic development. However, for textbooks to make a maximum contribution, their development requires scarce resources--both financial and human. We have discussed here some of the elements of what can be called a "textbook system." It is surprising that only limited research has focused on textbooks to guide the formation of public policy. However, we have good reason to believe that textbooks can be related to educational development and change. The following should be considered by policy-makers in formulating textbook policies:

> Textbooks must be seen as an integral part of any educational development; planners must ensure that the implications for the development, publication, and distribution of texts are taken into account in the inception of any plan for educational change.
>
> The financial elements of textbook development must be incorporated into any educational planning documents.
>
> The issue of who should produce textbooks must be confronted by educational planners. In some countries, textbooks are produced by government ministries; in other countries, they are put out by parastatal concerns; and in still others, by the private sector or by multinational corporations.

The implications of deciding who should produce textbooks are considerable for the publishing industry as well as for the development, distribution, and costs of textbooks.

Textbooks must be integrated into the grade structure of the educational system and appropriately sequenced within that structure.

The issue of "who should pay" is a major policy decision. In many nations, textbooks are provided free of charge to students. In others, the user absorbs some or all of the costs of books. The policy implications of deciding who should pay are considerable in terms of who has access to books and its implications for the poor.

Policies relating to the content of textbooks are important and frequently formulated on an ad hoc basis. The content of books, whether they be in mathematics, literature, national history, and the like, is a very important question which has implications in terms of the effectiveness of the text and in terms of the relation of education to national policy goals.

While some policies can be formulated, with the current state of research on textbooks, clearly there is much that we do not yet know about textbook development, distribution, and impact. We would hope that the following brief agenda includes topics worth considering as efforts are made to produce the best possible textbooks for the rapidly expanding school systems of the Third World.

Every Education Ministry should have appropriate staff concerned with all aspects of textbook development having appropriate expertise on the curricular, learning, production, and fiscal aspects of textbooks at the relevant levels of the school system. One of the responsibilities should be research on how texts are being used and what suitable changes and innovations should be made.

In many parts of the Third World, regional cooperation in the preparation and production of textbooks may prove successful particularly in scientific fields, it might be possible to produce books for use in more than one country if language is a common element. Even where languages differ, it might be possible to prepare different texts for a common set of pictures and other common production elements in order to save considerable sums. Regional cooperation, which is presently rare, may yield significant results.

In the rush to ensure that textbooks are available in the rapidly expanding schools of the Third World, relatively little analysis has been done on the consequences, planned and unanticipated, of the messages in textbooks. The books not only have specific messages in terms of their content, but have more subtle and difficult to discern indirect messages. These messages are important to understand since they have a direct impact on educational development. Research to evaluate textbooks must be an important part of the agenda of any textbook project.

Textbooks are educational tools that also have important political and social messages. These messages are frequently poorly understood, yet the consequences for the society may be significant. There have been analyses of how textbooks portray gender relations, the state, class and race relations, and other topics. Such analyses are important for understanding the messages being communicated in textbooks and also for suggesting possible alternative approaches.

The conditions under which textbooks become effective means for instruction are not well understood. There has been little research conducted on how teachers use texts in Third World settings and even less research on how specific text formats and contents affect learner outcomes. In order for texts to become effective, research on teacher practice, textbook format and use, and learner outcomes is important.

The economics of textbooks is poorly understood. There is currently a good deal of discussion concerning whether users should pay directly for texts or whether they should be supplied free by the state. There are cogent arguments on both sides of this issue. Other economic aspects of textbooks are also worthy of consideration. For example, the interrelationships between textbooks and the publishing industry are important and not well understood.

Conclusion

We have discussed a range of concerns about textbooks in this essay and are convinced that textbooks deserve much more attention from educators, policy makers, government officials, and the public. In the Third World, textbooks are among the most important educational inputs. If there is an insufficient number of books, the education of children will suffer. If the books are not relevant to the subject or the country, there will be discontinuities. If scarce resources are wasted on ill-advised projects or production is handled inefficiently, there will be fewer books available. Texts are among the commonplace elements of a school, yet they are often not taken seriously. We believe that textbooks are important and that they deserve careful research and analysis.

NOTES

1. Philip Coombs, The World Crisis in Education: The View from the Eighties. (New York: Oxford University Press, 1985).

2. Steven P. Heyneman, Textbooks and Achievement: What We Know. (Washington, D.C.: The World Bank, 1978).

3. For a discussion of colonial schools, see Philip G. Altbach and Gail P. Kelly, eds., Education and the Colonial Experience. (New Brunswick, New Jersey: Transaction, 1984).

4. See Philip G. Altbach, "The Distribution of Knowledge in the Third World: A Case Study in Neocolonialism," in P. G. Altbach and G. P. Kelly, Education and the Colonial Experience, (New Brunswick, N.J.: Transaction, 1984), pp. 229-251.

5. For an elaboration of some of these points see, Philip G. Altbach and S. Gopinathan, "Textbooks in the Third World: Challenge and Response," in P. Altbach, A. Arboleda and S. Gopinathan, eds., Publishing in the Third World, (Portsmouth, New Hampshire: Heinemann, 1985), pp. 13-24.

6. Jorg Becker, "The Geopolitics of Cultural Paper: International Dimensions of Paper Production, Consumption and Import-Export Structures," (Unpublished paper prepared for the Unesco World Congress of Books, London, England, 1982).

7. See Altbach,"The Distribution of Knowledge in the Third World," op. cit.

8. See, for example, Karen Biraimah, "The Impact of Western Schools on Girls' Expectations: A Togolese Case," in Gail P. Kelly and Carolyn M. Elliott, Women's Education in the Third World, (Albany: SUNY Press, 1982), pp. 188-202.

9. See Mbuyi chapter in this volume.

10. See Ernest Stabler, Education Since Uhuru: Kenya's Schools. (Middletown, Connecticut: Wesleyan University Press, 1969).

11. Azubike Kalu-Nwiwu. "Education and National Integration: A Study of Nigerian Secondary School Texts." (Unpublished Ph.D. dissertation, State University of New York at Buffalo, 1988).

12. See Mukherjee and Ahmed chapter in this volume.

13. See Mbuyi chapter in this volume.

14. See Charles Price Ridley, Paul Godwin and Dennis J. Doolin, The Making of a Model Citizen in Communist China. (Stanford, California: Hoover Institution Press, 1971).

15. See Kwong chapter in this volume.

16. See Shorish chapter in this volume.

CHAPTER 2

TEXTBOOKS IN DEVELOPING COUNTRIES: ECONOMIC AND PEDAGOGICAL CHOICES

Joseph P. Farrell and
Stephen P. Heyneman

INTRODUCTION

During the past few decades, particularly since the great epoch of decolonization between the mid-1950s and mid-1960s, there has been a massive expansion of formal schooling in developing countries, fueled both by parental demand and by national aspirations for political, social, and economic development. Since World War II, universal primary school enrollment has been achieved in thirty-five of the richer developing countries, including Argentina, Gabon, Malaysia, Trinidad, and Tobago. In the thirty-six poorest nations in the world, primary school enrollments as a percentage of the school-age population grew from 80% in 1965 to 91% in 1983, with corresponding secondary level figures being 23% and 31%. Maintaining this rapidly expanding enterprise is very expensive. In the typical developing nation, education accounts for approximately 15% of public recurrent expenditures, but the figure often is as high as 30%. There are twice as many elementary school teachers in developing nations now as there were in 1960. There are two and a half times as many secondary teachers and almost four and a half times as many tertiary-level teachers. Each of these teachers must be trained, placed, paid, re-trained periodically, and eventually maintained in retirement. A corresponding increase has been required in school furniture, equipment, and reading materials. But despite this impressive quantitative growth, educational systems throughout the developing world are facing an unprecedented fiscal crisis, resulting from a world-wide economic crisis.

During the past decade government resources in developing countries have been severely strained by the fluctuation of oil and energy costs, slumping commodity prices, recession-plagued export markets, high interest rates, and the inflated value of the U.S. dollar. One result has been the "international debt crisis." In 1982, for example, 62% of the foreign exchange earnings from Brazilian exports had to be allocated to servicing the national debt. In Chile, the corresponding figure was 53%, in Ecuador, 48%, in Morocco, 43%, in the Ivory Coast, 32%, in Zambia, 22%, and so on throughout most of the developing world. And the situation has deteriorated in many nations since then.

One reaction to this crisis has been "structural adjustment"; developing nations, whether on their own initiative or under pressure from the International Monetary Fund, have begun to change their macro-economic policies; often with surprisingly quick results. For example, in 1981 the balance of payments as a proportion of Gross National Product of the oil-importing developing countries stood at about -5.1%. Three years later this deficit had been cut in half to -2.1%. These fiscal improvements have, however, not come free of cost. They are the result of sacrifices across all levels of government and across all sectors. Highways, railways, and ports are no longer maintained as they once were, and as they need to be, if national transportation infrastructures are not to collapse. Pharmaceuticals can no longer be found in rural health centers. Subsidized fertilizers and pesticides are less available to farmers. Food prices for urban consumers have increased. Hardest hit of all has been the largest public sector--education.

Because of the fiscal pressures, the proportion of the GNP allocated to education has been on the decline, as has the share of education spending in government budgets, while enrollments have continued to increase. In Latin America per student spending fell by about 45% in real terms between 1970 and 1978 and the decline has continued since then. Declines have been even more precipitous in Africa. In Somalia, for example, the share of education in the national budget fell from 12% in 1975 to 6% in 1983. During that same period in Nigeria the share of education in the national budget fell from 16% to 9%, and in Kenya from 19% to 15%. Between 1970 and 1980 per student educational spending in the least developed nations of the world fell by an average of 34%. During the same decade, per student spending in Organization for Economic Cooperation and Development countries rose by 46% from $1229 in 1970 to $2257 in 1980. Thus, the gap in educational spending between the world's richest and poorest nations has been steadily widening. In 1960, OECD countries spent 14 times more on each of their primary school students than did the poorest nations. By 1970 the gap had increased to 22:1, by 1980 it had reached 50:1.

Where have the educational spending reductions occurred in poor nations? In some cases teachers' salaries have not kept up with inflation, but generally teachers' salaries have not been the main source of expenditure reduction, usually owing to the poltiical power of teachers' organizations. In Latin America, for example, teachers' salaries remained almost constant with inflation between 1960 and 1979. In other middle income developing nations teachers' salaries were about three times the national GNP per capita in 1960 and about three and a half times GNP per capita in 1979, an increase of 15%. Educational expenditure reductions have largely been imposed on that category of the education budget which has no politically organized interest group to defend it, nonsalary expenditures: money for chalk, maps, furniture, laboratory equipment, and textbooks. As a share of education budgets nonsalary items fell in one of every two Latin American countries between 1970 and 1978. By 1979 nonsalary expenditures in primary education represented only 4% of recurrent educational expenditures in Africa and only 9% in Asia compared to 14% in OECD nations. Already low nonsalary expenditures have been squeezed even further. In the early 1980s, Bolivia spent only US 80 cents on nonsalary inputs for each of its primary school students. Comparable figures for some other poor nations were Malawi--$1.24; Indonesia--$2.24; Thailand and Brazil--$4.00; Mexico--$5.64; Algeria--$896. These figures contrast sharply with Sweden and other Nordic countries, for example, which can afford to spend US $300 annually on equipment and reading material for each primary student.

In Uganda in 1970 there was an average of one book for every three elementary school children. But over the next ten years there were no new reading materials available, and by 1980 the ration had slipped to one book for every twelve students. In 1960 the United States published five times more titles (per million inhabitants) than Africa. Twenty years later, the United States published seventeen times more titles than Africa, eight times more than Asia, and five times more than Latin America.

The fiscal pressure upon the availability of textbooks is particularly important because the evidence is now clear that textbook availability is one of the most important predictors of academic achievement among students in developing nations.[1] Levels of available reading materials strongly determine the kind of education experience a nation is able to provide for its children and youth. Table 2.1 indicates the reading material usually available for students at various levels of per-pupil expenditure on classroom materials, and the typical learning outcomes. Countries able to spend about $1.00 per student on classroom materials are at the lowest level in the quality of their education. Their students are likely to be limited to rote memorization of simple, often inaccurate, information. Countries able to spend about $3.00 per student are able to provide significantly broader and more effective educational experience. Countries able to spend from $40.00 up to $300.00 per student may anticipate producing students typically able to investigate new ideas, to recognize strong and weak supporting arguments, and to become fully productive participants in a rapidly changing economy. Thus, developing nations that are unable to stem or avoid the decline in available textbook resources are likely to suffer a further decline in already low levels of educational achievement. Nations that are unable to finance an increase in available textbook provision are likely to be foregoing a critical opportunity to increase levels of learning in their schools.

What then is to be done? How can developing nations avoid or stem a decline in educational quality? How can they acquire more reading materials for classroom use? How can they diminish the increasingly wide educational gap between themselves and richer nations? It seems unlikely that a solution to this educational quality crisis will come from a major worldwide economic recovery, at least in the near term. With a few exceptions commodity prices are in a semi-permanent slump; prices of industrial and other necessities which must be imported do not appear to be on the decline; international "hard" currencies are still very strong; the debt crisis in many developing nations does not appear to be nearing a resolution; instead of being in an era of increasingly free trade we appear to be heading toward increasing protectionism, particularly in the wealthiest nations; these words are being written shortly after the beginning of the stock market "crash" of 1987, the outcome of which is unclear but does not give much grounds for optimism. In an era of stagnant or declining government revenues, the likelihood of significant increases in overall educational budgets is small in most developing nations.

Table 2.1: Stages of Development in School Quality

Annual Cost/primary student in classsroom materials ($US)	Indicator	Product	Example
Less than $1.00	One textbook/class with some exceptions the teacher has the only available book. Pupils expected to copy the text from the blackboard and memorize.	Rote memorization of unsophisticated and poorly interpreted information	Uganda Liberia Haiti
$3.00	One textbook/student. Each student has access to one book in each subject. Comparatively little prerequisite teacher skills beyond those required at the above stage.	Major expansion information and the efficiency of presentation; little progress on self-generated skills of investigation.	Philippines People's Republic of China
$40.00	Several different textboook titles available for each student; pupils in lower grades work on	Latitude of educational programs based upon individual student ability;	Malaysia

Table 2.1 continued

	locally designed exercises. Teacher picks and chooses from among the best or most appropriate available materials. Requires significant intellectual independence on the part of teachers	significant increase in the mastery of cognitive skills.	
$200.00	Fifteen titles per student in supplementary reading material or forty books total per student in addition to a wide variety of curriculum packages, reference books, maps, dictionaries, film strips, lesson tapes, documentary films, and computer-assisted instruction. Significant managerial skills required on the part of teachers at all levels of education.	Self-generated habits of learning; ability to investigate new ideas and to recognize strong and weak supporting arguments; major improvement in cognitive creativity; wide exposure to culture as well as science.	Japan U.S.A. Sweden

Source: Stephen P. Heyneman (unpublished).

If countries are going to halt or avoid the decline in the quality of education, they will likely have to find the resources from within the education sector itself. They are going to have to spend more wisely than in the past, make increasingly difficult choices, and challenge some widely held assumptions and traditions in attempts to achieve their most important objectives. In textbook production and distribution there will be new and complex challenges. Authorities will have to find ways to produce more materials for the same or less cost. This may mean using competitive (sometimes international) suppliers rather than public monopolies, or narrowing the range of subject matter, or finding new ways of financing the production of reading materials, or altering the "quality" standard for texts (for example, use of color, thickness of paper, number of illustrations). It may require a complete reorganization of the way textbooks are published and manufactured. This chapter outlines some of the major choices and options available to authorities responsible for the publishing, manufacturing, and distribution of textbooks. This material is based upon a considerable body of experience in the development of national textbook programs that has accumulated over the past ten to twenty years. Before considering the specific issues and choices, that experience will be briefly reviewed.

Experience with Textbook Development

As evidence about the importance of textbooks to the educational process has accumulated, and in spite of the deteriorating macro-economic climate, more and more nations have mounted major textbook development and provision programs. For example, in the 1982/83 school year, just over four million textbooks covering 94 titles were produced for the schools of the Yemen Arab Republic; three years later, the figures had risen to over eleven million textbooks covering 275 titles. In the mid-1970s, the Philippines embarked on an ambitious multi-year program to produce roughly one hundred fifty million textbooks, aiming to provide one book for every two primary students in each of the core curricular areas. Over two decades, Mexico has carefully built up a system for providing free textbooks to all of its primary school students. Even a nation as poor as Ethiopia managed, between 1975 and 1985, to print and distribute almost forty million school textbooks. At the top of the scale, the most populous nation in the world--China--produces and distributes each year over two billion school texts.

International donor agencies have also been increasing their support for textbooks. UNESCO has been sustaining a major international effort through its Division for Book Promotion and International Exchanges; for example, the works published in their series Studies on Books and Reading. In a recent "General Operational Review of Textbooks" prepared by the World Bank, it was noted that between the Fiscal Years 1979 and 1983, one out of three Bank education projects (twenty-nine of ninety) had textbook components. In Fiscal Year 1983, almost half the education project included textbook componenets, with total costs of about US $50 million.[2]

In some cases, textbook provision is one part of a major educational reform effort. In others, textbook provision is the project. It should be noted that in almost all cases, the international donor agency contribution represents only a small proportion of the total cost of a textbook program, and where the international contribution represents a high proportion of the total cost, the project is in an early stage of developing a provision system that the national government is committed to sustaining from its own resources over the long term.

Thus, over the past ten to fifteen years, nations throughout the developing world have been investing scarce resources in textbook provision, with assistance from the international donor community. As a result, billions of textbooks have been produced, and millions of school children who would previously have had to learn without books, now have access to them. This is a considerable accomplishment. Nonetheless, there are still millions of school children in the developing world who have no textbooks at all, or an insufficient number of books, or books which are inappropriate for their age level. Furthermore, many of the existing textbook provision programs have encountered serious problems.

It has become evident that mounting a large-scale textbook provision program in a developing nation is an extremely complicated and risk-prone venture, with implications well beyond the educational sector itself. Creating, producing, and distributing textbooks involves many parts of a nation's infrastructure, including the publishing industry, the educational establishment, writers, and government departments. International organizations and multinational publishing corporations are frequently involved. Copyright laws--seldom well understood or obeyed--further complicate matters. Production of textbooks requires substantial amounts of imported paper and technologically advanced printing facilities. It also requires planning, development, funding, testing, and distributing, as well as coordination of educational, governmental, publishing, and printing resources. As Philip Altbach has noted:[3]

> The keys to effective textbook development are not massive fiscal expenditures or crash programmes, but rather careful co-ordination, attention to the articulation between the educational system and the publishing industry, linking curricular development and the expansion of enrollments to textbook requirements, and the involvement of the necessary expertise in the development of relevant and high-quality textbooks. The textbook situation in any country depends on the state of the publishing industry (including printing capacity, the availability of paper and the distribution network), the presence of competent authors (and the research and testing facilities to ensure relevant textbooks), and the educational system.

Developing a sustainable textbook provision system is much like developing a complex new industrial sector and the complexity is equally forbidding, whether the system is managed by the public sector, the private sector, or a combination of the two. One must establish, train, and administer (or hire) separate teams of people to undertake each of the following general classes of activity and establish an administrative system to coordinate them:

• design and write books starting with curriculum guidelines and finishing with copy ready for manufacture;

• manufacture books including acquisition of raw materials (paper, ink, film, binding materials, etc.) printing, and binding;

• distribute books, getting them from the point of manufacture to all the classrooms in the nation, even the most remote, on time and in good condition;

• provide ancillary support including complementary teaching materials (such as chalk, lab supplies, etc.) and training teachers how to use the books;

• evaluate and resupply/revise books as required.

What has proven to be critical is a view of textbook provision as a long term investment in a total system rather than a "one shot" arrangement. The range of issues that have to be addressed and for which responses have to be coordinated is indicated in the following list of questions that we sent to the authors of a series of national case studies on textbook development.

1. On what grounds (financial, pedagogical, philosophical) was the decision taken to mount a major textbook provision program?

2. What provisions have been made to ensure that the program continues beyond the first round of book distribution? Is there a permanent organizational entity within the Ministry of Education or within another part of the government? Why was this particular structural arrangement chosen? How is the program financed to ensure its long-term sustainability? Is there an annual appropriation from general revenues, a special protected fund, a revolving fund based upon parent or student payment for books, foreign assistance, or some combination of the above?

3. How are textbook manuscripts developed and approved for use in school? What mechanisms are used to ensure correspondence between curriculum guidelines and textbook content? Who sets the guidelines and how are they communicated to textbook developers? Who are the textbook authors - practicing teachers, university faculty, curriculum specialists, or others? What are the mechanisms for editing, field testing, and evaluating manuscripts? What are the mechanisms for final approval of manuscripts for publication?

4. What is the language (or languages) of publication? If more than one, which books are published in which language(s) and why?

5. Was the decision taken to a) import books, b) publish locally, c) print locally, or some combination of a), b), and c)? If a combination, which books are imported, which are published and printed locally, and why?

6. For locally published or printed books, is the work done by a state agency, a parastatal agency, private commerical firms, or a combination of the above? On what grounds were these decisions taken?

7. How are books distributed to students? What are the physical transport and storage problems and how have they been resolved? Is final distribution through schools, commercial outlets, or some other entity?

8. Who pays for the books? Are they supplied free by the government, paid for or rented by parents, or is there some other arrangement?

9. What evidence is available about the use of effectiveness of books in classrooms? Are students able to take books home with them or are they kept in school? What is the expected lifetime of the books?

10. What is the program's management structure? What is the range of responsibilities of the central coordinating office and where is it located administratively? What provisions are there for coordination and control between the central office and other agencies involved in textbook design, production, and distribution? What problems have been encountered in management, coordination, and control and what has been done to solve the problems?

11. What provisions are there for training classroom teachers, textbook authors, editorial staff, publishing staff, graphic artists, designers, manufacturing staff, and other staff?

12. How are paper supplies obtained? Have there been any serious difficulties obaining paper?

13. What is government policy about copyright on locally produced textbooks and on copyrighted material from other countries? Have there been any serious problems or conflicts over copyright?

14. What provision is there for regular evaluation and revision of textbooks? Who evaluates and how often? What kinds of evaluation are used? How are the results fed back to textbook developers?

Given this complexity, it is not surprising that major problems have been encountered in many textbook provision programs. A review of World Bank experience noted the following general classes of difficulty:[4]

• inadequate attention to the financial feasibility of the book provision systems;

• providing support for book purchases or printing without concomitant support to ensure suitable educational content, adequate teacher training, or effective distribution;

• failure to establish appropriate institutional arrangements for managing the full book system.

In review of textbook publishing organizations throughout the Third World, a UNESCO study noted the following common misunderstandings:[5]

• underestimation of the size and complexity of the task;

• lack of adequate publishing advice in planning operations;

• inadequate management resources;

• confusing the functions of printer with those of publisher;

• lack of understanding of the difficulties and time required to produce educationally satisfactory manuscripts related to prescribed curricula;

• failure to consider textbook publishing as an integral and basic part of a total national book publishing industry.

Another UNESCO study concluded that there was a lack of awareness of basic economic facts of book publishing in many developing nations, sometimes even among publishers themselves.[6]

One central lesson can be derived from all the experience to date: providing books to schools where there is little or nothing to read may seem like a simple undertaking, but it is not. Every developing country--from China to Guinea--wants to design, manufacture, and distribute its own textbooks. But this desire needs to be analyzed carefully. Instead of producing books locally from scratch, it may be cheaper to import technical experience, equipment, and raw materials (especially paper) from Western Europe or North America. The publication process demands substantial experience in editing, production, printing, testing, and distribution. Six to ten years is normally required to develop a new generation of textbooks for primary-school grades one to six. Given the necessary skills, this may be economical for books on local history, civics, and literature; but in mathematics and the sciences it may be cheaper to adapt already published materials. Furthermore, it is often more economical for countries to publish their own textbooks than to print them. Printing in large quantities requires specialized and expensive machinery, a constant supply of raw materials, and various maintenance skills; publishing requires editorial and design skills but the hardware for manufacture need not be local.

The problems noted above provided the rationale and context for a seminar co-directed by the authors of this chapter, that was held at the Economic Development Institute of the World Bank, in Washington, D.C., April 9 to 25, 1986. The seminar brought together twenty-five participants from twenty-two developing nations, eighteen consultants, eight staff members from the World Bank, and many other observers to consider what has been learned from roughly two decades of experience in the development and implementation of large-scale national textbook programs. The participants from developing nations were all senior government or para-statal officials with major responsibilities for their national textbook provision systems. The twenty-two nations represented ranged from very small (such as Losotho and Honduras) to very large (such as Brazil and China) and from very poor to middle-income nations. Both market economies and centrally planned economies were represented, as well as all major regions of the developing world. (Appendix A provides a complete list of the nations represented.) The depth and range of experience among these participants was an extremely important resource for the seminar.

During the seminar all aspects of textbook provision were examined--from obtaining raw materials for paper production to the delivery of tested texts to remote schools, and from the training of teachers to the establishment of a system for evaluation, revision, and resupply. At each step seminar participants and consultants examined the available alternatives and their consequences, drawing upon both specially prepared background papers and, most importantly, their own experience. In the remainder of this chapter we note the major issues and choices that were identified and discussed in the seminar, and provide a synthesis of the main conclusions reached. It should be noted that the material presented here does not represent primarily the views of North American or Western European "academics," or donor agency officials (although such individuals were used as resource people for the seminar); rather, it is principally a distillation of the accumulated wisdom and experience of the seminar participants who are responsible "on the ground" for the development and success of their own national textbook provision systems.

Key Issues and Choices

1. *An Overriding Constraint: Readership Size*

A fundamental condition that contrains almost all other choices is the size of the prospective readership for a given textbook. In private commerical publishing, this is referred to as "market size," but we have used a more general term because the basic principles apply equally to government publishing in a non-market setting. Simply put, the larger the readership for a particular book, the greater will be the total cost of producing it, but all else being equal the smaller will be the cost per book (unit cost).

Readership size is itself influenced by a number of distinct factors. First, obviously, is the total school-age population of the nation. Second is the enrollment ratio at any given grade level. Even in developing nations which enroll almost all age-eligible children in grade one, there is typically a high drop-out rate during primary schooling; thus the readership size for a grade six or seven text may be half (or less) than that for a grade one text, and the readership for secondary level texts may be very small. Added to this is the degree of specialization of the book. In most nations, the curriculum is common throughout primary schooling and often through at least part of secondary schooling. In such cases, the readership for a given textbook is the total enrollment at the particular grade level. But at some point the curriculum becomes diversified--different students study different subjects--and then the readership for a given book becomes a fraction of the total grade level enrollment. This frequently produces serious difficulties and hard choices at the upper secondary level and even more serious difficulties at the university-level. At this point, the total population of the nation becomes very important. For example, a university level physics textbook serves a very specialized audience, but in a large nation such as Brazil or India, the total readership may still be large enough to justify locally produced texts; by contrast, a small nation may have no choice but to use imported texts.

Another factor affecting readership size is language of instruction. Clearly, the greater the number of languages in which books must be produced, the smaller the readership for any given language version, and the greater the cost per book. Small multilingual nations face very difficult choices from the early primary level on. But even large multilingual nations frequently find that at the secondary level, where enrollment ratios are low and the curriculum diversified, a switch to single-language publishing is the only economcially viable option.

The problems created by failing to consider readership size are illustrated by the case of Lesotho in the early 1970s. This nation's total population is under three million. The government set high quality specifications for textbooks that were published and manufactured by local private firms. Because of the small market and the high quality standards, the book prices were high, beyond what most parents in a poor nation could afford. Consequently, few school children had books. Dropout rates were high and enrollments declined. Moreover, because sales were low, the commercial publishers could not recover their costs. However, in Lesotho a subsequent textbook program, that has taken readership size into account, is successfully overcoming these problems.

Generally, for large (and/or more affluent) nations the constraints imposed by readership size less difficult. However, in some cases even very small and very poor nations have found imaginative ways to work within these constraints, such as pooling resources across national boundaries and adapting foreign texts. For example:

• Three small West African nations, Senegal, Cote d'lvoir, and Togo, share textbook publishing and printing costs. Their Nouvelle Editions Africains are used in all three nations.

• Several British Commonwealth nations have negotiated with an international publisher to provide history texts. The books for all of the nations contain a standard set of chapters dealing with international history, combined with chapters that deal with each nation's own particularly history. The resulting books are both locally relevant and low cost, even in very small markets.

• The small island states of the English-speaking Caribbean have combined efforts to produce economically manageable texts even in specialized subjects like home economics.

• Many small nations (Sierra Leone is an example) have successfully combined local development and production of general primary tests with adaptation of foreign tests for more specialized, small readership subjects at higher schooling levels.

2. A Basic Macroeconomic Decision: State vs. Private Sector

In all nations, government tends to intervene strongly in the textbook provision process. Even in the most market-oriented economies such as the United States and the nations of Western Europe, government, and government agencies (whether at the central, state/provincial, or local level) attempt to regulate and control textbook provision. In other words, in the area of textbook provision there is no such thing, empirically, as a wholly free market. Nations differ in the degree of state intervention, the locus of state intervention (i.e. centralization vs. decentralization), the mechanisms of state intervention, and the extent to which the state formally owns (directory or through para-statals) the various agencies of textbook production and distribution. The range of choices available to a nation regarding private and public sector participation is very wide. In her review of textbook provision programs assisted by the World Bank, Searle notes "the diversity of patterns in which alternatives are combined. This diversity is an important finding because the existence of such a variety of possibilities complicates the task of designing or modifying a book provision system".[7] Even more significantly, this diversity indicates that there are few predeterminable choices between private and public sector.

Table 2.2 notes the patterns of state and private sector participation in the preparation, printing, and distribution of primary tests in twenty-one nations represented at the seminar. There are ten distinct patterns among these twenty-one nations. The most common pattern (five nations) is a combination of state and private sector participation in all three stages. The next most common pattern (four cases) is exclusive state participation. In only one case was the private sector exclusively involved in all three stages, and here the government exercised considerable control through regulation of the private sector. These three patterns account for just under half (ten) of the twenty-one nations. The remainder are scattered across seven other patterns or combinations of state and private sector participation.

Clearly, the empirically viable policy questions have to do with the appropriate degree of, loci of, and mechanisms for state control or regulation in a given set of national circumstances. Thus understood, the question of the appropriate balance between state and private sector in textbook provision was a central theme of the seminar. No universally applicable pattern was sought for or found. Cases were

Table 2.2: State and/or Private Sector Participation in Three Stages of Primary School Textbook Provision Among Twenty-one Developing Nations

Preparation	Printing	Distribution	No. of Cases
State & Private	State & Private	State & Private	Five
State	State	State	Four
Private	Private	Private	One
State	State & Private	State & Private	One
State	State & Private	State	Two
State	State & Private	Private	One
State	Private	State	One
State & Private	Private	State	Three
State & Private	State & Private	State	Two
State & Private	Private	State & Private	One

Source: Country reports from seminar participants

examined where the state presence was overwhelming, either because a political-economic decision had been taken that disallowed the development of a private sector or because a private sector textbook enterprise was seen as non-viable. Where the two sectors coexist (as happens most frequently), there are many instances where a strong state presence has clearly inhibited the growth of the private sector. In many nations, the development of a viable local general publishing industry is dependent upon private sector access to the textbook market. However, there are other instances where strategically organized state intervention has assisted the development of the private sector. It was noted that private sector publishing is frequently cheaper than government publishing (although government publishing sometimes appears cheaper because accounting systems disguise some costs), but other cases were examined where government publishing was clearly the cheaper alternative. Again, one must judge in terms of the real alternatives available at a given time and place. In short, pedagogical and economic pragmatism should be the guide rather than ideological predisposition toward either the private or the public sector.

3. Local vs. International Publishing: To Protect or Not?

All nations insist upon state influence over school curricula and consequently upon textbook content. A natural extension of this normal public prerogative is often to asume that textbook design and manufacturing should be done by local firms.[8] The line of reasoning is similar to that for any other enterprise in which there is perceived to be a national interest--namely that local jobs are at stake; that a local enterprise has a comparative advantage; that local capacity (not currently extant) requires experience and therefore 'protection' in its infant stages; and that foreign contracts consume scarce foreign exchange. Such arguments are put forward in many domains of manufacturing and commerce, often with great passion. The nation's future "depends" on having these products manufactured locally; its culture and its pride are at stake, and so on.

It became clear during the seminar that local control is distinguishable from local ownership. Many nations have opted on economic grounds for off-shore publishing or printing of textbooks (indeed much of the manufacturing of both textbooks and general books for developed nations is done in developing nations) while maintaining a satisfactory degree of control over textbook content and design. Given such experience, the choice between local or international publishing and/or printing should be based upon economic analysis. In some cases, full origination or adaptation by an international firm is the most sensible alternative. In others, the use of local publishers and/or printers is either the economically most sensible approach or the only available alternative, especially where the language of instruction is unique to a nation. If the decision is taken to use local industry, the question of whether or not to "protect" that industry inevitably arises.

Protection can take many forms: taxes on foreign imports; incentives for local production like contractual advantages and so forth; subsidies such as use of government postal services for distribution; or outright prohibition of foreign products. If protection is required, it implies that local sources are not competitive with international sources. Whatever form protection may take, and however good the reason for it, protection has a monetary cost. The relevant questions are: How much is that cost? Who is asked to pay? Is the justification for the additional cost acceptable?

One other general principle needs mention: there is never enough money in an economy to accept all claims for protection simultaneously--those from manufacturing, agriculture, services, etc. If all claims for protection were to be accepted, it would bankrupt any economy. Consequently, when is protection justified in the production of textbooks in developing countries?

In addressing this question, countries are likely to find that the case for protecting local publishing is usually stronger than that for protecting local printing. In some countries, local printing is above international market costs because of the separate protection of local paper manufacturing industries. In these instances, the claims of the Ministry of Education for permission to use international printing can be pitted against the claims of the Ministry of Agriculture or of Industry in favor of local manufacturing. It doesn't matter which ministry causes the protection; what matters is the magnitude of its effect, namely, the increased cost of the textbooks. In other cases, particularly small economies, the purchase of international paper is in such small quanities and the cost of maintaining expensive equipment is so high compared to its level of utilization that a comparative advantage is unlikely vis-à-vis an international printer. Therefore the two procedures (publishing and printing) should always be analyzed separately for their costs and benefits.

Even local publishing is not always the most cost-effective. There are more Bahasa authors in Jakarta than in London, and so books in Bahasa are likely to be cheaper, as well as better, if published locally. But this is not inevitable. International publishers in London can also find good Bahasa authors, as can good local publishers in neighboring countries. And it is often an open question whether design and layout experts, also necessary for publishing, are at a comparative advantage simply because they are local.

There is also the question of subject matter. Certain subjects (such as science and math) "travel" better than others (such as local history or geography). Readership size is important. There is more likelihood of developing a local publishing capacity (and therefore more "infant industry" justification) with large readerships. Some nations such as India, Colombia, and Mexico have developed such a thriving publishing industry that books have become an export product. It would be in the interests of these developing countries to reduce protective barriers on the importation of international textbook manufacturing. To protect or not to protect is not simply a north/south issue.

The most problematic question is that of "cultural control", the assumption that to control content, the product must originate locally. It goes beyond the quality of appropriateness of the product itself in that international firms, whether in other developing countries or in industrialized countries, can be responsive to demands by curricular authorities. The product is declared unacceptable for political reasons. The question then becomes one of expediency. If the education budget is fixed or in decline, how much of a sacrifice are locally produce materials worth? If the unit cost of a textbook is increased by 30% is it worth 30% of the children not having access to a book?

4. The Advantages and Disadvantages of Copyright

While national and international copyright provisions are an essential incentive to the production and dissemination of knowledge, they are viewed by many people in developing nations as symbols of existing international inequalities and as impediments to their acquisiton of knowledge. It was observed that national attitudes toward copyright change over time: as nations develop their own publishing industry, they tend to view copyright provisions more favorably. Empirically, the number of nations who do not belong to an international copyright convention is decreasing, but at the same time "piracy" of books is increasing, that is fewer nations engage in piracy but they are doing so on a greater scale. International copyright law is extremely complex. In any international negotiations about textbook provision, developing nations should acquire specialized legal advice.

5. *Who Pays?*

In most developed and many developing nations, it is assumed without question that textbooks should be provided free to students. However, it was discovered that in many nations (including, to the surprise of many at the seminar, China) students or their parents are expected to pay for their books and that, in some countries, even very poor parents are willing to pay at least a small sum for textbooks. Indeed, in some nations a revolving fund or student fee payment is the only possible way to finance a sustainable textbook provision system. Experience with revolving funds has been mixed: some appear to be working well, others have failed. Investigation of the conditions necessary for success is warranted. However, the question of equity remains: what does one do about children whose families are so desperately poor that they cannot afford even a very modest book fee? Partial subsidization may be appropriate. Thus, some nations successfully operate combined systems, selling or renting books in wealthier areas and providing them free in poorer regions.

6. *The Politics of Textbook Content*

Educators tend to regard their work as apolitical. This is far from the truth. Decisions about curricular content, and therefore textbook content, frequently reflect deep-rooted political conflicts within a nation. In relatively open political systems, textbook content often represents delicate compromises among groups with different ideological positions or different religious beliefs and practices or different ethnic and tribal backgrounds. The experience in the United States, that was examined in the seminar, documents the pedagogical and economic difficulties this can create even in a very rich nation. Inappropriate or insensitive decisions can provoke political conflict or lead to rejection of textbooks by some groups. In one-party states, textbook content is usually carefully shaped to reflect the prevailing ideology. In such cases, sudden political shifts or regime changes can render suddenly obsolete a large part of a nation's stock of textbooks, requiring massive and expensive rewriting and production.

7. Potential Conflicts Between Curriculum Developers and Textbook Publishers

While curriculum development and textbook publishing are distinct enterprises, there is a general need for closer collaboration between them. Those responsible for curriculum development often have little idea of the cost of implications of the specifications that they develop for textbooks and other teaching materials. Instances can be found where the formal specifications for types and quantities of texts, exercise books, etc. are way beyond what the nation could possible afford. Frequently, specifications are laid down for book length, paper quality, book size, and type and quantity of illustrations that greatly magnify the cost of producing the textbooks or that require technology unavailable locally. Early and continuous collaboration between curriculum developers and textbook publishers is required to produce books that are both pedagogically sound and economically afforable.

8. Paper Supply

Contrary to what was believed a few years ago, there is no worldwide shortage of paper, nor does it appear likely that one will develop. Compared to prices for other products, cultural (book quality) paper prices over the past several years have tended to remain stable or decrease slightly. Nonetheless, developing nations frequently pay more for paper than is charged to customers in developed nations, even after differences in shipping costs are taken into account; furthermore, there are times when certain types of paper are very difficult to find on the international market. Careful planning of paper acquisition could result in significant cost savings and so help to reduce book prices. Particularly important is to buy in large lots. Some experiments are underway with "paper buyers' clubs" to realize the savings that arise from bulk buying. However, savings from such buying can sometimes be squandered by increased warehousing costs or by losses due to improper warehousing. In some nations, local paper production has proven to be an economically viable alternative, but in a few cases it has resulted in prices higher than those on the international market. Developed nations may be able to play a useful role in assisting with paper acquisiton by jointly establishing some form of "Paper Bank," perhaps along the lines of the Paper Supply Project financed by Canadian International Development Agency in Canada.

9. Textbooks as Part of a Package of Interventions

Although an adequate supply of textbooks is essential for effective learning, simply placing books in schools will have little effect if teachers have not been trained how to use them and if there is a shortage of other ancillary learning materials (workbooks, exercise books, pencils, chalk). An effective textbook provision system must take into account all of the elements of a total instruction package. Beyond this, it is clear that if children learn to read effectively in school but have nothing to read when they leave school, literacy will soon decline; consequently, the investment in textbooks, and indeed much of the total national investment in education, will be lost. Textbook provision programs should be conceived as part of an overall "reading materials development strategy." In the words of a spokesperson from one of the nations which has successfully pursued such an overall strategy: "We have created a nation of readers." Those responsible for textbook provision systems should never lose sight of the fact that "a nation of readers" is the ultimate goal.

Summary

Coupled with population growth and with expanding educational opportunity, the decline in national financial resources has had a double impact on the classroom. Student numbers are increasing at a time when per-student resources are declining. Salaries of teachers and other educational personnel, while not lavish, are often the only part of the education budget being maintained. Decline in student resources is particularly evident in the nonsalary budget categories; that in other words, just those ingredients have proven to be most effective in the achievement of learning objectives. The availability of reading materials is the single most consistent correlate of academic achievement, and yet the availability of reading materials appears to be the category of the educational budget most at risk. So what is to be done?

In any such fiscal or management crisis, there are basically two options. One is to generate additonal resources by instituting savings elsewhere. Since increases in national revenues are unlikely and the reordering of intersectoral priorities tends to be idiosyncratic, perhaps savings can be found within current educational allocations. Can they be found within educational salaries? Can parents or communities finance a higher proportion of the revenue? Can the curriculum be narrowed down so that it includes only the most important subject? Can the time in school be reduced or the class size increased? These are possibilities.

The other option is to seek savings within the budget category at risk. To do this requires an analysis of the way in which textbooks are conceived, developed, manufactured, and distributed. It requires that previously held assumptions--for example, about the appropriate role of the public or private sector--be questioned if other alternatives are less costly. It requires questioning whether local production is a necessity and whether reading materials should be distributed free. It requires that all phases of the process be open to scrutiny and professional debate.

Before such questioning occurs, agreement needs to be reached on the normal objectives of the textbook enterprise--namely, that all students should have access to effective materials, delivered on time, at an affordable cost, and (as far as possible), locally developed. But there are trade-offs within these objectives, and their implications need to be clarified.

The point is that developing countries have a scarcity of reading materials not only because of the current economic crisis but also because current policies toward textbook development are not always the most cost efficient. Although improvements can be made in developing and developed countries alike, solutions to the educational quality crisis in developing countries cannot be restricted to seeking resources from outside. Solutions must come from within us as well as from without. This chapter has explored some of the areas of textbook policy that require examination in the light of this crisis.

NOTES

1. See Stephen P. Heyneman, Joseph P. Farrell, and M. Sepulveda-Stuardo, Textbooks and Achievement: What We Know. World Bank Staff Working Paper No. 298. Washington, DC: The World Bank, 1978; and Stephen P. Heyneman and Dean Jamieson, "Student Learning in Uganda: Textbook Availability and Other Factors," Comparative Education Review 24(No. 3, 1980), pp. 206-220.

2. Barbara Searle, "General Operational Review of Textbooks," Washington, DC: The World Bank, Education and Training Department, Operations Policy Program Unit, 1984, p. 3.

3. Philip G. Altbach, "Key Issues of Textbook Provision in the Third World," Prospects 13(No 3, 1983), p. 316.

4. Searle, op. cit.

5. Douglas Pearce, Textbook Production in Developing Countries: Some Problems of Preparation, Production and Distribution, (Paris: Unesco, 1982), pp. 20-21.

6. Datus Smith, Jr., The Economics of Book Publishing in Developing Countries, (Paris: Unesco, 1977), pp. 7-8.

7. Searle, op. cit., p. 11.

8. Although they are related, the issue of whether publishing or printing should be local or international is separate from whether they should be public or private. Here we are referring only to the decision on whether to protect a local private industry. This assumes that the public sector has already made the decision not to monopolize, and that local private enterprises exist.

APPENDIX A

Nations Represented at the Seminar

Brazil
China
Colombia
Ethiopia
Ghana
Guatemala
Honduras
Kenya
Lesotho
Malawi
Nigeria
Papua New Guinea
Peru
Philippines
Portugal
Sierra Leone
Somalia
Syria
Tanzania
Turkey
Uganda
Yeman Arab Republic

CHAPTER 3

TEXTBOOKS IN THIRD WORLD HIGHER EDUCATION

Philip G. Altbach and S. Gopinathan

Introduction

Textbooks are central to the curriculum in higher education, just as they are integral to education at the primary and secondary levels. Virtually every course, especially at the undergraduate level, uses one or more texts. Along with the input of the instructor, the texts are crucial to learning. Introductory textbooks, particularly, help to define a field for the students. While a textbook often does not reflect original research, it is one of the major means of synthesizing a field of study, of codifying knowledge in a field. Creative textbooks can sometimes shape scholarship and even move a discipline in a new direction. The worldwide influence of Paul Samuelson's economics textbooks is but one example.[1] Where well stocked libraries are unavailable to undergraduate students, as is often the case in Third World higher education systems, the text becomes the most important--and sometimes the only--reading material used by the student. Textbooks are universal, they are influential, and they constitute a key element of the educational experience of every student.

Yet, in comparison with other aspects in the educational process such as curriculum, very little attention is paid to textbooks. It is often assumed that once the curriculum is created textbooks will magically appear. In countries where there is a well developed academic and publishing infrastructure, textbooks are published and the marketplace works to select a few dominant texts in particular subject areas. However, in the Third World, the provision of textbooks in higher education continues to be a serious problem, one generally ignored by planners and teachers alike until a crisis occurs. There has been minimal research on the preparation, publication, and distribution of textbooks for higher education in any country, industrialized or Third World. This is surprising given the fiscal and substantive importance of texts. It is the purpose of this chapter to shed light on some of the many aspects of textbook development and use in higher education, focusing mainly on the Third World. This is a pioneering venture in that we deal with the role of the textbook in the broader context of the higher education enterprise, and seek to point out the many and complex ramifications of textbook preparation and publication. In a sense, this is a broad discussion of a crucial, yet heretofore neglected, aspect of postsecondary education.

Though there are many similarities in the writing, manufacture, and dissemination of textbooks at the elementary, secondary, and university levels it is vital that we recognize, at the outset, differences between them.

For example, higher education in the Third World is for the most academically able, those destined to be the intellectual elite of the nation. Their teachers are an even rarer group, often the best qualified in the nation, and in the social science areas and in some areas of the sciences and humanities, capable of making, if not original contributions, at least critiquing received wisdom. Often they have had the advantage of travel and training abroad, a sharpened awareness of standards and rigor, and knowledge of changes and trends in their discipline, at least more so than school teachers. Thus it may be argued that the way they view knowledge and its transmission is considerably different from the way elementary and secondary school teachers view it.

The function of knowledge from a university perspective needs to be clearly understood before we can grasp the significance of university level texts. Review and critique of the material are likely to be as important as transmission. A university's commitment to research, nominal though it may be in some institutions, nevertheless exerts a strong symbolic influence. The individual lecturer is encouraged to (and often does) supplement basic texts with his own notes as a way of introducing new research. Indeed, students in undertaking experiments, assignments, and projects are reflecting a model of research activity. Further, in countries with strong anti-colonial traditions there is often pressure to produce nation-centric materials in history, economics, sociology, and literature and other courses. There is much less of this sort of effort at the school level.

It is necessary to analyze the current status of university texts to see if they indeed meet the needs of their audience. In many Third

World universities the enrollment is large and academic requirements, at least at the undergraduate level, are often low. The quality of institutions varies with private and some key state universities, leading the pack. Academic salaries are low, with little incentive for research and publication. Paradoxically, textbook writing can flourish in such an environment, as an incentive to make money or to overcome the limitations of poor libraries, but obviously quality is often the victim. In these circumstances, where mastery of content is the main goal of students, textbooks become both vital and limiting.

Despite these problems, qualitative improvements have been made. The development of postgraduate training, at home and abroad, has resulted in the accumulation of theses and dissertations, especially in the social sciences. In turn this has led to the systematic introduction of indigenous scholarship into the universities. This scholarship contributes to the best postsecondary publishing. True, these books are often beyond the grasp of undergraduate intellect, but they provide to the faculty necessary data and analysis. It is this accumulation of knowledge via research that makes the later writing of standard textbooks possible.

We are likely to see many similarities in any discussion of textbooks in a comparative framework. There are common issues of development, articulation with the curriculum, the economics of publishing and the like. Yet, each nation has its own set of special circumstances. In the centrally planned economies of Eastern Europe and the Soviet Union, for example, all publishing is done by the state, and there the philosophy of publishing and books is distinctive.[2] In the United States, all textbooks are published by private sector firms, and most decisions on postsecondary textbook use are made by individual instructors, thus making for a highly decentralized and complex system. As noted above, in most countries, there are significant variations between most aspects of textbooks at the primary and secondary level and higher education. Even in countries where school books are produced by the state and are tightly controlled in terms of preparation and production, the publishing of higher education texts is often less centralized. There is typically more autonomy in the production of postsecondary textbooks than is the case for schoolbooks.

What is a Postsecondary Textbook?

The need for books in universities and other postsecondary educational institutions is complex and particularly difficult for Third World nations to fulfill. Textbooks are more difficult to define at this level than they are for schools. In many subjects, texts are prescribed for specific use in class as the key source of information in addition to the lectures given by the professor. For such traditional uses, textbooks can be prepared for specific academic levels in ways not dissimilar to the preparation of books developed for schools.

However, university-level texts are more often selected on an institutional rather than a national basis, and traditionally the individual teacher or the academic instituion exercises more control over the content and orientation of instruction than is the case for schools. Postsecondary textbooks typically pay more attention to the subject matter than to pedagogical approaches and thus are more often content oriented than school texts. Postsecondary texts are also more frequently written by individual scholars than is the case for school texts although there is a trend, in countries such as the United States, toward committee-written "managed texts." In addition to the traditional postsecondary textbook, there are many other types of materials that students use in postsecondary education. Reference books of all kinds are crucial to higher education, and these are frequently an integral part of a course of study. Supplementary textbooks, particularly in more advanced subjects, are common. These books provide important additional information to students and are frequently chosen by the individual instructor based on his or her evaluation of student needs and the adequacy of the basic text. In many countries, students use "guides" or informal supplementary books to help in passing examinations. These publications, called "cram books" in the United States, are not sanctioned by the educational institutions but are frequently an important part of the learning process. As in the schools, postsecondary students in some fields also use workbooks and other "disposable" printed matter in some of their classes. These books need also to be considered as part of the textbook equation.

Textbooks in the Third World: Special Problems and Key Issues

The developing countries of the Third World differ greatly in terms of their ability to produce textbooks. Some nations, for example, have highly developed private sector publishing enterprises which have little difficulty producing appropriate books for colleges and universities. India, the Philippines, Korea, Taiwan, Mexico, and Argentina are examples of Third World nations with a considerable capacity for higher education textbook production. In these countries production is left largely to the private sector. Some other countries have a mix of public and private sector publishers involved in textbook development, while in still other nations, such as China, book production is done almost entirely by the state. Countries with large university systems typically have an easier time producing textbooks because of a significant and potentially profitable internal market. On the other hand, nations with small populations almost inevitably have to import textbooks, particularly in specialized subjects. A large academic system also means that there is likely to be a sufficient number of potential textbook authors available.

Despite these, and other differences, there are some important common elements among Third World nations, and thus a broad discussion of Third World text problems and developments is relevant. First of all, it is probably the case that university-level textbooks are even more important in the Third World than they are in industrialized nations. In the Third World, the basic infrastructures of higher education are typically less well organized than in the industrialized nations, and the universities are typically under considerable pressure. Library resources are frequently very limited, or even nonexistent, and access to libraries for undergraduate students may be a particular problem. Relevant and up-to-date journals and data bases are very rare indeed. In many countries, laboratories for science courses are rudimentary and supplies difficult to obtain. Where higher education has expanded rapidly and where opportunities for postbaccalaureate study are limited, it is likely that qualified instructors will be in short supply; this is common in many Third World nations.

In these conditions of scarcity, textbooks take on an even more important role. They are frequently the main reading material available to students, providing both organization and substance to the curriculum. In some respects, the textbook may be the basic curriculum. The bulk of the information obtained by the student may well be from the textbook, and the instructor may use the book to structure the course. In academic systems that are very examination oriented, test questions may be taken from available textbooks. There is frequently a strong relationship between examinations and texts.

State vs. Private Sector Publishing

A number of issues are commonly raised in discussions concerning postsecondary textbooks. These issues are crucial to any textbook industry and thus need discussion.[3] The question of who is to publish textbooks is a controversial one in many Third World countries for the issues have many ramifications. There is, first of all on the part of the state, a distrust of the private sector and a feeling that undue profits are being made on textbooks. Increasingly, school textbook publishing is going into the hands of government agencies throughout the Third World, and many argue that postsecondary books should also be published by public agencies; a secondary motive for government involvement at this level is the belief that without government direction little improvements will be made to textbook shortage problems. In some countries, public or parastatal agencies have a role in higher education text publishing. In Malaysia, for example, the Dewan Bahasa dan Pustaka (Language and Literature Agency) played a leading role in ensuring that college texts were available in the national language, Bahasa Malaysia, when English was dropped as the medium of instruction in the universities.[4] At present, both the Dewan and private sector publishers, including several multinational firms like Heinemann and Oxford University Press, are involved in textbook publishing. In Nigeria and Ghana, experiments with parastatal publishers have been attempted in which new publishers with elements of state control and with significant funding from the government have been set up with varying degrees of success.[5] In centrally planned countries such as Cuba, Vietnam and China, all publishing is in the hands of the state.

Historically, the multinational firms have played a key role in postsecondary text publishing in the Third World. Not only have they pioneered the publication of scholarly books (frequently from theses and dissertations) but they have had a direct role in textbook publishing. The multinationals have imported books, both scholarly and text, from the metropole and this has been a mainstay of their business. They have, in recent years, published many textbooks in the Third World, sometimes as in West Africa, seeking to serve a regional market. In some Third World countries, the multinationals remain a major or even a dominating force in the production of postsecondary textbooks. Their entrenched position in the import and export of books, in their very considerable expertise in publishing, and frequently in their market share has given the multinationals a considerable advantage.[6] Many in the Third World have argued that it is necessary to dislodge the multinationals in order to prevent foreign control over an important "cultural industry" and to encourage indigenous publishers.

Indigenous publishers have to contend with government publishing as well. Indeed, in the Third World, texts, which constitute the bulk of local publishing, have become the mainstay of the new publishers. In many countries as government agencies have tried, not always successfully, to provide cheaper and more relevant textbooks for primary and secondary schools, this major market share has been taken away from private sector publishers. Frequently, the higher education market, which is more varied, smaller, and more difficult to control, was left to the private sector publishers. At present, there is a mix of public, foreign, and private input into the postsecondary text market in much of the Third World. In countries where governments have moved into text publishing, they have deprived the private sector firms of their one remaining predictable and relatively lucrative sector of the market. This makes it even more difficult for private sector firms to publish trade books, scientific volumes, and journals. However, in some countries with small postsecondary markets and with weak private-sector publishing industries, government initiatives have proved necessary. In a few instances, the universities themselves have gone into the textbook publishing business in order to produce books needed by their own students.[7] It can be seen that the simple question of "who should be responsible for postsecondary textbooks?" is in itself a complex one, with ramifications that extend beyond the specific concerns of textbook publishing.

Foreign Books vs. Indigenous Materials

The use of foreign books has also been a perplexing question in the Third World. In those Third World nations formerly under colonial domination, the large majority of the books used in primary and secondary schools and in higher education were from abroad, typically from the colonial power, whose publishers controlled the book trade and often reaped considerable profits from sales of books in the colonies. Countries like Ghana, Nigeria, Kenya, India, Singapore, and Malaysia were jewels in the British publishing crown. Even in non-colonized countries such as Thailand and Japan, many foreign books, often in translation, were used in higher education. The contemporary role of books produced overseas has become controversial. Textbooks produced in the metropolitan nations (especially Britain, the United States, and France) are readily available and they can immediately fulfill curricular needs in rapidly expanding Third World university systems. In some fields, notably mathematics and the "hard" sciences, many would argue that the origin of textbooks does not make much difference since the content of knowledge is universal. Others point out that the use of local examples and, in the life sciences, data from the immediate region is important and that such material is not generally included in books produced in the industrialized nations.

Educators have commented on the lack of direct relevance of books that were designed for another educational system and for countries at very different levels of economic and political development. The underlying assumptions of texts produced in the industrialized nations may be quite different than the prevailing perspectives in the Third World on methodological or political issues. There is universal agreement that the problems of using foreign textbooks in the social sciences and history is much more problematical than in the natural sciences. Foreign books are generally significantly more expensive to purchase than locally produced volumes and the expenditure must be made in scarce foreign exchange. They also deprive the domestic book industry of a lucrative and important market.

It seems quite clear that in fields requiring a large number of books, such as the basic sciences, the development of locally produced books in most markets would be both economically and pedagogically viable. However, in smaller academic fields needing only a limited number of books with a high level of specialization, it is quite possible that the continued use of imported books may be both cost effective and educationally justified. It should also be possible for one Third World country to use textbooks from other Third World nations, either directly imported or in adapted formats. Countries such as India and Mexico produce large numbers of texts for higher education and it is possible that the content and perspectives of these books might be relevant for other Third World nations. In the case of India, the books are also significantly cheaper than books from the industralized nations. With few exceptions, primary and secondary texts are now locally developed and printed. There is a trend in this direction for postsecondary texts as well, but there are still many texts in a large number of Third World nations which are imported. Given high costs for developing indigenous text, it is likely that imported books will continue to play an important role.

The Role of Overseas Assistance Programs

An additional factor in this debate is the role of overseas assistance programs in book exports and development. Virtually all of the major industrialized nations have book aid policies and typically the largest segment of such programs relate to university-level textbooks.[8] In the past several decades, the United States, the Soviet Union, Britain, and France have had the largest programs. There are several different models for textbook assistance. The British, through the English Language Book Scheme (ELBS) print books in Britain specially earmarked for sale at discount prices overseas. Hundreds of titles of standard British textbooks have been distributed through the ELBS. The American aid programs frequently reprinted American textbooks in English in the Third World countries involved or, in some instances, translated the books into local languages. These books were sold at greatly discounted prices. Another American program saw subsidiaries of American publishers reprint their texts in Hong Kong or Japan for sale at subsidized prices in the Third World. The Soviet Union typically translated standard Soviet texts into a variety of Western and Third World languages, printed the books in the USSR and sold them at subsidized prices in the Third World. Hundreds of titles and millions of copies of texts have been distributed in the Third World through these aid programs. While Third World nations have often welcomed book aid as a means of quickly providing inexpensive books to rapidly expanding higher education systems, there has recently been much criticism of the programs. Third World publishers have claimed that the foreign books undercut their own publications and actually hinder the emergence of domestic textbooks. Some educators have criticized the inevitable orientation toward the industrialized nations found in the books and have commented on their lack of relevance to local conditions.[9] It is clear that foreign involvement in Third World university textbooks, through the operation of the multinational publishers or through book assistance programs, has been a powerful influence over the years and remains a matter of considerable importance and controversy.

The Language Issue

Related to the use of foreign books is the highly complex language question. Textbooks do not create a language policy, they reflect decisions made about language by governments or educators. However, language issues impinge on the development and provision of textbooks in significant ways. In most formerly colonized areas, the medium of instruction in higher education was the language of the colonial power, and in many Third World countries, notably in Africa, the metropolitan language continues to be used. Where a European language is used in higher education, textbooks can be imported from industrialized nations using the language and the direct problems of textbook production are not very serious. However, as we noted earlier, reliance on imported books has its limitations. The imported books typically do not reflect the situation in the Third World, the examples may be irrelevant, and the level of presentation is linked to the pedagogical considerations of the country in which the book was published. Thus, while obtaining a postsecondary textbook in virtually any field is possible when a European language is used, the suitability of the book for the Third World is very much in question.

Several countries have attempted to overcome the language problem through translation but only Japan has succeeded. Typically, the problem has been one of finding competent translators and in completing translations in time to keep up with rapid developments in the field. In countries like Malaysia, where the language of translation is relatively underdeveloped, this has proved to be an additional problem. Malaysia's Dewan Bahasa has all but abandoned translation as a viable means of producing suitable manuscripts, opting instead to persuade authors to write original texts in the national language. Though taxing and not without problems there is a chance that a relatively original work will be produced.

A special problem faced by publishers of university textbooks in the indigenous languages is the relative underdevelopment of the language, especially in the scientific and technical fields.[10] This is a problem that affects languages as developed as Hindi as well as relatively underdeveloped languages like Bahasa Malaysia. India established a Commission for Scientific and Technical Terminologies that has evolved terminology in major scientific areas. CSTT has so far published 31 definitional dictionaries containing over 45,000 definitions. Without this massive effort India would not have been able to do as much as it has already done with postsecondary textbook publishing.[11]

If there is a necessity to publish textbooks in local languages, then problems are significantly magnified. As noted earlier, the development and publication of an indigenous textbook is a long and expensive effort. In many instances, experienced academics are more used to working in a European language than in their own, and this creates further difficulties. Providing appropriate remuneration to textbook writers in local languages is also a problem, since in many cases the audience for the books is fairly small (relative to the school textbook market) and funds to pay royalties are scarce. Countries, such as Malaysia and Indonesia, which have shifted to indigenous languages for higher education, have found the provision of textbooks one of the most difficult challenges in making the transition. When the decision is made to use indigenous languages for higher education, it is almost always necessary to provide funds for textbook development and publication. And even where the language of higher education has been local for a long period of time, such as in the Middle East or Indonesia, students at advanced levels continue to use books in Western languages in order to have access to complex information and to keep abreast of current developments. In some faculties, the language of instruction is Western, often in part because of the lack of text and research materials in local languages. In a number of Arabic-speaking universities, faculties in engineering, science, and medicine often operate in English.

For the minor Third World languages, including many in Africa, it is unlikely that textbooks in any but the most basic courses at the postsecondary level can be provided in local languages. For major languages, such as Swahili, Indonesian, or most of the languages of the Indian subcontinent, the provision of postsecondary texts for most undergraduate specialities is not an impossible task. Spanish and Portuguese, widely used Third World languages, are in the fortunate position of being able to easily utilize materials from a number of countries. While most would agree that the use of indigenous languages at all levels of education is important and that the worldwide trend is in this direction, it is nonetheless inevitable that in terms of advanced textbooks and scholarly and research materials, virtually all Third World nations will continue to be dependent on writings in the major Western languages produced in the industrialized nations. In addition, for Third World writings to be recognized internationally, they will have to be translated into Western languages.

Infrastructural Problems

Those concerned with planning higher education in the Third World frequently do not consider the problems of textbook development and publication. The practical issues involved are considerable. It is necessary to possess a viable publishing industry if textbooks are to be effectively produced. It is also necessary to have adequate distribution mechanisms, sufficient paper, and a cadre of writers. The basic infrastructures of publishing are crucial. It has often been said that a publisher is simply a coordinator of the activities of others, and there is a good deal of truth to this statement. However, the other elements of the publishing equation must be present to coordinate. In most of the Third World, printing facilities are now available although equipment may not be modern. Basic printing presses and the expertise to use them are required. A particular problem for text printing in indigenous languages is that printing facilities in these languages may be scarce even if capacity in Western languages is available. Adequate supplies of paper are sometimes a problem. Specific kinds and qualities of papers are frequently needed for textbooks, and these are frequently in short supply. Further, paper, especially when imported, is expensive and it constitutes a much higher proportion of the cost of a book in the Third World than it does in industrialized nations. Paper is a basic element of the infrastructure of publishing, and one that is frequently overlooked by planners. Sometimes printing presses that are suitable for newspapers or for general business printing are inadequate for textbooks, particularly if the texts require large printings.

The coordination functions provided by publishers are very frequently in short supply. This is a special problem when textbook development is taken over by government agencies that have little experience in publishing. It is seldom recognized that the process of book publishing is highly complex. Publishing enterprises not only need skilled editors, but also book designers, copy editors, production managers and the like. These skills are usually in short supply in the Third World. Skilled personnel are necessary not only to ensure that a book is able to proceed through the process from manuscript to printed volume but also to ensure that costs are controlled, that the book is published in the shortest possible time, and that the presentation of the material is of the highest possible quality given the constraints of cost and the available facilities. Book publishing does not necessarily require the most modern equipment, but it is a complicated process that does require a high level of skill and coordination. Some countries lack the skilled personnel necessary in publishing while others do not utilize the publishing skills available in the private sector. Without question, the skills of publishing personnel are one of the most important parts of the infrastructure of book publishing.

A final element of the infrastructure is book distribution. It has been said that distribution is the weakest element of Third World publishing. In order to get postsecondary textbooks from the publisher to the intended users, a distribution mechanism is needed. Textbook distribution is an easier task than general book distribution because the approximate market for texts is known and it is possible to target the places where the books will be needed, but there must be an established mechanism for distribution. In most Third World nations, students purchase their own books, and thus commercial factors are involved in book distribution. Also, the distribution of books is inadequate and so it is often quite difficult to ensure that higher education texts will reach their intended readers on time.

Bypassing the commercial distribution channels for textbooks at the postsecondary level has generally not been successful. It is possible to set up "cooperative bookstores" at a college or university and sometimes these are quite successful, but it is seldom possible for academic institutions or government agencies themselves to successfully deal with textbook distribution.

Thus, even if textbooks can be written, it is necessary to have in place the appropriate infrastructures of publishing if the manuscript is to be turned into a book. Those responsible for textbook development frequently ignore the complex set of skills and mechanisms needed to produce a book. Physical equipment like presses, supplies such as paper, and the skills of publishing personnel are all mandatory. In addition, a distribution apparatus is also needed. In many Third World nations, private sector publishers or multinational firms have the basic skills needed for` publishing, and they can participate in textbook development. Government agencies frequently lack the necessary skills and equipment, yet they are increasingly involved in text production and distribution. Clearly, an assessment of facilities, skills, and agencies needs to be made so that the infrastructures can be as effectively mobilized as possible.

Promoting Authorship

The author is the key element of text development at the postsecondary level. As we noted earlier, Third World academic authors work under difficult conditions. In general they work part-time on their writing, often burdened with heavy teaching loads, out dated syllabi and an examination-dominated system. Frequently, textbook writing is seen by their peers and university administrators as not quite respectable--research-based articles or monographs are considered to have higher prestige. Library resources are often limited and access to the most current literature in a field is a particular problem. Third World authors seldom have appropriate research or secretarial help, and it is unusual for publishers or academic institutions to provide assistance or funding for textbook writing. Thus, Third World textbooks are often well behind scientific developments worldwide.

It is often difficult to convince the top scholars in a field to write textbooks because of the low prestige attached to them. Yet, there is hardly a more important academic task than writing needed textbooks for key fields. In most countries, textbook writers come from the ranks of professors who are able to write and have a desire to contribute to their fields--and also want to earn extra income. Third World textbook authors frequently adapt their writings from books published in the West. This means that the basic orientations to a field and sometimes ideological assumptions and methodologies are taken from foreign models. The specific examples are usually from the local situation and this is important in terms of making a field relevant to students in the respective country. When authors are writing textbooks in indigenous languages, adaptation is perhaps even more common. This strategy, which makes books available faster, also decreases the originality of many Third World textbooks.

The author stands at the center of the textbook equation. If the author is not at the top of his or her field, and does not have the ability to present material--and ideas--clearly, then the text will not be of top quality and the loss to the academic system is considerable. Clearly, the need for the preparation of textbooks is not given a high priority in the academic hierarchy; what suffers is the quality of education available.

Postsecondary textbooks constitute a specialized kind of writing and of publishing. They must, therefore, be seen as distinct from general or scholarly publishing. The process of generating textbooks is unique, as is the means of selecting books. A textbook author may differ from a scholarly book author in that he or she may not be a researcher. There are particular skills needed for writing a textbook such as clarity in writing style, the ability to synthesize a subject and to bring together the work of others, and a concern with the relationships between the book and the broader aspects of the educational enterprise.

Case Studies in Textbook Development

It is useful to look in some detail at the experience of two Third World countries in developing postsecondary textbooks. Our purpose here is to indicate some of the various approaches to textbook production and distribution and not to provide a complete analysis of all approaches.

India, with the world's third largest higher education system, has considerable experience in postsecondary textbook publishing and possesses a successful indigenous textbook publishing industry. Books are produced in English and a dozen or more Indian languages that are used in higher education in various parts of the country. As noted earlier, Indian textbooks are used in other Third World nations, and thus reach an international market. Although the publication of textbooks for primary and many secondary schools has increasingly been taken over by government agencies, most postsecondary textbook publishing remains in the hands of the private sector.[12]

In general, the Indian universities develop their own syllabi; textbook authors and publishers compete for "recognition" by selection committees in the universities. Since the Indian universities are institutions that "affiliate" up to 150 colleges and some have more than 100,000 students, the book market for these institutions is considerable–India has more than 3 million university students. While there is little overt coordination among the universities, the syllabi in many fields are similar and thus some textbooks have a national market or at least a regional language market. Typically, a selection committee will authorize the use of several books in a particular field, depending on whether the books deal with the particular topics covered in the syllabi and whether they fit in with the university-wide examination system. Publishers are free to develop books that they feel will meet the needs of the universities. Authors will frequently approach publishers with ideas for textbooks, and a textbook author can earn large sums from a successful text. The publishers typically pay higher royalties on texts than on general books, often up to 25% royalties on the list price of the book, especially for books in English and in Hindi, the two major languages of higher education.

There are several important variations on this private enterprise theme. For a number of years, the foreign aid agencies of the major powers have published university level textbook titles for India. Since the early sixties the United Kingdom has subsidized the publication of 720 titles, the United States 1,620 and the Soviet Union about 400 titles. In some instances these books were translated into Indian languages, but they were mostly published in English. The foreign aid programs provided India with needed books, particularly during the early years of the expansion of higher education, but the programs also had some negative implications for the development of local publishing capacity.

Government initiatives also have been a part of the textbook scene in India, particularly as there has been criticism of foreign programs and as higher education has slowly shifted from English to the various Indian languages as the main languages of instruction. With government encouragement, a number of the Indian states have moved to provide texts in their state languages, and the central government has also participated financially in programs to provide Indian language translations of English university textbooks. The central government has provided funds to each of the Indian states for textbook development; as early as 1970, ten million rupees was given to each state to assist them in the production of university-level books in the regional languages. According to J.C. Sharma, the scheme is implemented through Book Production Boards set up by the state governments. Through December 1986 some 7,600 books (1,950 in Hindi and 5,650 in other Indian languages) had been published in about

30 subjects by State Granth Akademies or Text book boards, covering basic and applied sciences, social sciences, and humanities. For the most part, government efforts have at least been partially funneled to the private sector, which handles most of the actual publishing.[13]

The government has also taken several other steps to assist both parastatal and private sector publishers to make university-level texts more readily available. It has in particular recognized the problem of persuading good academics to write college textbooks. The University Grants Commission, for instance, attempts to promote indigenous authorship through offers of fellowships for the preparation of manuscripts on approved subjects by university lecturers. The government has also recognized that in some core discipline areas, medicine for example, it would be preferable to have a number of core texts published and it has commissioned the National Book Trust to prepare a number of them. The National Book Trust has also been implementing a scheme to subsidize university level books since 1970 and 756 titles have been subsidized to date.

At the upper levels of the university system, India still relies on books from abroad. In the sciences, most of the volumes used by researchers are Western books in English. Postgraduate students typically use Western books, but in the social sciences, and especially history, India is close to being self-sufficient at all levels, including advanced research monographs.

With its large internal market and its well established indigenous publishing industry, India has achieved a high level of self-sufficiency in the production of postsecondary textbooks. India has the necessary infrastructures--printing capacity, paper production (although there is also a good deal of imported paper and prices are quite high), and a substantial number of authors able to write textbooks in virtually all fields of study. Some of the Indian languages still suffer from a lack of titles in key academic fields, with particularly acute problems in languages like Assamese and Sindhi. And Indian textbooks often tend to be derivative of Western volumes. Nevertheless, after more than a quarter century of publishing development, India has built up an impressive textbook industry to service the tertiary sector.

Malaysia can be contrasted with India. It is a much smaller country (15 million population) with a much smaller internal market and with only about 40,000 students in post-secondary education. In addition, the expansion of its higher education system began only in the 1960s, and this growth encountered a number of problems, including a severe shortage of textbooks in most disciplines. Added to the complexity was the decision, in 1960, to shift the language of education from English to Bahasa Malaysia, a language in which virtually no scientific books had been written. Strained political relations with Indonesia, which uses the same basic language, meant that Indonesian books were not welcome in Malaysia. Until the shift to Bahasa Malaysia, most of the textbooks used in higher education were imported from abroad--mostly from England and the United States. A much smaller number were written by local authors (Malaysian or Singaporean) and published in the region in English, typically by one of the multinational firms active in the area; in some instances local books published as scholarly monographs became university texts. A good example of this is K. J. Retnam's Communalism and the Political Process in Malaysia, first submitted for a Ph.D. to the University of London, and one of the first scholarly books to be published by the University of Malaya Press in 1965. With a small academic system and the use of substantial numbers of expatriate professors, the market for locally produced texts was small and the potential pool of local authors very limited.

When English was replaced, the textbook equation changed dramatically. It was no longer possible to simply import books from abroad. Local books had to be provided. One of the key problems of Malaysian higher education now, after two decades of the use of the local language, is a shortage of textbooks and a continuing shortage of advanced level texts in Bahasa Malaysia. Both the government and academic institutions recognized the problem and have moved to develop a sufficient number of textbooks. A number of programs have been established. A government funded agency, the Dewan Bahasa dan Pustaka, has responsibility for developing books in all fields in the local language. It has played a key role in sponsoring textbook development and has published more than 300 titles in most academic fields. The Dewan assesses the need in particular fields and then commissions authors (almost always university teachers) to write books or, in some instances, to translate Western books into the local language. The Dewan then publishes the books and sells them through normal commercial distribution channels. Several of Malaysia's universities are also directly involved in the development of textbooks. The Science University, has been particularly active in this field. Based on its own needs, a university committee develops ideas for books and then contracts with members of its academic staff to write the books. The University Press publishes them. An innovative aspect of the program is using modern computer-assisted typesetting and simple offset printing to produce "preliminary editions" for quick use at the university which can later be updated and refined based on student reactions.

In spite of these advances Malaysia faces many problems in producing university-level texts. The language is relatively underdeveloped and there is insufficient consensus on terminology. The scope of the enterprise is large; it has been estimated that the higher education system currently needs between 2,000-3,000 textbook titles in Bahasa Malaysia. Other problems include the "dearth of competent local authorship, translators and editors, the economic and production problems of short-run editions, the high costs and the limited market."[14]

Conclusion

This essay has only attempted to outline the major features of the issues and opportunities concerning the provision of university textbooks in the developing world. While some features are common with school text publishing, in many vital ways the problems are unique. No less than the quality of intellectual and cultural life is involved in the adequate provision of text materials; shared global disciplinary norms and the urge to localize and indigenize provide tensions frequently overlooked by planners who, with few exceptions, are not adequately alert to the needs of university education. Thus, while the picture is not altogether gloomy, and there is a pool of experiences that developing countries can draw upon, the situation is critical enough to warrant more concerted action and indeed more research.

NOTES

1. Paul Samuelson's influential undergraduate textbook, Economics (New York: McGraw-Hill, 1985) now in its twelfth edition, has been translated into many languages and sold throughout the world. It has influenced students in many nations. It has been one of the main forces in determining the undergraduate economics curriculum in the United States. Of course, Samuelson's influence outside the United States has meant that American economic concepts have been exported through this influential book.

2. See Gregory Walker, Soviet Book Publishing Policy (Cambridge: Cambridge University Press, 1978), pp. 108-112.

3. Philip G. Altbach and S. Gopinathan, "Textbooks in the Third World: Challenge and Response," in P. G. Altbach, A. Arboleda and S. Gopinathan, eds., Publishing in the Third World (Portsmouth, New Hampshire: Heinemann, 1985), pp. 13-24. See also "Textbooks in Developing Countries," Prospects, 13 (No. 3, 1983), pp. 315-372.

4. Lim Chee Hong, "An Urgent Need in Malaysia for Books in the National Language," Scholarly Publishing, 17 (April, 1986), pp. 216-223. See also H. H. Ahmad, "The Publishing Program of the Dewan Bahasa dan Pustaka," in B. Lim, ed., Publishing in Southeast Asia, (Kuala Lumpur: Association of Southeast Asian Institutions of Higher Learning, 1975), pp. 87-96.

5. Eva Maria Rathgeber, "The Book Industry in Africa, 1973-1983: A Decade of Development?" in P. Altbach, A. Arboleda and S. Gopinathan, eds., Publishing in the Third World, (Portsmouth, New Hampshire: Heinemann, 1985), pp. 57-75. See also E. Oluwasanmi, E. M. McLean and H. Zell, eds., Publishing in Africa in the Seventies, (Ile-Ife, Nigeria: University of Ife Press, 1974).

6. John Nottingham, "Establishing an African Publishing Industry: A Study in Decolonization," African Affairs, 68 (April, 1969), pp. 139-144. See also Keith Smith, "Who Controls Book Publishing in Anglophone Middle Africa?" Annals of the American Academy of Political and Social Science, 421 (September, 1975), pp. 140-150.

7. Lim Chee Hong, "Academic Publishing in Malaysia with Particular Reference to the Universiti Sains Malaysia Press," in S. Gopinathan, ed., Academic Publishing in ASEAN, (Singapore: Festival of Books, 1986), pp. 33-39.

8. For an overview of American programs and plans, with a discussion of several other foreign efforts, see William M. Childs and Donald E. McNeil, eds., American Books Abroad: Toward a National Policy (Washington, D.C.: Helen Dwight Reid Educational Foundation, 1986).

9. Philip G. Altbach, Publishing in India: An Analysis, (New Delhi: Oxford University Press, 1975), pp. 62-72.

10. For a discussion of the issues that emerge when a country shifts to the use of an indigenous language in postsecondary education, in particular for academic life and publishing, see S. Gopinathan, "Intellectual Dependency and the Indigenization Response: Case Study of Three University Disciplines in Two Third World Universities" (unpublished Doctoral Dissertation, State University of New York at Buffalo, 1984).

11. J. C. Sharma, "Languages of India and Publishing," Asian Book Development Newsletter, 18 (No. 1, 1987), pp. 3-6.

12. For an account of recent developments in Indian publishing see O. P. Ghai, "Indian Publishing: Yesterday, Today and Tomorrow," and Abul Hassan, "The Book in India: Change in Continuity," both in Indian Book Industry, 34 (September 1986).

13. J. C. Sharma, op.cit., p. 6.

14· Datuk Hassan Ahmad, "The Role of the Dewan Bahasa dan Pustaka in the Advancement of Indigenous Academic Publishing in Malaysia," in S. Gopinathan, ed., Academic Publishing in Asean: Problems and Prospects, (Singapore: Festival of Books, 1986).

CHAPTER 4

THE POLITICS OF TEXTBOOK SELECTION AND CONTROL: THE CASE OF INTERWAR INDOCHINA AND WEST AFRICA

Gail P. Kelly

This chapter focuses on textbook production, selection, and control in interwar French Indochina and West Africa in the period of 1918 to 1938. This case study relates textbook production, selection, and control to teacher cultures and the political context of the schools. French colonial governments and the educators who served them created very different textbook policies and practices in Indochina and West Africa. In one context, the French followed laissez-faire policies on questions of textbook development and use; in the other context a bureaucracy to develop, sponsor, and censor textbooks and tightly control their use arose. I will argue throughout this chapter that textbook supply and development policies were very much a result of complex interactions between the schools and their political environments. Increasing the numbers of textbooks available to the schools was not in the 1920s--nor is it today--reducible to a technical set of issues; rather, the ways in which texts are developed and made available relate directly to preexisting teacher cultures within the schools and the relation of those teacher cultures to political opposition to the state. Textbook policies derive from policies of teacher control, they are not simply a question of a pedagogical efficiency.

The Context

France had virtually completed conquest of West Africa and Indochina by the turn of the 20th Century. The French presence in West Africa began in the 18th Century with the establishment of footholds in the coastal areas of Senegal that were, in the spirit of the French revolution, incorporated into France as departments. The conquest of the remainder of West Africa, which formed most of the colonial territory, took place at the end of the 19th century. By 1905, Sénégal, Soudan (contemporary Mali), Dahomey, Upper Volta,Guinée, Ivory Coast, Niger, Dakar and dependencies, and Mauritania had been placed under the authority of a government of French West Africa situated in Dakar. Each was considered a colony (for a while several were military territories) governed by a Lieutenant Governor situated in the capital of each colony. French West Africa was a federation. Education was the responsibility of each colony, but until the 1920s, under the leadership of Georges Hardy, who was inspector of education, the government in Dakar took initiative in setting policy. For example, most of the African teachers who were in service in the interwar years were trained at the École William Ponty in Sénégal. Education legislation was initiated by the center as well. All major reforms emanated from Dakar and were re-enacted in the decrees of the Lt. Governors with little deviation.

Indochina was as much a French artifact as was West Africa. It consisted of Cambodia, Laos, and the three states of Annam, Tonkin, and Cochinchina which had formed the pre-colonial nation-state of Vietnam. Cambodia and Laos became French protectorates. Vietnam from 1858 to the 1880s waged a losing battle against colonial occupation. By the turn of the century, the Government General was firmly entrenched in Hanoi. The five states--Cambodia, Laos, Cochinchina, Annam, and Tonkin--formed French Indochina. As in French West Africa, educational legislation was initiated from Hanoi and was re-decreed in the five pays of the federation, albeit sometimes with great opposition and footdragging on the part of the protected governments. The bureaucratization of education in Indochina had little parallel in West Africa. The government of Indochina in 1917 established an office of public instruction which superintended the primary and post-primary schools.

The school systems of French West Africa and Indochina took final shape in the years immediately following World War I. School organization in the two colonial federations diverged. In Indochina, the

1918 Code of Public Instruction organized the full gamut of elementary through higher education.[1] Elementary education consisted of a three year course (the cours enfantin, the cours préparatoire, and the cours élémentaire). It was provided in the mother tongue. Primary education was three years in duration and provided in French while post-primary schooling consisted of a four year primary-superior cycle of studies followed by three years of secondary education. In Indochina, a university crowned the system. Its faculties in the early 1920s numbered eight; in the 1930s after much reorganization, the university was reduced to three faculties. The school system in Indochina relied heavily on competitive examinations administered centrally for matriculation into succeeding levels of education and for degree conferral (individual schools did not award degrees). Schools offering primary, primary-superior, and secondary studies administered entry and matriculation examinations on their own in addition to state-administered degree tests.

Education was nowhere nearly as well developed in West Africa as it was in Indochina. In Indochina, emphasis was placed on providing the full range of schooling; in West Africa government concerns focused solely on the extension of rudimentary education in the French language. Until the mid-1920s, education consisted of three levels of primary education: a three-year preparatory course equivalent to Indochina's cours préparatoire given in village schools; a four-year elementary school that repeated the preparatory course of the village school and taught the cours élémentaire; and a four-year regional school that offered a program of studies similar to the cours moyen of Indochina.[2] After 1924, the schools were reformed and the cours supérieur was added to the regional school program. After 1924 primary superior education was organized which offered general studies, a preparatory course for those planning to become teachers and enter the École William Ponty (a teacher training school which had been organized in Sénégal in the late 19th century); and a vocational course. Unlike Indochina where a university formed the apex of the system, in West Africa a series of vocational schools served the federation. These schools included institutions for midwives and medical assistants, teachers, river pilots, and mechanics. After 1920, students preparing to be teachers in the École William Ponty were required to attend primary superior school before sitting for the Ponty entry examination, and medical and veterinary students were expected to complete a preparatory course of three years at the École William Ponty before entering their courses. In West Africa, there was no secondary education outside the program offered in Sénégal at the Lycée Faidherbe in St. Louis and the secondary course in Dakar. These two programs were part of French metropolitan schooling and were open only to the children of French citizens and African originaires of the four French communes in Sénégal.

Centrally administered examinations did not characterize West Africa's school system the way they did the schools of Indochina. In West Africa, individual colonies like Upper Volta, the Ivory Coast, or Sénégal could and sometimes did administer primary certificate examinations. But individual colonies like Soudan were under no obligation to administer or require examinations for purposes of degree conferral or matriculation. Individual schools administered examinations if school places exceeded demand for them.

The distribution of education in West Africa and Indochina diverged. In Indochina, particularly in the three states which had constituted the precolonial state of Vietnam (Annam, Cochinchina, and Tonkin), the schools reached one out of ten school-aged children; in West Africa the schools accommodated 4.7 out of every 1000 children. In 1938 in Tonkin, Cochinchina, and Annam 287,037 students went to school: of these 150,812 were in elementary schools; another 129,020 were in primary school, 4,552 attended primary-superior schools and 400 were in the secondary course studying for the baccalaureate. Another 2,253 students attended post-primary vocational schools. About 630 students were in the university.[3] In West Africa, 56,135 students went to elementary and primary school; another 717 went to primary superior school, 220 were enrolled in École William Ponty and 501 students went to post-primary technical/vocational schools.[4]

The curricula of the schools of West Africa and Indochina were developed by the French with the full recognition that curricula used in metropolitan France's schools were inappropriate to the schools of West Africa and Indochina. French school texts were deemed inappropriate as well. In both areas education officials--in West Africa the Inspector of Education situated in Dakar and his staff; in Indochina the Director of Public Instruction and his staff of school inspectors situated in Hanoi--encouraged the development of texts that would prevent metropolitan teachers in service in colonial schools as well as their "native" counterparts from importing French education wholesale.

While the educational and political leadership of both colonies insisted on developing texts for the schools, how that development proceeded diverged in West Africa and Indochina. In West Africa, a laissez faire policy emerged by the 1920s; in Indochina centralized, bureaucratic procedures for textbook development and adoption were pursued.

Textbook Policy in West Africa

Textbook policies in West Africa tended to focus on providing African teachers a series of texts that would provide them with guidelines on how to produce an African curriculum. Before World War I, French cadres on loan from the metropole dominated in the schools; through much of the interwar years they were a strong presence. At no time were these metropolitan teachers less than one-fourth of the teaching staff of French West Africa. As late as 1933, they contributed 36% of all education staff in service.[5] In the first decade of the 2Oth Century, French teachers tended to use ones that they had relied upon when teaching at home. Georges Hardy, the first Inspector of Schools for West Africa (who probably had the strongest influence that any one individual was able to exert on the school system), emphasized that teachers should place their efforts in gathering knowledge of local customs, learning local songs and tribal dances, and developing local history so that these might be incorporated into the schools.[6] In 1912, Hardy created a pedagogical journal, the Bulletin of Education for French West Africa (it was later called African Education), to diffuse this knowledge to teachers. Under Hardy's editorship, the journal published ethnographies, songs, historical materials, and folktales, as well as teaching tips.

The Inspectorate of Education in Dakar under Georges Hardy's leadership saw its role as creating a new curriculum. The Inspectorate encouraged its staff to write texts to accomplish this task, but it never insisted that teachers use either the texts the Inspectorate created in the 1910s or those it had encouraged its staff as individuals to write in later years. Such policies meant that there was no captive market for any one text and that private entrepreneurs were free to develop texts on their own for the African market. School inspectors ended up writing for a profit. As early as 1911, initial reading primers were developed to assist in the teaching of French in village schools. J. L. Monod, a school inspector who was posted in Soudan and later in other parts of West Africa, wrote a series of such primers. In 1911, his first and second Booklet of the Soudanese School Boy: Language, Writing and Reading appeared. Several years later in 1926 and 1929, revisions of these texts appeared under the title The Black School Boy and were marketed to all of French West Africa.[7] Louis Sonolet, a former school inspector, and A. Pérès, a school director in service in West Africa, wrote another primer which Armand Colin published in France in 1915.[8]

The problem with this approach to school textbook development, as Hardy soon noted, was that only primers appeared. There were no books to teach hygiene, singing, geography, and history. In 1915, Hardy undertook to sponsor a series of texts that were published under the aegis of the Bulletin of Education for French West Africa which was published in Sénégal. Initially, the Bulletin itself converted entire issues into school texts. For example, in 1913 the November issue was André Leguillette's History of French West Africa.[9] By 1915 the Bulletin published texts that did not appear in the journal: in 1915 it issued a French composition book written by J. Toulze, Director of the Regional School at Tivaouane,[10] as well as a drawing text.[11] In 1916, it printed Singing in the Native School.[12] This text provided words and music for songs intended as alternatives to European songs French teachers used to teach Africans the French language. The book included songs "To Work," "The Mosquito," "Mamadou the Vain," "My Village," and "Hymn to France." Each song was developed in accordance to the principles of educational adaptation spelled out by Georges Hardy. Hardy himself wrote a text on the geography of West Africa. This text was intended as a teachers' manual as were an agriculture and a hygiene text published in 1917 and 1918.[13] The final text the Inspectorate commissioned and published in Senegal was J. L. Monod's Instructions for Teaching Personnel Who are Assigned to the Schools of West Africa.[14] This text outlined the curriculum of the schools and stressed the differences between the West African course of study and that of French schools. It contained lesson plans, a number of songs, complete with music and drawing lessons.

For the first two decades of the 20th Century, the tendency was to centralize education; after World War I school reform in West Africa emphasized decentralization. While the inspectorate in Dakar continued to publish its pedagogical journal, its active role in textbook development ended. School inspectors and school directors, encouraged by the Inspectorate in Dakar, did continue to write a number of books which were published in France by firms like Armand Colin and Librairie Delagrave in Paris and Istra in Strasbourg. Several of these firms sponsored series. Andre Davesne, an Inspector of Education for French West Africa, contracted with Istra to write a series of texts for French West Africa. His texts about Mamadou and Bineta consisted of an initial reading primer, an intermediate reading text, and a writing and composition text designed to teach French in the primary grades.[15] The book was destined for the students of black Africa, including French

Equitorial Africa. J. L. Monod edited a series of texts in the 1920s for Delagrave. His series included re-editions of his earlier Soudanese School Boy, basic primers, as well as a history text and a geography book intended for all grade levels of the elementary and primary grades.[16] Louis Sonolet and his colleague A. Pérès also wrote a number of texts for Armand Colin. One of the texts in the series was a thinly disguised version of Monod's 1921 Directions to Teaching Personnel Beginning in West African Schools which had been the last work published by the Inspectorate in Dakar.[17]

The schools of West Africa were chronically short of texts. Private publishers did not supply texts for each and every course the schools taught or for all grade levels in large part because there was such a small school population. Most of the texts that appeared were reading primers destined for the first five years of education, where the most students were by 1938 this market consisted of 56,135 students, three-fourths of (whom were in the first three years). The majority of texts were initial reading primers like Monod's widely used Black Student. This particular text introduced the alphabet, consonants, vowels, and words in isolation. Other than teaching the sounds and some vocabulary in French, very little of substance was included. It was only in the upper levels of schooling, the cours moyen, where rudiments of hygiene, African history and geography, and mathematics were supposed to be taught.[18] And for these subjects, very few texts were developed. For example, only two geography texts appeared for use in the entire school system in the interwar years: Rousseau's geography course for French West Africa that was published in the 1920s and a second cours moyen text issued in the mid 1930s.[19] One history textbook made its way onto the market: Monod's adaptation of Delafosse's earlier history of French West Africa was published in 1926 by Delagrave.[20] Texts for a wide range of school subjects were simply unavailable, mathematics, science, agriculture, and hygiene, to name a few, on any level. Teachers often did without texts, particularly on the primary level, and lectured from the many materials made available through the Bulletin of Education for West Africa. Many of the monographs on African history and geography, on folkways and customs, proverbs, and the like, became classroom material for the post-primary schools. When teachers could find a supply, French texts were used for lack of anything else.

The textbook policy pursued in French West Africa left the choice of the text pretty much up to the teacher and what he (rarely she) could find. The student notebooks available to us from West African schools indicate that much instruction was oral. When the schools used texts, one text was used to teach all school subjects. For example, the full primary school in Ouagadougou in Upper Volta (now Burkina Faso) in the 1929/30 school year, used but one text, Moussa and Gi-gla, The Story of Two African Boys, in the cours moyen.[21] This text, a basic reader, was meant to teach reading, composition, geography, history, civics, morality, science, rudiments of hygiene, etc. Quite cleverly the author had organized the text around the travels of two primary school boys throughout the federation. As Moussa and Gi-gla roamed, they discussed plants, animals, trade, history of local peoples, government structures, and debated moral questions, and concluded by singing the praises of France as one marched off to join the Senegalese sharpshooters and the other returned home to become a farmer. The student notebooks from the school at Ouagadougou indicate not only that this was the only text in use for all subjects, but also that the book was used for two grade levels. The text was the basis for writing compositions and student essays were modeled on the individual chapters of the book. While the upper grades of the primary school at Ouagadougou used a text developed for West Africa, the early grades of the elementary school in Conakry appeared to use no books at all. Students copied lessons the teacher wrote on the blackboard in their notebooks.[22]

Scarcity of texts of any sort and the lack of texts in most school subjects left a lot to teacher discretion. The student notebooks indicate that in some schools students learned very little and were taught very little. In other schools, often in the same area, instruction was more rigorous either because the teacher had managed to find a text or had decided to teach more and was able to, because he was an experienced teacher. Education in West Africa was uneven. The schools in Ouagadougou and Bobo-Dialoasso in relative backwaters, seemed more rigorous than the schools in Conakry that served a more sophisticated, urbanized African population who had greater exposure to French.

While in West Africa, much was left to the individual teacher; in Indochina nothing was left to chance or to teacher discretion. The schools of Indochina served a population of close to 260,000 in 1938 (five times that of West Africa). A market place for textbooks existed, at all levels, and private entrepreneurs found it profitable to meet the demands of the school system. However, in Indochina, the government chose not to trust textbook development to private initiative; rather, as I will now describe, a tightly controlled system of textbook development and distribution was established in the early 1920s and remained in force throughout the interwar years.

Textbook Policies and Practices in Indochina

West Africa's schools became decentralized by the 1920s; reforms occurring at the same time in Indochina took a decentralized school system and centralized it, vesting control of education in the hands of an Office of Public Instruction in Hanoi. The Office of Public Instruction was set up by legislation enacted in 1918. It replaced a loosely structured Inspectorate, similar to that which existed in West Africa during the interwar years. The Office had a director appointed by the Governor General and a number of school inspectors attached directly to it. These inspectors, unlike many in West Africa, were full-time professionals (in West Africa the inspectors for the most part were school directors who moonlighted in this capacity). The Office had a rather large staff and a number of bureaus.[23] The secretariat was responsible for school publications, texts and curriculum formation, among other things. It published pedagogical journals which reprinted school law, including the laws mandating texts that could be used in the schools as well as those banned both from the schools and from teacher possession, and issued monthly lesson plans, composition topics, mathematics problems, science projects, and the like. The office's Bulletin of Public Instruction also contained a pedagogical section that ran articles on how to teach. It did not, like its West African equivalent, run long substantive monographs teachers could incorporate into the curriculum.

The Secretariat had a textbook commission that initiated, printed, and censured textbooks. It was the Secretariat, through its commission, who proposed the lists of approved texts that became decrees with the force of law. Texts were not recommended as in West Africa; they were legislated.[24]

The textbook commission in Hanoi was composed of three inspectors who were full-time staff of the Office of Public Instruction, and the Director of the School of Education at the Indochinese University in Hanoi (this individual often had served as a school inspector or Director of Public Instruction prior to taking up the post of director of the school). Also sitting on the Commission were three "native" teachers (who usually were Vietnamese and taught in the primary schools of Hanoi) recommended by the Director of Public Instruction, a prominent Vietnamese, and a senior-ranking French teacher who had reached the rank of professor "first-class".[25]

The textbook commission was advisory and its recommendations both for texts to commission and for texts to be approved for classroom use had to be endorsed by the top leadership of the Office of Public

Instruction, the political administrators of each of the five states of Indochina (in Tonkin, Annam, Laos and Cambodia, the Résident; in Cochinchina, the governor), and the Governor General of Indochina. Usually the Résidents of each state appointed advisory committees on school texts. Serving on these committees were the Chiefs of the Local Education Services, school inspectors, and representatives of the political administration and the political security police. In Indochina, in short, there was a specialized bureaucracy put into place with a number of checks on its actions from outside the education bureaucracy. In Indochina, textbooks were subject to political control as well as pedagogical control; in West Africa, neither form of control was formally exerted on the development of instructional materials.

Between 1918 and before 1924, when the Office published its first texts, the Office selected textbooks written by a number of school teachers and by school inspectors that were privately produced in Vietnam. These texts were submitted to the Office. If approved, they made their way into the many decrees that were issued listing texts that would be used in the schools. Some of these texts found their way onto banned lists as well.

In the 1924 school year, three Vietnamese teachers were released from their classrooms and assigned to the Office of Public Instruction in Hanoi. Their task was to write a series of initial reading primers and texts in Vietnamese for the early grades. They were instructed by the Director of Public Instruction to consult curricular guides printed in the government's three pedagogical journals, texts currently approved for use in the schools, and French textbooks. The books were first written in French, scrutinized by the education inspectors and the newly formed textbook commission, and, only if approved, translated into Vietnamese and printed.[26] By 1926, these teachers had produced nine texts which were approved for classroom use. These three teachers had developed other texts that were completed by Frenchmen employed by the Office of Public Instruction. By 1929, over 4 million copies of textbooks had been produced by the Office of Public Instruction, most of them were destined for the primary and elementary grades. As of 1930, the number had risen to 4,884,000 for all grade levels.[27] In the depression years of 1931 to 1936, the Office did not issue its own texts. Rather the textbook commission served as a censorship bureau and chose school texts from among those texts written by a number of entrepreneurs and published by private presses in Vietnam for profit. In 1936, the Office resumed its direct publication of texts. In 1936 alone, 371,838 copies of textbooks were sponsored by the office; in 1938 another 476,237 copies of textbooks were printed.[28] By 1938, the Office of Public

Instruction was responsible for close to 8 million copies of textbooks for all levels of education. Clearly the volume of textbook publication was far greater for Indochina than it was for West Africa.

Not only was the volume of textbook production greater in Indochina than it was in West Africa, the range of books produced under the centralized, highly controlled textbook selection, production, and distribution system of Indochina was much wider than under the decentralized, laissez-faire system in West Africa. Table 1 presents a listing of the number of books in each subject field published in Indochina by the Office of Public Instruction between 1924 and 1930. The Table provides a breakdown by linguistic medium since the schools of Indochina taught in Vietnamese, Cambodian and Lao in the first three years of schooling, as well as a breakdown by year of schooling. The table shows that close to 96% of all texts were published in the Vietnamese language destined for the schools of Annam, Tonkin, and Cochinchina where close to 90% of all school enrollments were concentrated. Textbook production for Cambodia and Laos was limited to reading primers and general science texts for the second and third grades. For Cambodia, a French text was issued as well as a history and a geography text for the second and third grades.

Texts were developed and made available in Vietnamese, as the table shows, for the full range of school subjects--reading, moral education, general science, mathematics, hygiene, history and geography, French, and physical education, as well as Chinese characters. By and large, the greatest effort was in the production of reading primers (23.01% of all texts) followed by moral education (18.82%). The texts were relatively evenly distributed across the first three years of education. Of the 3,933,000 volumes the Office of Public Instruction printed up to 1930, about 37% were for the first grade, 34% for the second grade, and 28% for the third grade.

Table 4.1 understates the volume and range of textbooks used in the schools because it reports only those texts the Office of Public Instruction directly commissioned, produced, and circulated to the schools. The Textbook Commission approved a large number of texts produced commercially for the school market. It relied on the private sector to produce school texts in the deep depression years 1931-1935 more heavily than it did in the period 1924-1930 and after 1935. Publishers in Hanoi, Haiphong, Saigon, and other Vietnamese cities competed with one another for the textbook market. Many were Vietnamese entrepreneurs like Nguyen-Van-Vinh who published a daily newspaper as well as books. Throughout the interwar years, there was

Table 4.1
Textbooks Produced by the Indochina Office of Public Instruction By 1930

School Subject	First Year	Second Year	Third Year	Total
Reading				
Vietnamese	360,000	300,000	160,000	820,000
Cambodian	40,000	20,000	5,000	65,000
Lao	10,000	10,000	...	20,000
Total No.	410,000	330,000	165,000	905,000
% all texts produced	10.42%	8.39%	4.195%	23.01%
Moral Education				
Vietnamese	360,000	240,000	140,000	740,000
Cambodian	...	...	...	...
Lao	...	...	...	...
Total No.	360,000	240,000	140,000	740.000
% of all texts produced	9.15%	6.10%	3.56%	18.82%

Table 4.1 continued

School Subject	First Year	Second Year	Third Year	Total
All Purpose Arithmetic, General Science, and Geography				
Vietnamese	320,000	...	...	320,000
Cambodian	...	...	...	...
Lao	...	...	...	...
Total No.	320,000			320,000
% of all texts produced	8.14%			8.14%
Arithmetic and The Metric System				
Vietnamese	190,000	140,000	...	330,000
Cambodian	10,000	...	...	10,000
Lao	...	...	...	...
Total No.	200,000	140,000		340,000
% of all texts produced	5.09%	3.56%		8.65%

Table 4.1 continued

School Subject	First Year	Second Year	Third Year	Total
General Science				
Vietnamese	...	220,000	100,000	320,000
Cambodian	...	15,000	10,000	25,000
Lao	...	5,000	5,000	10,000
Total No.		240,000	115,000	355,000
% of all texts produced		6.10%	2.92%	9.02%
Hygiene		400,000		400,000
Cambodian		10,000		10,000
Lao		...		...
Total No.		410,000		410,000
% of all texts produced		10.42%		10.42%

Table 4.1 continued

School Subject	First Year	Second Year	Third Year	Total
History and Geography				
Vietnamese	...	220,000	145,000	365,000
Cambodian	...	10,000	10,000	20,000
Lao	...	...	...	...
Total No.		230,000	155,000	385,000
% of all texts produced		5.85%	3.94%	9.79%
French				
Vietnamese	130,000	100,000	90,000*	320,000
Cambodian	3,000			3,000
Lao	...			
Total No.	133,000	100,000	90,000	323,000
% of all texts produced	3.38%	2.54%	2.29%	8.21%

Table 4.1 continued

School Subject	First Year	Second Year	Third Year	Total
Physical Education				
Vietnamese		40,000		40,000
Cambodian				
Lao				
Total No.		40,000		40,000
% of all texts produced		1.02%		1.02%
Chinese Characters				
Vietnamese	45,000	40,000	30,000	115,000
Cambodian	...	...	...	...
Lao	...	...	...	...
Total No.	45,000	40,000	30,000	115,000
%of all texts produced	1.14%	1.02%	.8%	2.93%
Total N texts				
Vietnamese	1,405,000	1,260,000	1,065,000	3,730,000
Cambodian	53,000	45,000	35,000	133,000
Lao	10,000	15,000	5,000	30,000

Table 4.1 continued

School Subject	First Year	Second Year	Third Year	Total
Total No.	1,468,000	1,320,000	1,105,000	3,933,000
# of texts in Vietnamese	95.60%			

Source: Indochine française. Direction générale de l'Instruction publique. Les Manuels scolaires et les publications pedagogiques de la Direction générale de l'Instruction publique. (Hanoi: Imprimerie d'Extrême-Orient, 1931) ff p. 22.

tension over the government's insistence that it control book publication for the school market and private entrepreneurs who wanted the government out of the publishing business.[29] As early as 1918, the Resident Superieur in Tonkin complained that individual school inspectors, in cohoots with private publishers, had cornered the school market by writing books, and seeing, for a price, that they were approved by the Commission in Hanoi. Such corruption, the Résident implied, could be done away with only if the Office published texts not for profit or if the authors of texts came from outside the Education Service.[30]

Textbooks were big business and private entrepreneurs sought to get into the market monopolized by the Office of Public Instruction. Several entrepreneurs tried to produce and market "look alike" texts. In 1927, for example, Nguyen-Van-Vinh published a Vietnamese reading primer that was hardly distinguishable from the one distributed by the Office of Public Instruction. His text sold at a higher price.[31] The Governor of Cochinchina tried to support Cochinchinese entrepreneur's bids to produce texts. In 1928, the Governor of Cochinchina insisted that textbook contracts be given to the Syndicate of Printers and the Cochinchinese Chamber of Commerce.[32] He did so despite the fact that the business interests he represented proposed charging two to three times more than the government per volume.

The private sector did produce a large number of texts for the Vietnamese school market despite the Office of Public Instruction's initiatives to monopolize the textbook market. These books were written on a wide range of subjects for elementary through secondary education. They were written individually and proposed to the Textbook Commission prior to publication. When and if approved, their titles were published in the Official Government Journal, enshrined as law. For example, on February 17, 1928, a decree approved 39 books for use in the schools.[33] Some of these books were Vietnamese language texts like Cao-Hai De's Moral Education text, Tran-Van-Kem's Vietnamese Grammar Text, Duong-Qung-Ham's Selected Readings in Vietnamese, Vietnamese History, and the like. Others were French language history, mathematics, geography, science, and literature texts written by French school inspectors (for a profit). Such were Taboulet and Imbert's History of France, Assan-Achou, Pandolfi, and his colleagues, The Teaching of French, and Mr. and Mrs. Brachet's mathematics and geometry texts. Private initiative did cover the entire range of subjects and insure a mix of both Vietnamese language and French language texts and a mix of texts for all grade levels.

While the Office of Public Instruction took the lead in publishing texts for the first three years of education, it produced very few texts for the post-primary sector. The upper level texts were left to the private publishers. The Office of Public Instruction retained approval rights. Many of the books on the list of approved texts decreed on February 17, 1926, for example, were post-primary school texts.[34] J. Lan, for example, wrote five botany texts which were approved for school use. Galloudec and Maurette wrote a geography text, Vayrac's collection of French prose and poetry was approved as well. In the matter of texts for the post-primary school, the textbook commission behaved like a censorship board. It did not take the initiative that it took on the primary level. The market was quite small, less than 5,000 students were enrolled in 1938 in post-primary schools. Yet, private entrepreneurs published books for this small a market, more than was the case for the 56,000 or so students in West Africa's primary grades.

The Textbook Commission censored textbooks and banned several from the school system. Sometimes the government banned texts for technical reasons. Many private presses were none too careful in questions of prose and grammar. At its meeting of May 2, 1929, for example, the textbook commission rejected a number of books because of frequent misspellings, grammatical mistakes, and lack of correct diacritical marks.[35] Such cases arose as late as 1938. However, technical questions were not the only basis for banning texts from the schools. The textbook commission by law could ban any publication from the schools, whether it be a text or periodical literature, that "it considers contrary to public morals, public order or to established institutions or capable of corrupting youth."[36] The Commission did ban a number of texts. In 1928, for example, the textbook commission forbade the use of four books by Tran-Van-Tam, a former teacher from Haiphong. His History of Annam, according to Thalamas, the Director of Public Instruction: "has . . . tendencious remarks capable of slandering established institutions."[37] The remarks in this instance were comparisons between republican and monarchial regimes that were hardly favorable to monarchies. Again in 1929, the Commission rejected Tran-Tuan-Khai's Annamite Fables, written in Vietnamese. The Commission gave as its reason: "The work contains allusions with political undercurrents . . ."[38] In other words, it was seditious.

The censorship, while exercised by the Commission, did not prevent the development of a range of textbooks for all grade levels and for all subjects the schools taught. It did not dampen the enthusiasm of the entrepreneur in the development of texts; it simply meant that the knowledge the schools distributed was tightly controlled.

Teacher Control and Textbook Policy

This chapter has described the differences in textbook policies pursued by France in West Africa and in Indochina in the interwar years. In West Africa, a laissez-faire policy was pursued. The state did not initiate textbooks after World War I. Individual school inspectors acted as entrepreneurs, wrote textbooks for the African schools, and worked with individual publishers to produce them. The state did not undertake to create a monopoly for any publisher; nor did it even seek to commend a text for school use. It simply left textbook selection up to individual teachers and production of the textbooks up to the publishers and their assessment of the market. No attempt was made to control strictly the flow of knowledge into West Africa's schools. In Indochina, on the other hand, the state sought to control texts. At the lower grade levels, where there was a mass school system, it sought to create, publish, and disseminate its own textbooks and exerted its right to select and sanction knowledge produced elsewhere. The state did not encourage entrepreneurs to produce texts for the school market; rather, it tried to limit their activities and bring them into compliance with state educational policies. Paradoxically, a policy which sought to control school knowledge in Indochina resulted in a far greater number and range of textbooks produced for school use than a policy that sought to leave school knowledge up to the teacher in West Africa. In Indochina, particularly in the Vietnamese states, texts were widely available in most school subjects, including physical education, moral education, science, botany, and drawing. In West Africa, the laissez faire policy that put no limits on texts and their contents resulted in the production of fewer texts and a very limited range; most school subjects went without textbooks.

I will explore two possible explanations for why textbook policies and their results in the two French colonies varied the way they did. The first relates to the scale of the system, the second to the teachers in service in the schools.

It would be easy to attribute textbook policies and their practices to the scale of the system. The schools of West Africa served at most, particularly on the primary level, one-fifth the population of the schools of Indochina (56,135 in the primary grades in 1938 versus over 300,000 in Indochina). There was simply a greater market in Indochina for textbooks than there was in West Africa, and the greater market meant that textbooks in the subject areas were economically feasible. This explanation on the surface seems a logical one, but on greater scrutiny it cannot alone account for the shape of textbook policies. While in West Africa there was a small school population which might have deterred private publishers, it is doubtful that the small market tells the entire story. In Indochina, there were many privately developed textbooks destined for post-primary education which had considerably fewer students than did the West African elementary and primary schools. In all 4,552 students attended primary superior school in Indochina in 1938 and another 400 went to secondary programs (against over 56,000 students in the elementary and primary schools of West Africa). Despite the small number of students in post-primary schools in Indochina in 1926, at least ten privately published books were adopted by the Office of Public Instruction for classroom use at these levels; in 1927 a similar number were adopted.[39] These books covered subjects as diverse as botany, history, and moral philosophy. Despite the risks of having books rejected for school use in Indochina, texts were developed in far greater number even for post-primary education than was the case in West Africa. In West Africa, where there were no risks that a text once developed would not be used, private entrepreneurs did not step forward to fill the demand for texts. Free market mechanisms had less of an impact on textbook production than did government policy.

The pattern of textbook policy and practice in the two colonies was heavily influenced by the extent to which teacher control was a pressing concern to school administrators and colonial government officials. The entire mechanism for selecting, censoring, and developing texts in Indochina arose because school inspectors saw teacher control as a political issue, in the context of a society that was literate and had a pre-existing book culture. Henri Russier, a school inspector in 1915, reported to the governor general that there was a growing number of publications in the Vietnamese language of a politically suspect nature. Many of these were finding their way into the classrooms.[40] The following year, Roume, another French school inspector, echoed Russier's concerns and suggested that legislation giving the government the exclusive right to determine what texts should enter the classroom be promulgated. The Roume suggestions became the basis for subsequent textbook policy.[41]

Roume's and Russier's fears that alternative knowledge might enter the classroom unless the government moved to control textbooks were not without basis. The schools the French established were not the first in the three Vietnamese states. The school system that the 1917/1918 Code of Public Instruction codified was a replacement for a widespread mass educational system that taught in Vietnamese written in Chinese characters. These schools were staffed by Vietnamese teachers who had aspired under an independent Vietnamese government to state service and national leadership. The ideal of the teacher in pre-colonial Vietnam was that of a practitioner who was independent arbiter of school knowledge and who acted on the basis of his conscience and knowledge to bring about a "correct" moral social order.[42] It was this model of the teaching profession that textbook policies sought to control.

In West Africa, the secular schools the French introduced were an entirely new institutional form, and they did not seek to undermine pre-existing institutions. The schools coexisted with Koranic schools as well as bush schools and did not seek to replace them. The school system in West Africa initially relied on French teachers who were trained in metropolitan norms. They were socialized to use state-mandated curriculum and were career professionals on loan from the metropole. They shared the government's vision of appropriate teacher's roles and so did the Africans who eventually became the elementary teachers in the system. The model upon which the teaching profession was based in West Africa was an exclusively French one. Competing models such as those that existed in the three Vietnamese states of Indochina, were absent. Thus, the need to strictly control teaching behaviors via textbooks was less pressing.

The model for teachers in West Africa was a model that emphasized teacher roles as pedagogical in nature and as representing the state. Nowhere is this clearer than in Georges Hardy's The Two Routes, a manual Hardy wrote for the graduates of École William Ponty who were assuming school posts for the first time.[43] In this book, Hardy emphasized how teachers were moral examples of French authority and prestige. He provided advice on how teachers might dress, what kind of house they were to live in, and how they should relate to Europeans. Much of his advice sought to convince the new graduates that they should be deferential to Europeans, keep out of politics, and not take more than one wife. Although Hardy's work produced an uproar (the elite found it demeaning, to say the least), its very existence indicates a lack of models for African teachers other than the ones the French brought to Africa.

In the three Vietnamese states of Indochina there were alternative models to the French imposed ones. In pre-colonial Vietnam, teachers were not only perceived as independent arbiters of knowledge, but also as leaders in questions of public morality and politics. Socialization into such norms was the exclusive form of training for a sizeable proportion of the teaching force: in 1921/22 academic year, 40.1% (or

1122 teachers) had no French training; by 1937/38 this proportion had fallen to 31.9% of all teachers. The proportion of teachers trained in normal school to French visions of teacher roles in 1921/22 was 22.2% of teachers in service; by 1936/37 they were 19.2% of all teachers.[44] (In contrast, in West Africa by 1935/36 school year, 69% (or 577 out of 834) of African teachers were normal school graduates trained by École William Ponty.[45] In addition, another 291 teachers in the system were French metropolitan cadres on loan from the metropolitan teaching corps. Twenty-five percent of the teaching force in West Africa was French. In Indochina, French metropolitan cadres were a minuscule part of the teaching force, concentrated in post-primary schools and in the university. Lack of direct socialization of teachers was a bigger problem in Indochina than it was in West Africa.

Not only was a sizeable proportion of the teaching force in Indochina lacking in any socialization into the profession according to French norms, those who received normal training tended to be from aspiring urban elites who entered teaching because alternative professions were closed to them in colonial society. Many such individuals became disgruntled and were involved in various anti-colonial organizations. The Vietnamese Nationalist Party, for example, which was associated with an attempted uprising in 1929, was heavily dominated by teachers, many of whom had normal school training.[46] It is little wonder that French inspectors found them suspect and sought to control what these teachers taught by controlling the books they used and the books they and their students might read. Such heavy handed policies became the norm in a society that had strong intellectual traditions and reverence for the written word. There was a lively publishing infrastructure in Indochina which the state sought to control. The free market for books existed in Indochina, and the government, unlike its counterpart in West Africa, feared that market and sought to control its entry into the schools. In West Africa, the free market could be encouraged because there was no publishing infrastructure that could respond to the demand. The only publisher for texts in West Africa was the government and the government got out of the textbook business by 1920. The publishers of textbooks for West Africa were in France and the demand for books was mediated by French school inspectors. The market was not particularly free. The informal control by the inspectors like Davesne and Monod was no less effective than bureaucratic censorship and publishing modes adapted in Indochina in controlling what was taught in schools. The teacher without text was not a horrifying spectre in West Africa, since teacher culture was French created, and the French were the sole repository of knowledge.

This study has implications for the ways in which we think about textbook policies and practices in the contemporary world. All too often we think of the problems of textbook creation and supply as technical issues. This case study has shown that textbook creation and supply is highly political. It suggests that the extent to which textbooks are made available and widely distributed goes beyond pure economics, but rather is related to teacher cultures and the extent to which knowledge not sanctioned by the state is likely to enter the classroom. It also suggests that state intervention in the matter of textbook creation does not necessarily encourage textbook production, but rather it serves to control that production, as well as in-class teacher behaviors.

NOTES

The following abbreviations have been used below:

AOM -- Archives de France d'Outre Mer
JOIF -- Journal Officiel de l'Indochine Française
JOAOF -- Journal Officiel de L'Afrique Occidentale Française

1. Gouvernement général de l'Indochine française. Code de l'Instructional publique, 21 déc. 1917 et 1921 (Hanoi: Imprimerie d'Extrême-Orient, 1921).

2. This discussion of the schools of French West Africa is based on the following sources: Exposition Coloniale internationale de Paris. Commissariat de l'Afrique Occidentale française, L'Enseignement en Afrique Occidentale Française (Paris: Librairie Larose, 1931); Gouvernement général de l'Afrique occidentale française, Service de l'Enseignement, Textes portant reorganisation de l'Enseignement en Afrique occidentale française, ler mai 1924. (Gorée: Editions du BEAOF, No. 57, 1924); Circulaire du Gouverneur général sur l'Enseignement (signé Carde), JOAOF 20e Année, No. 1008 (26 janv. 1924), pp. 69-71.

3. Gouvernement général de l'Indochine française, Rapports au Grand Conseil des intérêts économiques et financiers et au Conseil de Gouvernement, Deuxième Partie: Fonctionnement des divers services indochinois. Session Ordinaire de 1938. (Hanoi: Imprimerie d'Extrême-Orient, 1938), Tables 5 and 9.

4 . Gouvernement général de l'Afrique occidentale française, Annuaire Statistique de l'AOF (1933-38) p. 29.

5. Ibid., p. 25.

6. See especially, Georges Hardy, Une conquête morale: L'Enseignement en AOF (Paris: Armand Colin, 1917).

7. J. L. Monod, Premier Livret de l'Ecolier Soudanais--Langage Lectures, Ecriture. Paris: Librairie Ch. Delagrave, 1911; J. L. Monod, Deuxième Livret de l'Ecolier Soudanais--Langage et Lecture. Paris: Librairie Ch. Delagrave, 1911. The second edition was put out in 1926 and 1929 under the titles Primier Livret de l'Ecolier Noir. Lecture Ecriture - Langage. (Correspondant au programme des Ecoles de Villages de L'AOF) (Paris: Librairie Delagrave, 1924) and Deuxième Livret de l'Ecolier Noir. Langage et Lecture (Correspondant au Programme de langage des écoles de villages de l'Afrique française de l'Ouest). (Paris: Librairie Delègrave, 1926).

8. L. Sonolet et A. Pérès. Methods de Lecture et d'Ecriture de l'Ecolier africain. (Paris: Librairie Armand Colin, 1915).

9. André Leguillette, Histoire de l'Afrique occidentale française. Editions du Bulletin de l'Enseignement de l'Afrique occidentale française. 2e Année, No. 9 (Nov. 1913).

10. J. Toulze, La Composition française à l'École indigène. Editions du Bulletin de l'Enseignement de l'Afrique occidentale française. (Gorée: Imprimerie du Gouvernement général, 1915.)

11. Le Dessin à l'Ecole indigène. Editions du Bulletin de l'Enseignement de l'Afrique occidentale française, 4e Année, No. 18 (Nov. 1915). (Gorée: Imprimerie du Gouvernement général, 1915.)

12. Le Chant à l'Ecole indigene. Editions du Bulletin de l'Enseignement de l'Afrique occidental française. (Gorée: Imprimerie du Gouvernement général, 1916.)

13. Georges Hardy, Géographie de l'Afrique occidentale française. Livre du Maître (avec collaboration de MM. Allier, Instituteur, Amaud, Administrateur des Colonies, Fages, Gallin, Gendron, Gomez, Instituteurs; Monod, Inspecteur des Ecoles de Haut-Sénégal-Niger; Toulze, Traore, Vaillant, Instituteurs.) Editions du Bulletin de l'Enseignement de l'Afrique occidentale française. Gorée: Imprimerie du Gouvernement général, Oct. 1913; G. Frommet. Memento d'Agriculture Soudanaise. Editions du Bulletin de l'Enseignement de l'Afrique occidentale française, 5e Année, No. 31 (Avril - Mai, 1917); D. Bec & A. Pérès. Memento d'Hygiène à l'usage des Instituteurs. Editions du Bulletin de l'Enseignement de l'Afrique occidentale française, 1918.

14. J. L. Monod (Inspecteur des Ecoles au Afrique occidentale française). Instructions au Personnel Enseignant qui debute dans les Ecoles de l'Afrique occidentale française. Editions du Bulletin de l'Enseignement de l'AOF. (Gorée: Imprimerie du Gouvernement Général, 1921.)

15. See A. Davesne. Nouveau syllabaire de Mamadou et Bineta (à l'usage des écoles africaines). Paris & Strasbourg: Istra, 1934; A. Davesne. Mamadou et Bineta lisent et écrivent couramment. Livre de français à l'usage des écoles africaines. Cours préparatoire, 2e Année et cours élémentaire. (Paris & Strasbourg, Istra, 1931); A. Davesne et J. Gouin. Contes de la Brousse et de la Foret. Paris: Istra, 1932; A. Davesne, Les Primieres Lectures de Mamadou et Bineta. Livre de Lecture et de Français à l'usage des Écoles africaines. Cours préparatoire, 2e Année (Paris & Strasbourg: Istra, 1934); A. Davesne & J. Gouin, Mamadou et Bineta Sont Devenus Grands. Livre de Français à l'usage des cours moyens et supérieurs des écoles de l'Afrique noire. (Paris: Istra, 1939).

16. Monod, L'Ecolier noir, op cit. J. L. Monod, Histoire de l'Afrique occidentale française d'après les travaux et les indications de Maurice Delafosse adapte aux Ecoles indigenes (Paris: Delagrave, 1926); R. Rousseau. Cours de Géographie à l'usage des Ecoles de l'Afrique occidentale française. (Paris: Delagrave, 1927).

17. See L. Sonolet, A. Pérès. Le livre du Maître Africaine à l'usage des Écoles et de Village. 2e Edition. (Paris: Armand Colin, 1923); L.

Sonolet et A. Pérès, Moussa et Gigla: Histoire de deux petits noirs. Livre de lecture courante (cours complet d'Enseignement à l'usage des écoles de l'Afrique occidentale française). (Paris: Armand Colin, 1926).

18. Gouvernement Général de l'Afrique occidentale française. Service de l'Enseignement. Textes Portant Réorganisation de l'Enseignement en Afrique occidentale française, ler Mai 1924. Editions du Bulletin de l'Enseignement de l'Afrique occidentale française (no. 57). (Gorée: Imprimerie du Gouvernement Général, 1924).

19. Rousseau, op cit. D. Faucher Blanchard and J. Spinelli. Cours de Géographie. La France et ses Colonies. Ouvrage Adapté specialement aux Ecoles de l'Afrique occidentale française, cours moyen. (Paris: Librairie Gedalge, 1930).

20. Monod, Histoire de l'Afrique occidentale française, op cit.

21. Cahiers de Roulement, Ecole Regionale de Ouagadougou, Année Scolaire 1930-31, cours élémentaire, lère Année, AOM, 46 PA, Carton 2. Cahier de Roulement, Ecole Regionale de Ouagadougou, cours moyen, 2e Année Scolaire 1930-31, AOM, 46 PA, Carton 4, Dossier 20.

22. See Cahier de Devoirs, cours élémentaire, 2e Année, Ecole Regionale de Garcons de Conakry, William Wilson, Année Scolaire 1930-31, AOM, 45 PA, Carton 4, Dossier 18 bis; Cahier de Devoirs, cours préparatoire, 2e Année, Ecole Regionale de Garçons de Conkry, Soriba Lamara, Année Scolaire 1930-31. AOM, 46 PA, Carton 4, dossier 18 bis.

23. This discussion of the Office of Public Instruction is based on Project de loi fixant l'organisation de l'Instruction publique aux colonies, 28 Oct. 1919 and Projet sommaire de l'organisation de l'administration de l'instruction publique aux colonies, 3 juillet 1919. AOM, Nouveau Fonds 259-2223 (1); "La Direction de l'Instruction publique en Indochine." L'Echo Annamite. ler Année, No. 70 (6 juillet 1920) p. 2. (This is a reprint of the Arrêté of 20 mai 1920 establishing the Office of Public Instruction in Indochina appearing in the Journal Officiel de France.) See also 20 juin 1921, Rapport au Gouverneur général suivi d'arrêtés: 1) portant modification au Règlement général de

l'Instruction publique, JOIF. 33e Année, No. 52 (29 juin 1921) pp. 1257-1271.

24. Initially the power to ban and sanction books for school use was in the hands of the Governor General of Indochina as specified in the Arrêté of 6 Avril 1917 (JOIF, 29e Année, No. 26 11 avril 1917, pp. 499-500). Transfer of power to select texts for classroom use occured in 1924 and is detailed in 14 oct. 1924, Arrêté portant creation à la Direction de l'Instruction publique d'une commission de reception de manuels scolaires et de tableaux muraux destinés à l'enseignement primaire elementaire indigène, JOIF, 36e Année, No. 8 (18 oct. 1924), p. 1999; 17 nov. 1928, Arrêté modifiant l'article 21 de l'arrêté du 27 janv. 1925 et l'article 269 du Règlement général de l'Instruction publique en Indochine, JOIF, 49e Année, No. 93 (21 nov. 1928) p. 3443; 10 mai 1926, Arrêté relatif á l'elaboration de manuels scolaires et de tableaux muraux destinés aux élèves des divers cours de l'Enseignement primaire franco-indigène, JOIF, 38e Année, No. 9 (15 mai 1926) p. 1302.

25. See Procès Verbal de la Réunion de la Commission des publications scolaires. No. 6576-E. Hanoi 2 mai 1929. AOM, Fonds du Gouvernement Général 51.239; 26 janv. 1934. Arrêté complètement les articles 262 et 265 du Code de l'Instruction publique. JOIF, 46e Année, No. 9 (31 janv. 1934) p. 275; See also 14 oct. 1924. Arrêté portant création à la Direction de l'Instruction publique d'une commission de réception de manuels scolaires et de tableaux muraux destinés a l'enseignement primaire élémentaire indigène, JOIF, 36e Année, No. 8 (18 oct. 1924) p. 1999.

26. See No. 18, 11 sept. 1924. Le Resident Supérieur, Directeur p.i. de 'Instruction publique en Indochine a M. le Gouverneur Général de l'Indochine. Signé Blanchard de la Brosse. AOM-GG 51.165; No. 698 G 2 oct. 1924. AOM-GG 51.165. The procedure is also outlined in "Manuels Scolaires de la Direction de l'Instruction publique," Bulletin général de l'Instruction publique, Partie générale, lOe Année, No. 9 (mai 1931) pp. 144-48.

27. Indochine francaise. Direction générale de l'Instruction publique. Les Manuels scolaires et les publications pedagogiques de la Direction générale de l'Instruction publique. (Hanoi: Imprimérie d'Extrème - Orient, 1931) ff. p 22 (Tableau).

28. Gouvernement général de l'Indochine francaise. Rapports aux Grand Conseil des intérets economiques et financiers et au Conseil de Gouvernement. Deuxième Partie: Fontionnement des divers services Indochinois (Hanoi: Imprimèrie d'Extrème-Orient, 1938) p. 142.

29. See No. 2151G, 28 nov. 1929. Le Directeur général p.i. de l'Instruction publique en Indochine a M. Le Gouverneur général. Signé Thalamas. AOM, Fonds du Gouvernement général 51.165.

30. No. 107. 1 mars 1918. Le Résident supérieur au Tonkin a M. Le Gouverneur général de l'Indochine à Hanoi. AOM, Fonds du Gouvernement général, 51.163.

31. See AOM, Fonds du Gouvernement général, 51.164 for details of Nguyen-Van-Vinh's textbook venture.

32. See Le Gouverneur de la Cochinchine à M. le Gouverneur général de l'Indochine. No. 262, 15 mars 1928 a.s. Protestations Syndicat des Imprimeurs de Cochinchine relative adjudication des fournitures scolaires à la Direction de l'Instruction Publique. AOM, Fonds du Gouvernement général, 51.172. This dossier also contains letters from the governor.

33. Extrait d'un arreté approuvant la liste additionelle des Publications scolaires qui peuvent être mises en usage dans les écoles publiques franco-indigènes en l'Indochine. JOIF, 38e Année, No. 14 (17 fév. 1926) pp. 468-469.

34. There were many other lists of approved texts appearing in JOIF whose "mix" was similar. See, for example, 15 oct. 1927. Extrait d'un arrêté approuvant la liste additionelle des publications scolaires qui peuvent etre mises en usage dans les écoles franco-indigènes de l'Indochine, JOIF, 45e Année, No. 13 (15 fév. 1933) p. 390.

35. Procès-Verbal de la Réunion de la Commission des publications scolaires. No. 6576-E. Hanoi, 2 mai, 1929. AOM, Fonds du Gouvernement général 51.239.

36. 17 nov. 1928. Arrêté modifiant l'article 21 de l'Arrêté du 27 janv. 1925 et l'Article 269 du Reglement général de l'Instruction publique en Indochine. JOIF, 40e Année, No. 93 (21 nov. 1928) p. 3443.

37. 3 Oct. 1928. No. 1508g. Le Recteur d'Académie, Directeur général de l'Instruction publique en Indochine a M. le Gouverneur général de l'Indochine. Signé Thalamas. AOM, Fonds du Gouvernement général, 51.266.

38. Procès-Verbal de la Réunion de la Commission des publications scolaires. No. 6576-E. Hanoi 2 mai 1929. AOM, Fonds du Gouvernement général 51.239.

39. See footnote 34.

40. No. 1822G. 7 déc. 1915. L'Inspecteur Conseil p. i. de l'Enseignement en Indochine a M. le Gouverneur général de l'Indochine. Hanoi. Signé Henri Russier. A. S. du depot obligatoire des manuels scolaires. AOM, Fonds du Gouvernement général, 51.163.

41. 3 janv. 1916. Minute a M. le Gouverneur général de l'Indochine. Signé Roume. AOM, Fonds du Gouvernement général. 51.163.

42. See Gail P. Kelly, "Teachers and The Transmission of State Knowledge: A Case Study of Colonial Vietnam," in P. G. Altbach, Robert Arnove and Gail P. Kelly (eds.) Comparative Education (New York: Macmillan 1982) pp. 176-194.

43. Georges Hardy, Les Deux Routes, Conseils practiques aux jeunes fonctionnaires indigènes Editions du Bulletin d'Enseignement de l'Afrique occidentale française (7e Année No. 40, nov. 1918) (Gorée: Imprimerie du Gouvernement général, 1919).

44. Gouvernement général de l'Indochine francaise. Rapports au Grand Couseil des interets economiques et financiers et au Conseil de Gouvernement. Deuxieme Partie. Fontionnement des divers service indochinois. (Hanoi: Imprimerie d'Extrême-Orient, 1922, 1938).

45. Gouvernement général de l'Afrique occidentale française. Annuaire Statistique de l'AOF, 1933-1938. Chaptre III. Enseignement Tableau I, p. 25.

46. See Gail P. Kelly, "Education and Participation in Nationalist Groups: A Study of the Indochinese Communist Party and the

VNQDD, 1929-1931." Comparative Education Review15 (June 1971) pp. 227-237.

CHAPTER 5

THE ORIGINS OF INDIA'S TEXTBOOK CULTURE

Krishna Kumar

"If textbooks are treated as a vehicle for education, the living word of the teacher has very little value. A teacher who teaches from textbooks does not impart originality to his pupils. He himself becomes a slave of textbooks and has no opportunity or occasion to be original. It therefore seems that the less textbooks there are, the better it is for the teacher and his pupils."

(M. K. Gandhi, Harijan, September 9, 1939)

Education systems differ in the mode of production and dissemination of textbooks as well as in the expected function and the actual use of textbooks by school teachers. A sharp contrast exists between countries where corporate interests are involved in the textbook business, and others where the state has overwhelming or even monopoly rights to publish school textbooks. How textbooks are supposed to be used is a matter of considerable difference between systems in which state officials merely recommend suitable textbooks or publish a list of approved texts, leaving schools free to select the ones they consider useful, and other systems where specific textbooks are prescribed and no deviation is expected. In the matter of how textbooks are actually used, we can broadly distinguish between two types of education systems. In the first type, the teacher has the freedom to decide what materials to use for developing a lesson. She is trained and expected to prepare her own curricular plan and mode of assessment. She has authority over what happens in the classroom, in what order, at what pace, and with the help of what resources, printed or otherwise. The second type of education system ties the teacher to the prescribed textbook. She is given no choice in the organization of curriculum, pacing, and the mode of final assessment. Textbooks are prescribed for each subject, and the teacher is expected to elucidate it, lesson by lesson in the given order. She must ensure that children are able to write answers to questions based on any lesson in the textbook without seeing it, for this is what they will have to do in the examination when they face one.

The Indian education system is of the second type. As far as the structuring of knowledge is concerned, the system offers a rather limited space within which the school teacher must move. Over the pacing and ordering of knowledge, and over its associations with certain texts, the teacher has very little autonomy. Textbooks hold a central place in the system. The term 'textbook culture,' which will be used throughout the paper, encapsulates certain common features of Indian school pedagogy which are as follows:

1. Teaching in all subjects is based on the textbook prescribed by state authorities.

2. The teacher has no freedom to choose what to teach. She must complete the prescribed syllabus with the help of the prescribed textbook.

3. Resources other than the textbook are not available in the majority of schools, and where they are available they are seldom used. Fear of damage to such resources (e.g. play or science equipment), and the poor chances of repair or replacement discourages the teacher from using them.

4. Assessment during each year and examinations are based on the textbook.

Apart from these manifest features, the textbook culture has a latent feature that relates to the distribution of authority in the system of education. Textbooks are prescribed by the highest bureaucratic authority governing all schools in a state, traditionally known as the Director of Public Instruction. This authority also has the power to appoint, promote, penalize, and transfer a teacher to any school. While the exercise of the powers involving appointment, promotion, and transfer takes place once in a while, the textbook is always present in the school as a symbol of bureaucratic control. It is used as a convenient yardstick to judge a teacher's speed and fluency. Apart from serving as a means through which the bureaucratic authority exercises its influence, it becomes the symbolic hub of the power structure that governs the teacher's daily routine.

This essay examines the historical circumstances, prevailing from the early nineteenth century onwards, under which the textbook-centered culture of Indian school education developed. The essay will first look at the broader socio-economic conditions associated with colonial rule, teachers' service conditions, their professional status, and their status in the wider society. It will then discuss the examination system, and the imposition of a foreign language, as factors that contributed to the growth of an obsession with the prescribed texts among students and teachers. The economic interests that shaped textbook policy are also taken into account. In the final section, the essay will present an overview of post-independence developments.

Nineteenth Century Origins

The textbook-centered character of school pedagogy in India is related to the historical circumstances under which India's present education system developed. More specifically, the roots of the textbook culture can be traced to early nineteenth century when the East India Company took certain definite steps for establishing an education system. The new system acquired a final, bureaucratic format in 1854 from Sir Charles Wood's dispatch. Among the major decisions taken by the colonial administrators during this period, the following are of special interest for us: (i) the new system would be governed by a bureaucracy at every stage from primary schooling onwards, and in all aspects including the structure of syllabi, the content of textbooks, and teachers' training; (ii) the new system would aim at acculturating Indian children and youth in European attitudes and perceptions and at imparting to them the skills required for working in colonial administration, particularly at its middle and lower rungs; (iii) the teaching of English and its use as a medium of instruction would be a means of this acculturation and training; (iv) indigenous schools would have to conform to the syllabus and textbooks prescribed by the colonial government if they wanted to seek the government's aid; (v) impersonal, centralized examinations would be used to assess students' eligibility for promotion and to select candidates for the award of scholarships.

The textbook culture originated in the operational meaning that these policies acquired under the socioeconomic and cultural conditions prevailing in India at the time. These conditions are not easy to characterize. The procedures applied by the colonizer to gain control of the indigenous economy, and later of the indigenous culture, became increasingly complex as the Indian response to colonization developed its contradictions originating in class interests and cultural instincts. In general, even as the native economy with its subsistence agriculture and village-based crafts crumbled under the pressure of taxation and foreign goods, new aspirations spread among the class of people who had profited by acting as middlemen between the English colonizers and the Indian population.[1] These aspirations acted as catalysts for the reception of the colonizer's worldview through education. Colonial education meant that its beneficiaries would begin to perceive themselves and their society as consumers of the knowledge supplied by the colonizer, and would cease to see themselves as people capable of producing new knowledge.[2]

Education was thus supposed to reinforce culturally what colonial policies were aimed at achieving economically. Colonial economic policies in India were aimed at creating a class of consumers of goods manufactured in the colonizer's home country. Steps taken to uplift the colony were not intended to establish a production economy (for this would harm the very purpose of establishing a colony in the first place), but rather to legitimize and consolidate administrative control. Colonial policies did not just leave the productive capacities of the Indian society untouched, they actually destroyed such capacities through direct means like the introduction of new land systems and the dumping of British machine-made goods, and through indirect means such as education involving training in unproductive skills and socialization in colonial perceptions.[3]

Teachers and Teaching

The imposition of a bureaucratically controlled system of education had a dramatic impact on the old vocation of teaching. Instruction in the basic skills was widespread in many parts of India at the time when colonial control of the economy was established. Religious schools were also common. Teaching as a vocation had a base in the caste structure and it had been known in the subcontinent for many centuries as a special form of social activity. Teachers had traditionally enjoyed reverence. Often, they combined priestly functions with teaching. In the indigenous schools surveyed by Adam in 1876, the teacher exercised autonomy in choosing what was worth teaching and in deciding how to teach it. Mostly, the curriculum consisted of acquaintance with culturally significant texts and the learning of skills useful to the village society.[4] In these matters most teachers went by conventions but they had the freedom to make choices.

The new system of centralized official control eroded the teacher's autonomy by denying him any initiative in matters pertaining to the curriculum. Not that the earlier situation offered many alternatives, but it did not impose choices as the new system did. Apart from the official curriculum and texts, the new system also imposed on the teacher the responsibility to fulfill official routines such as the maintenance of admission registers, daily diaries, records of expenditure, and testing. These routines became associated with the fear of punishment and monetary loss, particularly when student performance during inspection began to be used as a criterion for financial grants. The fear led not just to behaviors like sycophancy, self-debasement, and zealous waving of English flags at the time of inspection, but even to the tendency to give extra punishment in case there was any suspicion that a boy might have offended the inspecting officer.[5]

Teachers' behavior towards bureaucratic authority, including their behavior in the matter of sticking to the prescribed textbook, can hardly be properly understood without taking into account the enormous difference of salary and status between the teacher and the officer.[6] At the beginning of the century, a primary school teacher's salary was ten times less than the salary of a Provincial Education Service Officer, and at least four times less than that of a Subordinate Education Service Officer. In 1920, when a trained primary school teacher in the United Provinces had to start with Rs. 17 a month, a deputy inspector started at Rs. 170, and a sub-deputy inspector at Rs. 70. In Bombay, where teachers got a somewhat higher start, a trained primary teacher was given about Rs. 30 while the average for an officer of the Provincial Education Service was Rs. 486 and Rs. 114 per month for an officer of the Subordinate Education Service. Along with this striking difference in salaries went the contrast in power and status. A sub-deputy inspector had the power to mar a teacher's career and teachers were therefore inspired with awe.

In contrast to the new professions that emerged with the consolidation of colonial rule after the 1857 revolt, such as legal and medical practice, teaching soon acquired low status. Compared to civil service, school teaching meant a socially powerless low-paying job and, compared to the other professions, such as legal and medical practice, teaching projected a rather unspecialized image. A substantial part of the school teacher's daily routine, consisted of fulfilling official requirements such as maintenance of accurate records of admission, tests, and money. For a long time, maintaining carefully recorded stocks of prescribed textbooks and dispensing them for a small commission were among the official responsibilities of the teacher in several parts of British India.[7]

Had teachers been given a role in syllabus preparation, and had they been given the freedom to choose suitable textbooks, their identity could perhaps compete better with that of other professions which offered autonomy in professional matters. The possibility of such autonomy being granted to teachers could only arise out of a demand from the teachers themselves or as a result of reform in the policy of the education department. Poor salary and status kept the first route blocked, and the other was obstructed by vested interests. Such interests did not exist when textbook production first started under the auspices of a School Book Society in Calcutta in 1817, but as soon as schooling facilities expanded, particularly after mid-nineteenth century, vested interests developed rapidly.

A letter in the Statesman in 1868 complained that "every inspector has his own friends and prestiges to serve, and thus a good deal of jobbery is perpetrated in the name of uniformity in textbooks."[8] Missionary publishers were among the dominant interests in the textbook business and, as the century advanced, they were joined by firms importing or reprinting books published in England. Three major English firms, Oxford University Press, Macmillan, and Longmans, established offices in India in the early years of the twentieth century. The influence they carried in curriculum committees, consisting mainly of bureaucrats, was far stronger than what Indian publishing houses could muster.[9] This situation changed a little after Indian ministers were appointed for the education departments in the wake of administrative reforms in 1921. The average teacher's lack of freedom to choose textbooks remained unchanged. His role continued to be confined to helping children to learn (or rather memorize) whatever text had been prescribed by the department's bureaucracy.

The textbook culture was a joint product of the preexisting conventions and the conditions created by the colonial bureaucracy. Preexisting conventions consisted of archaic pedagogical practices that treated memorization as a mode of achievement. This is how W. D. Arnold, the Director of Public Instruction in Punjab during 1857-58, described the concept of learning he found popular among people when he came to Punjab:

> We found a whole population agreed together that to read fluently and if possible to say by heart a series of Persian works of which the meaning was not understood by the vast majority, and of which the meaning when understood was for the most part little calculated to edify the minority, constituted education.[10]

The phenomenon Arnold is describing had its roots in old conventions of mechanical reading and rote learning. These conventions apparently offered a suitable climate for textbook culture to flourish. Only if the new education policies had tried to relate learning to the child's real life and milieu would it have posed a threat to existing practices and orientations. This could have happened if teachers had received better compensation, both in terms of money and status, from the bureaucrats. The colonial administration chose not to increase its financial burden by increasing teachers' salaries. It left the teacher in a meek professional role that could only perpetuate the textbook culture.

Examinations and the Curriculum

The policy of impersonal, centralized examinations made a major contribution to the textbook culture. Examinations were impersonal in the sense that students were examined by someone other than the teacher. The idea of impartial assessment meant spot testing by the inspecting official and public written examinations at terminal points. In these examinations, secrecy had to be maintained over both the question papers and the identity of the examiners. With its aura of strictness and impartial treatment of all examinees, the examination system played an important role in the development of a bureaucratic system of education. To the English administrator, examinations, like textbooks, were a means of maintaining norms. As Shukla has pointed out, colonial policy used written examinations to evolve a bureaucratic, centralized governance of education.[11] The official function of the examination system was to evolve uniform standards for promotion, scholarships, and employment, and to thereby consolidate government control. In the social context, the examination system served the purpose of instilling in the public mind the faith that colonial rule was fair and free of prejudice. It imparted this faith by being impersonal, hence non-discriminatory in appearance, and by being wrapped in secrecy.

In practical terms, the examination system required students to rehearse endlessly the skills of reproduction from memory, summarizing, and essay-type writing on any topic. Students were examined on their study of specific texts, not on their understanding of concepts or problems. An early report by Kerr records that when the first uniform code of rules was prepared for government institutions in Bengal, the 'class-books' on which candidates for scholarships were to be examined were specified.[12] A little later, in 1845, an even greater narrowing of the syllabus was implemented by 'fixing' not just the particular textbooks but the exact portion of each which were to be studied for the next scholarship examination. Whatever could not be examined within the norms of the examination system (that is a written essay-type answer to be assessed by an examiner unknown to the student) was kept out of the curriculum, no matter how useful, relevant, and interesting it might be. This is how theoretical, especially literary, study acquired a dominant place in Indian schools and colleges. Literary study fitted nicely within the framework of textbook culture and written examination. Practical or vocational skills and subjects dependent on practical skills (such as the science subjects) were a misfit in the frame. For a long time they were not allowed a place in the approved curriculum and later on, when they were allowed a place, it was peripheral. Literature had an advantage over science in any case as it was perceived in the formative phase of colonial policy as a useful instrument of acculturation. As Chatterjee has mentioned, an important difference between the views of J. S. Mill and Macaulay, both influential theoreticians of the early nineteenth century colonial policies, was that Mill considered both European literature and science necessary for the education of Indian children whereas Macaulay favored literature.[13] It is Macaulay's view that prevailed even though Mill's position had its supporters among influential Indians like Raja Rammohun Roy. Emphasis on literary study set the stage for the textbook culture and once textbook culture was born, it reinforced the dominance of literary study and skills in the curriculum.

Another implication of the examination-textbook link was that the curriculum remained alien, even hostile, to the student's milieu. Since examination was centralized, it could only accommodate the most general kinds of information as opposed to information reflecting a specific milieu. In a country like India, where local milieux are so sharply varied, both geographically and culturally, the demands of a centralized examination system could only be met by a curriculum that transcends local or regional specificity. The nature of questions appropriate for essay-type answers complemented this tendency of the curriculum. The tendency was further strengthened by the dominant role that colonial perceptions played in the selection and representation of knowledge. At the height of the Victorian period, colonial perception of India consisted of broad impressions of the degeneracy of her culture and the destructive effects of her climate on the Indian character. As Welsh has shown, these impressions were reflected in school and college textbooks.[14] The sweeping nature of such impressions, that were both products and feeders of the Victorian tendency to form grand theories about why certain races were backward and certain others so far ahead, found a fitting medium in the textbooks prepared for a centralized examination system. At another level, only this kind of generalized 'knowledge' could be expected to fulfill the agenda of acculturating the Indian student in colonial perceptions and attitudes. Any specific or locally relevant knowledge of social affairs, politics, or even one's own life and one's surroundings was debarred.

A more specific case of how alienation of the curriculum strengthened the textbook-examination linkage and the textbook culture can be found in English as a school subject. The textbook written for the teaching of English used literary pieces whose idiom and images were mostly steeped either in the domestic world of the Victorian bourgeoisie, or in its counterpoint, the natural world of Wordsworth and his early contemporaries. Neither of the two worlds was accessible to the Indian student. Poems about the English spring or winter were as unrelated and strange to the Indian climate as were the happy family stories foreign to the Indian way of life. Texts of this kind could <u>not</u> be read for meaning: they could only be memorized. Conventional pedagogy of reading also contributed to the tendency to memorize, but the role of alien symbolism in making the texts unintelligible was more significant. Lester gives a useful description of how textbook literature encouraged the tendency to memorize lessons for reproduction at the examination:

> Stories in one-syllabled words that English children enjoy, tales of domestic life, of cars, of faithful dogs, of snow and skating, only muddled the minds of those who had never seen ice nor felt cold, who were trained never to let a dog, which ate filth, come near them. As for the pictures which accompany two syllable-worded stories about kettles and tea pots, puddings and turkeys and cozy fireplaces in the cottage kitchens where a table is spread for Sunday dinner, and chairs are drawn up while everyone bows the head to listen to the father asking the blessing, it seemed a mad, if not immoral, world that was being presented. The only thing to do was to learn it all by heart and repeat it rapidly when called upon.[15]

The precise effect of the examination system on the student's orientation toward education cannot be understood without taking into account the relationship between examinations and the opportunities for education and employment. The examination system served as a turnstile between the opportunities for education and the opportunities for employment. Although educational opportunities, in relation to the population, remained very limited throughout the colonial period, they outnumbered the opportunities for employment shortly after the new system of education was introduced. Colonial rule was not designed to, and never did, release the productive energies of the Indian society; the only opportunities for work that it could create were in the administrative domain. Already, by the last quarter of the nineteenth century, this domain was saturated. Despite the extremely narrow spread of education, people with certificates and degrees could not be accommodated in government jobs anymore. Examinations were now required to play a role far wider than that of maintaining norms within the education system. The new role was to keep eligibility for jobs under severe control by keeping the rate of failure high. Any lowering in this rate led to instant worry among colonial rulers.[16] The matriculate and the B.A. examinations, in particular, became watchfully guarded turnstiles to keep the numbers of those going past them under strict control. Loosening of the turnstile would mean invitation to social discontent arising out of joblessness among the eligible.

This function of examinations as an agency of social control resulted in a deep fear of failure among young people. The fear became part of the lore of childhood and the consequences of failure became a recurring motif in literature.[17] Fear of failure in the examination had repercussions both on classroom interaction and students' own strategies of preparation. When the main concern of both the teacher and student was to prevent failure at the examination, the best possible use of classroom teaching could only be to prepare students as meticulously as possible for the examination and this was done by confining teaching to the content of the prescribed textbook. On the student's side, the ability to consign vast amounts of printed text to memory became highly valuable. Metaphors of bodily storage of knowledge became a part of children's culture. Storage of knowledge for guaranteed reproduction in the examination notebook at the end of the year would hardly have been possible without the construction of a strong symbolic association between knowledge and the prescribed textbooks. In the biographical account of his Punjabi ancestry since the middle of the nineteenth century, Prakash Tandon recalls how in his grandfather's days, "the boys had coined a Punjabi expression, remembered even in our days, wishing that they could grind the texts into a pulp and extract knowledge out of them and drink it."[18]

The examination-textbook linkage became stronger as the system of education expanded and as the stagnation of work opportunities exacerbated the competitive character of the system. The linkage defeated all attempts to reform the curriculum and methods of teaching. Gradually, this defeat utterly diluted the spirit with which ideas and programmes of reform were voiced and heard. Commission after commission, starting with the Hunter Commission of the 1880s, bemoaned the stultifying role that examinations had begun to play. Similarly, the obsolete nature of the curriculum was criticized and exhortations were made to change it. Writing in 1910, Alston drew attention to his feeling that colleges had become rival cramming institutions, and he pointed out how absurd it was that politics, history, and economics were taught from single texts. "Books and not subjects are prescribed", he wrote, expressing his impatience with the narrowness of the curriculum and with the tendency among both students and teachers to identify the curriculum with the textbook.[19] Alston's irritation over the absurdity of the situation and the impossibility of reform is just one sample of what was to become the perpetual mood of educational discourse in India.

Finally, the use of English as a compulsory subject in the secondary school, and as a medium of instruction and examination could well be assigned an important role in the rise and perpetuation of the textbook culture. As a foreign language, English posed a dual challenge to the Indian student. He was first supposed to master its grammar and its basic vocabulary, and then to use this barely mastered medium for the study of other school subjects. English was not a part of the average student's ethos, nor could the average student ever hope to be exposed to a native speaker of English. Learning the language meant making the best use of the dictionary, the textbooks (especially the textbook for grammar), and classroom instruction that was devoted to the teaching of the textbooks and grammar. The famous Bengali scientist, P. C. Ray, described the place English held in the curriculum in 1913:

> A boy in an ordinary school from IV onward has to learn something of Grammar, composition, phrases, idioms, homonyms, synonyms, difference between 'shall' and 'will', etc. Now for the matriculation course over and above these, he is expected to have mastered the contents of at least a dozen

> standard books. Even on taking up his I.Sc. course, he is not exempted from the overwhelming burden of textbooks of English Prose and Poetry.[20]

Learning English under such circumstances could only mean an enormous and continuous effort, on a scale that would leave no time or energy to grapple with the subject matter of other school disciplines. Memorization of the textbooks of these other subjects was the only convenient way to avoid failure at the examination. As Annie Besant explained, the students "were struggling to follow the language while they should have been grasping the facts. Their only resource was to utilize their extraordinary power of memorizing by learning textbooks by heart and reproducing them in the examination."[21]

After Independence

Structures of pedagogical transaction, once established, do not give in to change easily. Colonial pedagogy outlasted colonial rule; and in independent India curriculum continues to be textbook-bound. While the system of education has expanded enormously since independence, it has not been able to shed colonial policies of prescription of textbooks and examinations. A major change has come in textbook production with the emergence, mainly since the 1960s, of state corporations that have monopoly rights over the publication of textbooks, especially for the elementary grades. The state has thus extended its role well beyond that of choosing suitable texts and prescribing them. The establishment of the National Council of Educational Research and Training (NCERT) in the early sixties further reified the state's responsibility in curriculum and textbooks by creating a permanent organizational base for these matters. Private publishers still have some interest in the business of school textbooks, but their clientele is restricted mainly to private, especially unaided, schools.

Improvement in the quality of textbooks has been an important area of discussion concerning textbook policy since independence. A frequently discussed aspect of improvement is the quality of production. Organization and accuracy of content and the quality of pedagogical exercises have also received considerable attention. Success along these aspects vastly differs from one school subject to the next. But the important question, from the viewpoint taken in this paper, is whether improvement in the quality of textbooks can directly translate into the weakening of textbook culture. One fact that might help us reflect on this question is that the origins of textbook culture had nothing to do with poor production of textbooks. There always were some good textbooks (limited, though they were, by the state of knowledge at the time) as there are now. But they could not transcend or alter the norms of teacher-pupil interaction, as these norms were shaped by larger socio-economic and cultural conditions. Within the narrower context of the education system, textbook culture was linked to teacher-preparation and evaluation. Even a dramatic improvement in the quality of individual textbooks cannot be expected to alter the textbook culture if these corners of the system remain unattended.

Teachers' training and examinations continue to be two weak areas of the system. Since school teaching has continued being a low-status profession, teachers' training remains a poorly rated academic field. The training of elementary level teachers in particular, and all school teachers in general, remains largely untouched by an academic grounding in modern child-centered pedagogy. Such grounding could possibly dilute the patterns of teacher-pupil interaction associated with the textbook culture. Another factor that could dilute these patterns was improvement in the physical condition of schools. Most Indian schools continue to have poor quality buildings and very little teaching equipment. In elementary schools, the only teaching aid universally available is the prescribed textbook. According to the Fourth All India Educational Survey, 40% of all primary schools have no blackboards, 53% have no play space, 71% have no libraries and 57% are without concrete structures.[22]

The tension between local versus national concerns that is characteristic of the broad political context, has also been a key feature of curricular reforms since independence. Reforms initiated by the government have mostly emphasized the generalized as opposed to the localized kinds of knowledge and symbols. This description would succinctly apply to the nature of curriculum reforms undertaken by the NCERT during these last 25 years of its existence. Earlier, the situation was somewhat ambivalent. During the 'fifties, curriculum policy was characterized by a conflict between the pull towards local relevance under Gandhian "basic education." Gandhi's plan for educational reform was defeated both by ideological opposition to his vision of a self-reliant rural society and by deliberate attempts to make implementation ineffective. Textbook publishing houses were among the lobbies that made such attempts.

The trend towards centralized, as opposed to localized, development of curriculum and texts favors the continued use of prescribed textbooks as the dominant tool of pedagogy and as a symbol of the prescribing authority. This has led to a new contradiction. Schools are now expected to assist in the development of the child's total personality, and not just impart the basic skills as schools did in the past. The new task demands the use of child-centered methods of teaching and decreased reliance on the prescribed textbooks. It also demands greater autonomy for teachers. This is the area where the new expectation from schools contradicts the pull towards further bureaucratization and centralized management. Autonomy for teachers would imply greater professional self-reliance, demand for higher status, and local control. The fear of such demands continues to force the education system to reject the option of truly professionalizing its teachers. Professionalizing the school teacher would not just mean superior academic training, it would also mean conceding to the teacher the right to autonomy in matters pertaining to the choice of materials for teaching and in the construction of the daily curriculum. It would also mean some chance of thinning the textbook culture.

NOTES

1. See Anil Seal, The Emergence of Indian Nationalism (Cambridge: Cambridge University Press, 1968), particularly the chapter on 'The Rewards of Education'. Also see R. E. Frykenberg, 'Education as an Instrument of Imperial Integration during the Company's Raj in South India', Indo-British Review 22 (June 1983) pp. 58-85.

2. This was not very different from the way colonial rule worked in other societies. See P. Altbach and G. Kelly (eds.), Education and Colonialism (New York: Longmans, 1978).

3. For a comprehensive analysis of the status and role of education in a colonial, non-productive economy, see Asok Sen, Iswar Chandra Vidyasagar and His Elusive Milestones (Calcutta: Riddhi-India, 1977).

4. See the Adam Reports whose new edition is entitled One Teacher, One School (New Delhi: Biblia Impex, 1983).

5. See, for instance, Rev. G. Milburn's article, 'Government and the Schools' in The Indian Review 15 (March 1914) pp. 341-342. Also see Arthur Mayhew, The Education of India (London: Faber and Gwyer, 1926).

6. The amounts mentioned in this paragraph are given in the Ninth Quinquennial Review (Vol. I), Progress of Education in India 1922-27 (Calcutta: Government of India, Central Publication Branch, 1929).

7. See A. P. Howell's report, 'Education in British India, 1870-71' in Selections from Educational Records of the Government of India, Vol. I (Delhi: National Archives, 1960).

8. The Statesman, January 1, 1868. Fraser's full name, never mentioned in his writings, was J. Nelson Fraser.

9. For one account illustrating the influence, see 'Notes and Jottings' in The Hindustan Review 16 (October 1903) p. 364.

10. See J. A. Richey, ed., Selections from Educational Records, Part II 1840-1859 (Delhi: National Archives, 1965) p. 301.

11. S. Shukla, 'Education, Economy and Social Structure in British India', Varanasi National Journal of Education, 1 (No. 1 & 2: 1978) pp. 112-125; 7-80.

12. J. Kerr, Review of Public Instruction in the Bengal Presidency (Calcutta: J. Thomas, 1852).

13. Kalyan K. Chatterjee, 'Mill and Macaulay on Indian Education', Indo-British Review 4 (No. 4, 1972) pp. 85-89.

14. Judith E. Welsh, Growing Up in British India (New York: Holmes & Meier, 1983).

15. Muriel Lester, Gandhi, World Citizen (Allahabad: Kitab Mahal, 1962) p. 37.

16. For example, see the item 'A Novel Resolution' in The Indian Review 16 (April 1915) p. 378, reporting the attempt made by E. R. Watson, a member of the Calcutta University Senate, to raise an alarm over the rise in the percentage of passes in the examination.

17. Two eminent examples are Premchand's 'Bare bhai saheb' (Big Brother), first published in 1933, and Chandra Bali Pathak's 'Pareeksha' (The Test), published in 1925 in Balsakha, a children's monthly.

18. Prakash Tandon, Punjabi Century 1857-1947 (Berkeley: University of California Press, 1968).

19. L. Alston, Education and Citizenship in India (Bombay: Longmans, 1910) p. 63.

20. P. C. Ray, 'Scientific Instruction through the Vernaculars', The Indian Review 14 (April 1913) pp. 345-346.

21. Annie Besant, India: Bond or Free? (Madras: The Theosophical Publishing House, 1939).

22. The Fourth All India Educational Survey (New Delhi: NCERT, 1982).

PART 2

Content and Curriculum

CHAPTER 6

GENDER AND TEXTBOOKS: AN AFRICAN CASE STUDY

Karen L. Biraimah

Textbooks, by their very nature, tend to control knowledge as well as transmit selected values and role models to students. When these textbooks are generated within a society for which they were designed, they often reinforce cultural values of the majority, concomitant with inequalities embedded within that society. Textbooks produced in one country, but used in another, make issues of knowledge control and transmission of values more complex. And when these countries were once linked through a colonizer-colonized relationship, attempts to understand the implications of textbook production and use often take on the added dimension of imperialism.

For several reasons, including lack of educational infrastructure and budgetary constraints, many Third World countries often rely on former colonial powers for educational expertise and technology, as well as the production and control of scholarly journals, textbooks and the like. This dependency on industrialized nations for the delineation and production of knowledge (commodified in textbooks) often transfers new roles and values to the recipient country.

To determine whether this dependency on western educational materials necessarily perpetuates a form of imperialism through the control of knowledge and transmission of selected values, this chapter will focus on the issue of gender roles and how they are transmitted to West African school children who read textbook produced in France. The chapter will explore patterns of gender-role allocations within the official textbooks of a West African secondary school, and ask whether these sex-role divisions of labor represent a reorientation in values when compared to actual gender roles within that society. If a significant difference between actual female labor force participation and the sex-role division of labor presented in the texts is found, then one could posit that these patterns of gender-differentiation exemplify a form of imperialism through the introduction of new values from industrialized nations to Africa.

The chapter concludes with a discussion of the need and means by which Third World countries might lessen the effects of educational dependency, while encouraging the development of indigenous textbooks more sensitive to the students' lived culture.

Methodology and Textbook Sources

All books used in this study were required texts for third year (or 4ème) students at a four year school that will be called Lome Secondary School. Textbooks were available in the 4ème subjects of mathematics, physics-chemistry, French, English, and history-geography, but unavailable for classes in natural science, homemaking, or sports (see Table 6.1).[1] To determine patterns of gender-role allocations within these official textbooks of Lome Secondary School, every exercise and illustration was reviewed, as well as the content of each book's written text. Categories describing characters' role assignments and activities were established only after the raw data were gathered and analyzed. No effort was made to fit the data to predetermined classifications.

All textbooks were relatively recent, being published between 1972 and 1974, with the exception of the physics-chemistry text which was published in 1961. All were published in France, with none of the texts being a direct product of Togo or French-speaking Africa, though the English, French, and history textbooks were specifically directed toward African students. Judging from surnames and credits, most of the authors and editors were French males.

Initially, it appears problematic why Togo would continue to allow school knowledge to be controlled by France nearly three decades after achieving independence. Though Togo has made some effort to produce a few educational materials locally, these remain, for the most part, bound mimeographed texts with limited circulation and use. The vast majority of school textbooks, as well as other publications available in local bookstores, continue to be products of France or other Western countries. A cursory examination of new school textbooks, that were

Table 6.1
Lome Secondary Schoo1 4ème Textbooks

Subject	Title	Author(s)	Place	Publishing Company	Date
1) English	English for French-Speaking Africa: Working with English	David Mills Boniface Zodéogan Tim Doust Barry Tomalin	Paris	Librairie Armand Colin	1974
2) French	Manuel de Francaise Domaine Africain	Jean-Louis Joubert	Paris	Bordas	1972
3) History	Histoire: Le Monde Contemporain	Institut Pédagogique Africain et Malgache	Paris	EDICEF	1973
4) Math	Mathematique: Serie Rouge	Michel Queysanne André Revuz	Paris	Fermand Nathan	1973
5) Science	Physics et Chimie	G. Legreneur M. Peyraud	Paris	Classiques Hachette	1961

Note: While Lome Secondary School has recently adopted revised editions of some of these textbooks, they remain, for the most part, products of French male authors published in France.

adopted too recently to be included in this study, suggest similar patterns of knowledge production and control by France. Most new books were simply the revised editions of textbooks discussed in this chapter. Though Togo may not be comfortable with this arrangement, there appear to be several reasons for continued dependency on Western nations. First, Togo's small population, approximately two and one-half million, suggests a limited readership which can make publication quite expensive. Second, the enormous costs involved in establishing and running a Togolese publishing firm may be quite prohibitive when school budgets are already strained. Togo, like many other African nations, is struggling to educate a population which is overwhelmingly youthful and rural (70% of Togo's population is under thirty years of age, while 87% of the inhabitants live in rural areas).[2]

Moreover, if textbooks continue to be published in France, the issue of language remains moot. Currently, all texts originating in Paris are published in French, with the exception of the English language textbooks. However, if publishing was conducted locally in Togo, the decision of which language(s) to use in the textbooks could easily become a divisive factor among various ethnic groups.

As these and other factors may extend Togo's reliance on French textbooks for an indefinite period of time, it is important to identify the types of messages and values that these textbooks transmit to Togolese school children. The following discussion will highlight the quantity and variety of male versus female characters found within the 4ème textbooks of Lome Secondary School.

Textbooks: Visibility, Personal Attributes and Activities of Male Versus Female Characters

When the subjects of each reading, illustration, and exercise within the five 4ème textbooks were catalogued by gender, two important trends appear. First, males were found at least twice as often as female characters. Seventy percent of all humans portrayed in the textbooks were males, while only 30% were females (see Table 6.2). Second, though females were only marginally represented in the liberal arts textbooks, they were virtually non-existent within the science and mathematics textbooks. A total of twenty-six females were identified within the 671 pages comprising the physics-chemistry and mathematics textbooks (there were a total of 4,498 human characters identified within the 4ème textbooks).

Table 6.2
Quantity of Subjects in Textbooks (by Gender)

Subjects	All Books No.	All Books %	English No.	English %	French No.	French %
All Subjects	4498	---	1768	---	1936	---
Female	1367	30%	635	36%	597	31%
Male	3131	70%	1133	64%	1339	69%
	History-Geo.		Mathematics		Physics-Chem.	
All Subjects	693	---	36	---	65	---
Female	109	16%	11	31%	15	23%
Male	584	84%	25	69%	50	77%

An analysis of the quantity of male versus female subjects suggests themes of gender differentiation, but to be meaningful it must be expanded to include a discussion of the subjects' attributes and actions. In the following discussion the personal characteristics and non-career activities of these subjects are analyzed to determine if messages regarding the differentiation of male versus female characters are being transmitted through the textbooks. Job allocations will be discussed separately.

Table 6.3 represents, quantitatively, the characteristics and activities of male versus female subjects transmitted through the five 4ème textbooks.[3] While males dominated every category except victim, a closer examination of individual attributes reveals very definite patterns of gender differentiation. Though twice as many male as female subjects were portrayed in the textbooks, females still represented over half of the characters described as being witches, poor, without rights, wives, or girlfriends. Men, in contrast to females' narrowly defined and rather negative roles, were associated with a broader cross-section of characteristics and activities ranging from rich to ugly, and from active sporting events to passive spectator roles.

However, to gain a real sense of the gender-differentiated messages being transmitted through the texts it is necessary to go beyond a quantitative analysis. The following excerpts from the 4ème textbooks clearly illustrate themes of treachery, wickedness, and greediness or female involvement in frivolous social or home/nurturing activities.

The theme that achievement oriented males should avoid treacherous and self-seeking females is well illustrated in the following excerpt from a chapter within the English textbook entitled "Ask Charity."

> Dear Charity,
>
> I am 16 years old. My girl-friend is taking "A" levels next year. She loves me very much but whenever she writes to me, she asks me for money. Last week she threatened that our love affair would end if I didn't send her any. Should I leave her? I wish you would tell me what to do.
>
> "Worried," Accra, Ghana

CHARITY: You'd better leave her quickly before she gets you into trouble.[4]

Table 6.3
Personal Characteristics and Activities
Present in Textbooks (by Gender)

Category	Female		Male	
	No.	%	No.	%
I. Personal Characteristics				
A. Positive	12	17%	59	83%
1. Handsome/Beautiful	8	24%	25	76%
2. Rich	2	7%	25	93%
3. Dominant	2	18%	9	82%
B. Negative	12	33%	24	67%
1. Disobedient	4	40%	6	60%
2. Lazy/Ugly	8	31%	18	69%
C. Villain	10	30%	23	70%
1. Thief/Prisoner	2	9%	20	91%
2. Witch/Warlock	8	73%	3	27%
D. Victim	39	50%	39	50%
1. Poor	23	88%	3	12%

Table 6.3 continued

2. Refugee	2	50%	2	50%
3. Without Rights	2	67%	1	33%
4. Victim	10	26%	28	74%
5. Slave	2	29%	5	71%
II. Activity				
A. Active	49	21%	190	79%
1. Travel	30	24%	94	76%
2. Sports/Games	1	2%	40	98%
3. Scouting	0	0%	1	100%
4. Festivals	10	37%	17	63%
5. Revolutionary	8	17%	38	83%
B. Passive	110	44%	139	56%
1. Passive Spectator	14	42%	19	58%
2. Sedentary	16	33%	33	67%
3. Social Gathering	25	38%	40	62%
4. Husband/Wife	36	52%	33	48%
5. Boyfriend/Girlfriend	19	58%	14	42%
TOTAL	232	33%	474	67%

Women's stupidity, greediness, and inherently wicked nature were also consistent themes used to explain the evils and unhappiness found within society. For example, a reading from the English text entitled "The Magic Calabash" (or gourd) depicts a female character, Tunde, who is prompted by her poor widowed mother to negotiate with an evil witch for a magic calabash. Her sister Ayo warned her:

> not to take a big one. But Tunde was greedy, so she grabbed the largest one she could find and ran home with it.
>
> When she got home, Ayo was afraid. "I begged you not to get a large one," she said. "Oh, don't be so silly, Ayo," said the widow. Tunde cut open the calabash but instead of silk, out jumped snakes and toads, cockroaches and scorpions. Tunde, Ayo and the widow ran for their lives, and they never came back to the house again.[5]

Not only were women portrayed as wicked, greedy, or treacherous, but they were also presented as individuals whose personal interests were limited to social gatherings or fashions. For example, in the article "Two Pages From Our School Magazine," girls are criticized for their over-indulgence in European fashions.

> In the old days everybody used to wear agbadas or cloths. But nowadays we have to follow the latest fashion. . . and worse of all, we think we ought to copy what people wear in Europe. For instance, in the old days women used to tress their hair, but now lots of girls think they need to wear wigs, if they want to be smart. I've even seen girls walking down the street in boots! They were so hot and uncomfortable![6]

Themes of marginality were not limited to fictional characters, but were also prevalent among the few female figures appearing in the historical discussions or recreations. For example, in the students' history textbook one colorful illustration depicted lavishly dressed Nineteenth Century "Bourgeois Ladies of Leisure" chatting and devouring pasteries. The accompanying text described them as "venting their numerous household cares" by making "frequent and elegant assaults on a stylish pastery shop."[7]

The theme of women as wives, daughters, and queens, whose sole purpose is to serve and be dominated by men was also underscored through much of the literature. For example, in a selection that recreates the daily life in the court of King Guézo of the Dahomey Empire, the male author illustrates the king's absolute power over his subjects through a description of his wife's subservient duties.

> A queen advanced on her knees toward the King, calabash in hand. She put down her burden, uncovered: a white folded towel and three medium calabashes, of which two were closed and filled with water. The woman placed the wide calabash under the hands of the King who extended his arms; she took one of the calabashes of water, swallowed three sips of this liquid, then carefully washed the hands of the King and rinsed them with water from the second calabash, after having taken several sips as before. She finally dried his hands with the white towel and withdrew.[8]

Females were also frequently showcased in victimized roles as illustrated in the following excerpt from the students' English textbook.

> A young married woman went swimming in the river one morning. She didn't notice the crocodiles were watching her. Suddenly,one of the crocodiles slipped into the water and caught her leg in its mouth. Another crocodile saw what was happening and attacked the first one, which let go of the girl to fight its attacker. While the two crocodiles were fighting each other, the poor woman swam slowly to the bank. Fortunately some people near the river heard her cries and carried her to hospital. The crocodiles stopped fighting when they saw their victim had gone. But when they went after her, the people threw stones at them.[9]

Women and girls were also portrayed as victims of poverty while men and boys were often cast in roles associated with wealth or productive activities. The first of two excerpts that follow emphasizes that sisters suffer more setbacks in a poor family than do their brothers, while the second excerpt suggests that young boys are involved in rewarding experiences.

> Once when I was eating in a restaurant in town, a little girl came up to me to give me some water to wash my hands with. When I talked to her, I found that her father had two sons who were in school, but that he hadn't enough money to send his daughter to school as well.[10]

"Ten Year-Old Schoolboy
Earns 40 Pounds a Month"

> While visiting Benin--the capital of the Mid-West State of Nigeria--I was delighted to meet a young schoolboy who can earn up to 40 pounds a month. He is not even a teenager yet, but in one holiday month he can make four large brass statues which sell for about 10 pounds each. "Will you go to secondary school?" I asked him. "Yes, I will," he replied, "and then I will go to university to study African culture."[11]

When the texts are evaluated for quantity and quality of male and female roles, we find women marginally represented within narrowly defined roles conveying themes of wickedness, victimization, or dependency. Males, in contrast, are found in numerous and varied roles emphasizing positive characteristics and active participation in life.

Textbooks: Occupations of Male Versus Female Characters

Though the 4ème textbooks presented people in a wide variety of activities ranging from simple patterns of daily existence to more complex human interactions involving attributes of dominance or passivity, this discussion will now isolate those human activities directly related to occupations in order to identify patterns of sex-role differentiation transmitted by the texts.

Though the majority of male and female characters found within the 4ème texts were not directly associated with a particular career or occupation, significant portions of the textbooks were devoted to job-specific activities. Twenty-two percent of all humans present were associated with a specific career or job (992 of 4,498), though males were depicted in job-related activities three times as often as females. Nine percent of all female subjects (117 of 1,367) and 28% of all male subjects (875 of 3,131) were presented in job-related activities. If the role of housewife is considered an occupation, then 11% of all female subjects (153 of 1,367) were cast in job-related roles.

Table 6.4, which summarizes the major job categories presented within the 4ème textbooks, emphasizes two themes; the marginality of females within the world of work, and gender-differentiation of appropriate tasks. Women were found in only 12% of all job-related roles, while males were featured in 88% of all work-oriented activities. Moreover, the few career roles that were allocated to women remained,

Table 6.4
Occupations Present in Textbooks by Gender
(Percent of Male v. Female occupations)

Category	Female No.	Female %	Male No.	Male %
I. Leadership	9	3%	258	97%
A. Political Leader	0	0%	146	100%
B. Royalty/Nobility	9	10%	78	90%
C. Social/Religious Leader	0	0%	27	100%
D. Scoutmaster	0	0%	7	100%
II. Medical/Scientific	7	12%	50	88%
A. Scientist	2	5%	40	95%
B. Doctor	0	0%	9	100%
C. Nurse/Midwife	5	83%	1	17%
III. Academic/Arts	8	4%	210	96%
A. Writer/Reporter	5	5%	94	95%
B. Artist/Musician	2	13%	14	87%
C. Teacher/Professor	1	3%	36	97%
D. Headmaster	0	0%	7	100%

Table 6.4 continued

IV.	Business/Commerce	39	40%	59	60%
	A. Administrator	1	5%	18	95%
	B. Office Worker	2	18%	9	82%
	C. Cottage Industry	24	57%	18	43%
	D. Market Vendor/Trader	12	46%	14	54%
V.	Trades, Transportation, Labor	31	34%	59	66%
	A. Skilled Trades	7	35%	13	65%
	B. Factory Worker	2	6%	29	94%
	C. Laborer	4	36%	7	64%
	D. Transport. Worker	1	9%	10	91%
	E. Flight Attendant	17	100%	0	0
VI.	Defense/Police	2	2%	131	98%
	A. Military Leader	0	0%	44	100%
	B. Police/Fire Officer	0	0%	5	100%
	C. Armed Forces (enlisted)	2	3%	64	97%
	D. Police/Fire (enlisted)	0	0%	18	100%
VII.	Less Skilled/Independent Trade	21	16%	108	84%
	A. Famous Explorer	0	0%	36	100%
	B. Farmer/Fisher	7	16%	37	84%
	C. Hunter	1	7%	14	93%

Table 6.4 continued

D. Childcare/Parenting	13	38%	21	62%
TOTAL	117	12%	875	88%

for the most part, within the "traditional" female domains of nurse, queen, market vendor, cottage industries and skilled trades (such as weaving and hairdressing), flight attendant, or childcare workers.

The data in table 6.4 indicate that male subjects were well represented in a wide variety of job classifications including political leader, scientist, teacher, business leader, factory worker, transportation worker, military leader, or hunter. This is exemplified by an analysis of male role allocations depicted in the illustrations and captions found in the students' history book. The following abridged list of male occupations represents the variety of jobs fulfilled by men.

1. Cowboys in "Raising Cattle in Argentina."[12]

2. Religious leader in "The Pope Receives the Keys to Rome."[13]

3. Assembly-line workers in "Two Examples of Mass Production."[14]

4. European explorers in "Stanley Finds Livingstone (1868)."[15]

5. Ambassador in "An English Ambassador in China in 1816."[16]

6. Japanese emperor in "Emperor Mutsu Hito (1867-1912)."[17]

7. Astronaut in "The Conquest of Space."[18]

8. Revolutionary leaders in "The October Revolution."[19]

9. Teacher in "French Schools in Timbuktu in 1913."[20]

10. Scientist in "Louis Pasteur in His Laboratory."[21]

This predominance of males in productive roles within the history text is reinforced in the physics-chemistry textbook where only male scientists were mentioned. Men such as Faraday, Bunsen, Bessemer, and Berthelot were credited with noteworthy discoveries, and were often described in extremely complementary terms as in the following excerpt describing Ampère.

> Curious and fruitful spirit, with superior intelligence, André-Marie Ampère was a scholar full of genius. He devoted himself to mathematics, natural science, chemistry and especially to physics.[22]

In contrast to this wide range of job allocations, female characters appeared in fewer and less diverse roles. Women were frequently present in occupations such as flight attendant, nurse, market worker, child care/parenting, laborer, or skilled trades, but were present less than 25% of the time in the remaining twenty-one job categories found within the texts. Sex-role differentiation and the limited nature of female occupations are made clearer when the following list of female role allocations depicted in the history text illustrations is compared to the previous list of male occupations.

1. Tending babies and children in "Peasants in Southern India."[23]

2. Farm workers in "Poor Peasants of Europe."[24]

3. Slaves in "The Cultivation of Cotton in the South."[25]

4. Factory worker in "Weaving Machines in 1850."[26]

Even in the relatively glamorous job of flight attendant, the nurturing and marginal role of women was reinforced. For example, the following excerpt from the English text titled "I Want to be an Air-Hostess" emphasized the duties of serving food and tending babies, while indicating that charm is a major reason for being hired, and marriage a definite cause for dismissal.

> (Male reporter interviewing an air-hostess.)
> ANNOUNCER: . . . and this evening our reporter, Badarou Ousmane, is waiting for us at the airport. Are you there, Ousmane?
>
> REPORTER: Yes, here I am at the airport with some charming young air-hostesses. Let me see, you've just got off that plane over there, haven't you?
>
> AIR-HOSTESS: Yes, that's right. I've just arrived on the flight from Abidjan.
>
> REPORTER: They say being an air-hostess is very exciting. Is that true?

> 1st AIR-HOSTESS: Mmm, I don't know. You have to work very hard.
>
> 2nd AIR-HOSTESS: Oh, but it's a fascinating job. You travel all over the world.
>
> 1st AIR-HOSTESS: Well, perhaps you do. But I haven't stopped working since nine o'clock this morning--serving dinner, giving out drinks, selling cigarettes, looking after babies. I'm worn out!
>
> REPORTER: How long have you been working here?
>
> GROUND-HOSTESS: Oh, I've been here for years. I joined Air Afrique in 1965. But I became a ground-hostess last year, when I got married.
>
> 1st AIR-HOSTESS: Yes, you must stay single if you want to be an air-hostess.[27]

When notable female historical figures were included, they were often described as someone's wife or mother, wearing a particular style of clothing, or linked to ineffective or cruel policies. For example, the caption below a full-length picture of Ranavalona I (former Queen of Madagascar), while mentioning that she was active in politics, also pointed out that she was the widow of King Radama I, and that her robes were inspired by European design. In the text that follows entitled "The Traditionalist Reaction: The Reign of Ranavalona I 1828-1861," Queen Ranavalona was depicted as reactionary, manipulated by lords, and the supporter of cruel practices during her reign.

> The reign of Ranavalona, widow of Radama, reacted against innovation; being pressured by the grand lords who feared loosing their priviledges, the Queen hunted foreigners and missionaries and returned to former customs which included secret societies who counted many victims among their exploits.[28]

Later in the same text a discussion of the history of China included a description of Empress Tsue Hi. She was portrayed as using "cruel and treacherous" means while attempting to restore the empire to its former greatness.[29] Though this description may indeed be factually correct, emphasis on historical figures such as Tseu Hi distort and limit a student's knowledge regarding the role of women in history and society.

Though some females such as Queen Ranavalona or Empress Tseu Hi were presented in positions of power, the majority of females depicted in the texts were relegated to low-status occupations. For example, based on the data in Table 6.5, females comprised a large portion of the business and commerce occupations (40% female) but when these occupations were grouped according to status, only 5% of the high-status positions were held by women. The bulk of the female subjects were involved in low-status jobs such as cottage industries (57% female), or market worker (46% female). Likewise, 83% of the lower status medical or scientific occupations such as nurse were assigned to women, while 96% of the doctors and research scientists were men. Overall, when all jobs presented in the 4ème texts were grouped according to relative status, women were cast in only 3% of all high-status occupations (20 out of 574 jobs).

Through this discussion of the 4ème textbooks, consistent patterns of sex-role differentiation and female marginality have been uncovered. Whether originating from quantitative data on the presence of female subjects within the books, or more qualitative analyses of subjects' characteristics, activities, or job allocations, messages limiting females to marginal or menial roles were consistently transmitted to those students who read the books.

While these findings may be significant when analyzing the degree of gender-differentiation found within a formal curriculum, the focus of this chapter is to determine whether the messages that originate in France, foster imperialism through the transfer of values and role models inconsistent with Togo's lived culture.

Women in the Togolese Labor Force

The discussion thus far has been concerned with sex-role divisions of labor transmitted through Lome Secondary School's textbooks. Yet a central issue in this chapter remains whether this labor force participation represents a significant change and reorientation in values when compared to actual gender roles within Togolese society. If a significant difference between actual female labor force participation and the sex-role division of labor presented in the texts is identified, then these patterns of gender differentiation found within the textbooks might exemplify a form of imperialism through the introduction of new values from France to Togo.

Table 6.5
High and Low Status Occupations Present in Textbooks
(by Gender)

Category	Female		Male	
	No.	%	No.	%
I. Leadership	9	3%	258	97%
A. High Status	9	3%	251	97%
B. Low Status	0	0%	7	100%
II. Medical/Scientific	7	12%	50	88%
A. High Status	2	4%	49	96%
B. Low Status	5	83%	1	17%
III. Academic/Arts	2	4%	210	96%
A. High Status	8	5%	151	95%
B. Low Status	0	0%	59	100%
IV. Business/Commerce	39	40%	59	60%
A. High Status	1	5%	18	95%

Table 6.5 continued

B. Low Status	38	48%	41	52%
V. Trades, Transport., Labor	31	34%	59	66%
A. High Status	0	0%	0	0%
B. Low Status	31	34%	59	66%
VI. Defense/Police	2	2%	131	98%
A. High Status	0	0%	49	100%
B. Low Status	2	2%	82	98%
VII. Less Skilled/Independent Trade	21	16%	108	84%
A. High Status	0	0%	36	100%
B. Low Status	21	23%	72	77%
HIGH STATUS TOTAL:	20	3%	554	97%
LOW STATUS TOTAL:	97	23%	321	77%
TOTAL:	117	12%	875	88%

To pursue this theme it is necessary to compare the textbooks' portrayal of female work force participation with the known labor force participation of women within Togolese society. To evaluate the textbooks' messages regarding the sex-role division of labor with known female work force participation within Togo, the 4ème female students at Lome Secondary school were asked what type of jobs were held by relatives and Togolese women within their communities. In this way the expectations within the textbooks can be compared to labor force realities (as known to the students), to determine if the books transfer goals and values incongruent with those of Togolese society.

While textbooks underscored the marginality of females, the families of the 4ème girls offered a source of career role models not necessarily reinforced through textbooks, while providing support and motivation for these girls to succeed in both their education and future careers. Though the parents were not usually employed in careers desired by their daughters (over 90% of the girls did not expect to have jobs like their parents), a variety of other relatives did have jobs that reflected the students' own career interests. These relatives also provided a breadth of career role models not transmitted through the textbooks. For example, beyond the careers of nurse/midwife, flight attendant, hair dresser, or childcare worker, the girls were aware of, and expected to be employed like relatives who were doctors, lawyers, laboratory technicians, engineers, architects, school directors, journalists, or political leaders.

Besides the career role models present within families, the girls were also aware of a wide range of jobs held by Togolese women within their communities. Table 6.6 reflects the type of occupations held by the secondary school girls' female relatives, and women within Togolese society. It also shows the range of female occupations represented within the 4ème textbooks of Lome Secondary School.

When these data are compared it becomes apparent that the girls' knowledge of female participation in the Togolese work force has little in common with those careers transmitted through the textbooks. For example, careers as nurse, teacher, and office worker represent nearly 40% of all known female career possibilities, and nearly all of the modern sector careers mentioned, while women with modern sector occupations within the textbooks are either flight attendants or participants in a variety of skilled trades, unskilled labor, or child-care services.

Table 6.6
Female Students' Awareness of Female Participation in the Togolese Labor Force (Compared with Female Occupations Occuring in Textbooks)

Occupation	Known Females* in Togolese Labor Force (%)	Female Occupations in Textbooks (%)
I. Traditional Sector	57.1	34.6
1) Street/Market Vendor	46.8	7.8
2) Cottage Industries	6.7	15.7
3) Food Services	1.1	0
4) Farmer/Hunter	1.4	5.2
5) Small Storekeeper	1.1	0
6) Royalty/Nobility	0	5.9
II. Modern Sector	42.2	42.0
A) Medical	10.7	3.3
1) Nurse/Midwife	9.9	3.3
2) Hospital Worker	0.4	0
3) Lab. Technician	0.4	0

Table 6.6 continued

B) <u>Professional</u>	<u>3.3</u>	<u>1.3</u>
1) Lawyer	1.4	0
2) Engineer/Scientist	0.4	1.3
3) Architect	0.4	0
4) Political Leader	1.1	0
C) <u>Education</u>	<u>12.8</u>	<u>0.7</u>
1) Teacher	12.1	0.7
2) School Director	0.7	0
D) <u>Communications/Travel</u>	<u>1.1</u>	<u>16.4</u>
1) Flight Attendant	0.4	11.8
2) Journalist/Broadcaster	0.7	4.6
E) <u>Clerical</u>	<u>15.4</u>	<u>2.0</u>
1) Secretary	8.2	1.3
2) Cashier	2.5	0
3) Telephonist	2.5	0
4) Typist	1.8	0

Table 6.6 continued

5) Accountant/Bookkeeper	0.4	0
6) Administrator	0	0.7
F) Less Skilled Occupations	0	18.3
1) Skilled Trades	0	4.6
2) Unskilled Labor	0	3.9
3) Armed Forces	0	1.3
4) Childcare	0	8.5
III. Housewife	0	23.5

*Occupations held by female relatives and women within the community.

Another inconsistency which occurs is related to traditional sector employment which ranges from 57% of the known female work force to 35% of the textbooks' transmitted career expectations. This variance might be explained by the fact that the known female work force includes many older and poorly educated market vendors, while the textbooks are aimed at a select group of educated girls who, by their very presence in secondary school, are not likely to be identified with traditional employment.

Women as full-time housewives or childcare workers is yet another major incongruity between what girls and the textbooks perceive as appropriate female work force participation. Though not one school girl mentioned housewife or childcare worker as the main occupation of any known relative or Togolese women, one-third of all textbook characterizations reinforced these role expectations.

In summary, the textbooks' transmitted role expectations for female students did not closely parallel the girls' own knowledge of female participation within the Togolese work force. The texts also emphasized the limited nature and sparse participation of females within the work force, while they fostered the role of mother and housewife as full-time careers. None of these expectations were reinforced by known participation of women in the Togolese labor force.

Conclusion

The purpose of this chapter was to examine a set of textbooks used by West African students, but produced in France, to determine if messages transmitted within these texts represented a significant change and reorientation in values compared with those of the students' lived culture. Furthermore, if those values, as represented by gender-role allocations within school textbooks, varied significantly from actual female labor force participation, then one might posit that continued dependence on former colonial masters for school textbooks simply reinforced a form of imperialism through the introduction of new values from industrialized nations to Africa.

The results of the textbook study discussed in this chapter suggest that students not only received gender-differentiated knowledge with regard to divisions of labor, but that these gender-specific messages did not necessarily conform to known labor force participation patterns within Togo. These textbooks, which originated in Paris and were, for the most part, the creation of French males, introduced new values and gender-role orientations to Togo, and those patterns of gender differentiation exemplified a form of controlled knowledge distribution.

Apple's work on the reproduction of inequality in education suggests that in-school processes direct different knowledge to different folks.[30] However, in the case of Togolese textbooks produced in France, this process may not simply involve the reproduction of societal inequalities, but may also include the legitimation of Western notions of sex-role divisions of labor that are not necessarily practiced in Africa. The patterns of female marginality and labor force participation found within these textbooks not only underscored themes of gender differentiation, but also introduced additional forms of gender inequality.

When these inequities are taken together with Kalia's suggestion that occupational roles presented in Third World textbooks may have even more impact on career expectations than textbooks used in more developed nations, several reforms in Third World textbook production are indicated.[31] First, there is a need to produce textbooks that more closely conform to the reader's lived culture, and not necessarily to the values and roles associated with industrialized nations. To this end, it will be necessary to encourage indigenous authors to create textbooks more sensitive to the cultural patterns of their readers. Second, those who author these textbooks should be aware of gender-differentiated patterns of labor force participation found within the target society, so that these inequalities are not blindly reproduced within texts. Finally, educational policy makers from Third World countries need to encourage the adoption and use of textbooks that not only reflect the indigenous culture, but also expand notions of gender equality.

Though the results of the study discussed in this chapter underscore the need for various textbook reforms, they also raise a series of issues that require further exploration. For example, why do countries like Togo continue to purchase textbooks from industrialized nations that neither reflect their societal values nor encourage gender equality? In particular, how do factors such as budgetary constraints, language, demographic features, and local textbook availability affect policy decisions that permit patterns of imperialism to persist through the continued use of Western textbooks?

And finally, further research is needed to assess student exposure to, and subsequent internalization of, messages found within these textbooks. In Third World countries that often experience severe budgetary problems, the ability of any textbook to transmit a set of messages may be curtailed by classroom shortages. Studies focusing on access to classroom textbooks should be coupled with analyses of student comprehension rates and levels of internalization to determine a textbook's potential for imparting notions of Western imperialism and gender inequalities.

Notes

1. David Mills, Boniface Zodéougan, Tim Doust and Barry Tomalin, English for French-Speaking Africa:Working with English, (Paris: Librairie Armand Colin, 1974). G. Legreneur and M. Peyraud, Physics et Chimie, (Paris: Classiques Hachette, 1961). Institut Pédagogique Africain et Malgache. Histoire: Le Monde Contemporain, (Paris: EDICEF, 1973). Jean-Louis Joubert, Manuel de Francais: Domaine Africain, (Paris: Bordas, 1972). Michel Queysanne and André Revuz, Mathematique: Serie Rouge. (Paris: Fermand Nathan, 1973).

2. Francoise Prigent, Petit Atlas du Togo, (Paris: Afrique Biblio Club, 1978), p.2.

3. It should be noted that the categories developed under Personal Characteristics and Activities are not necessarily broad in scope or well balanced, but simply reflect those attributes present within the textbook.

4. Mills, English for French-Speaking Africa, p. 87.

5. Ibid, p. 47.

6. Ibid, pp. 33-37.

7. Institut Pédagogique, Histoire, p. 90.

8. Joubert, Manuel de Francais, pp. 162-163.

9. Mills, English for French-Speaking Africa, pp.72-73.

10. Mills, Ibid, p. 105.

11. Mills, English for French-Speaking Africa, p. 106.

12. Institut Pédagogique, Histoire, p. 15.

13. Ibid, p. 23.

14. Ibid, p. 75.

15. Ibid, pp. 130-131.

16. Ibid, p. 164.

17. Ibid, p. 183.

18. Ibid, pp. 278-279.

19. Ibid, p. 209.

20. Ibid, p. 181.

21. Ibid, p. 58.

22. Legreneur, Physics et Chimie, p. 206.

23. Institut Pédagogique, Histoire, p. 14.

24. Ibid, p. 86.

25. Ibid, pp. 44-45.

26. Ibid, p. 67.

27. Mills, English for French-Speaking Africa, p. 19.

28. Institut Pédagogique, Histoire, p. 157.

29. Ibid, p. 220.

30. Michael W. Apple, Ideology and Curriculum (London: Routledge and Kegan Paul, 1979).

31. Narendra Nath Kalia, "Images of Men and Women in Indian Textbooks", Comparative Education Review, 24, (June 1980), pp. S209-S223.

CHAPTER 7

THE QUEST FOR NATIONAL UNITY: LANGUAGE TEXTBOOKS IN MALAYSIA

Hena Mukherjee and Khairiah Ahmed

Introduction

This chapter focuses on the extent to which textbooks in use in Malaysian secondary schools contribute to national unity. In 1984 the Department of National Unity in the Prime Minister's Department funded a University of Malaya Faculty of Education project designed to examine English and Bahasa Malaysia medium secondary texts in civics, history, geography, Bahasa Malaysia and English. This study is reported in the pages that follow.

Background

Malaysia is a plural society of 15 million people. Malays, the ruling elite, and other indigenous groups make up 55% of the population, Chinese about 30%, and Indians about 10%. All Malays are Muslims and Islam has been designated as the official state religion. Other religious groups include Buddhists (17% of the population), Christians and Hindus (7% each), and groups that practice ancestor worship and animism. Languages spoken include Malay, known as Bahasa Malaysia, the national language, which is the language of the Malay community; Mandarin and several Chinese dialects; Tamil and several regional Indian languages; English; and the languages and dialects of the indigenous population of Sabah and Sarawak. Malaya was a plural society at the time of independence. When it merged with Sabah, Sarawak, and Singapore (which left the group in 1965) in 1963 to form Malaysia, the plural nature of the society became even more complex.

Malaysia inherited a multi-tiered educational system at independence. The schools were a result of interactions between British colonial administration (1786-1957), Christian missionaries, local Malays, and the growing Chinese and Indian migrant communities, all of whom sought educational structures that would serve the social, economic, and cultural needs of each distinct group. Requiring recruits for the lower rungs of the British administration, English education developed catering to the needs of the urban Chinese and Indians, with special consideration for the Malay elite. The administration sponsored the Malay vernacular school system on the principle that its products would be better farmers and fishermen. Privately-sponsored Chinese schools looked to the Chinese mainland (where they had come from to work in the tin mines) for curriculum, teachers, and textbooks. Isolated on the rubber plantations where they had come as indentured labor, Tamils based their children's education on that of South India. The four parallel educational systems, marked by social, cultural and linguistic differences, have been repeatedly identified as the prime source of disunity in modern Malaysia.[1] As the post-war, post-independence economy grew, English education was sought after, being perceived as the major avenue promising access to higher education and to prestigious jobs in the modern, urban sector.

A decade after independence, wide disparities between rural and urban Malaysia became evident in income, educational achievement, and ethnicity. These inequalities lay festering until they came to a head in the traumatic race riots of 1969 which changed the course of Malaysia's political and socio-economic development in dramatic and far-reaching ways. Education was then identified as the major tool that could bring about long-term structural change that would redress existing inequalities. An immediate step was the phasing out of English-medium schools whose language of instruction was to be replaced by Malay. This also signalled a burgeoning demand for new textbooks in all subjects that would emphasize "social integration and more equitable distribution of income and opportunities for national unity and progress" with national unity declared as the "over-riding objective" in all facets of the nation's development.[2]

School Texts and National Unity

In the early 1970s, the government of Malaysia made a concerted effort to develop texts that would provide a Malaysia-centric perspective. A directive encouraging local writing and publishing emanated from the Textbook Bureau of the Ministry of Education. The

Bureau's call met with a burst of activity since the Bureau provides the schools with lists of books from which they can select classroom texts. The books published in the 1970s form the basis of this study. In it, we analyze lower secondary school texts (years seven, eight, and nine) in terms of their contribution to national unity. This level of schooling is seen as particularly significant since the drop-out rate after year nine is fairly high and for many students participation in the formal, state-sponsored system that aims to reinforce national goals is about to come to an end. The norms and values they are to be socialized into at this juncture of their lives is perceived to be of paramount importance. We selected textbooks from five subject areas: history, civics, geography, Bahasa Malaysia and English.[3] It is felt these subjects lent themselves more readily to the teaching and learning of content and attitudes related to national integration than texts in science and mathematics. It will be noted that Bahasa Malaysia and English form part of the core curriculum, unlike Mandarin and Tamil which are taught only where more than fifteen students in any one class request it. Malay language texts are particularly relevant to the aims of this study as political strategists see language as a major instrument of unification among Malays and non-Malays.

In all its pronouncements, the Malaysian government authorities have never defined what is meant by national unity or integration. The government has not stated whether assimilation is a means to attain national unity or whether a policy of cultural pluralism would be a more effective means toward that end. Project group members, finding it difficult to operationalize the term 'national unity' without imposing meanings of their own, decided on a broad definition of the term deriving that definition from major official education reports and development plans. Such documents refer to the national unity in multi-ethnic, multi-religious and multi-lingual terms and set forth the goal that every occupational sector and level of interaction is open to all, irrespective of race and social class.

What features of the curriculum materials used in Forms (Grades) 1, 2, and 3 promote or hinder the development of national unity in Malaysia? This is the broad research question directing this exploratory study. Promotion or hindrance are interpreted in terms of curricula content that decreased or increased the cleavages existing among the various ethnic groups, geographical regions, and social classes with a greater focus on the first two categories. Taking comprehension and intensive reading passages as units of analysis, texts are examined with the aid of a textbook analysis schedule.[4] Specific language exercises and single sentences are included when they are seen to be significant.

Selection of Texts Analyzed

Eighteen Bahasa Malaysia (Table 7.1) and 20 Language texts (Table 7.2) used in the seventh, eighth, and ninth years are examined. These titles were provided by Textbook Bureau officials of the Ministry of Education who indicated that they represented the most widely-used of approved texts in the country. One series in each language was published by the National Language and Literature Agency (Dewan Bahasa dan Pustaka). The rest were published either by locally incorporated representatives of overseas publishing houses (such as Longman, McGraw-Hill) or local firms. Writers of Malay and English texts are chiefly teachers in secondary schools and universities. All writers of Malay texts are Malays from peninsular Malaysia. Of the 20 English texts examined, 50% (ten texts) are written by foreigners. All the texts were written in the seventies leading one to infer that they were written in response to the demand for Malaysian-oriented texts. The speed with which some series have been developed seems to bear this out, for instance, five series of English texts out of seven had published titles for all three lower secondary levels in the same year.

We analyze the texts to see the extent to which they focus on all regions of Malaysia (we assume that a balanced treatment of all the country's regions would promote national unity), how they portray Malaysia's various ethnic groups, the extent to which they promote interaction among ethnic groups of a positive nature, how the texts present the range of social class strata in the country, and if they promote cross-cultural awareness.

The Inter-Regional Dimension

The term 'region' was used loosely in this study to denote contrasting areas in peninsular Malaysia such as the west coast and east coast and to distinguish between peninsular Malaysia and the states of Sabah and Sarawak. The central mountain range that runs from north to south in the peninsula represents more than a physical divide. More accessible to international waterways and trade, the west coast of Malaysia has developed more rapidly than the east with its urban centers becoming important foci of development and modernisation, as well as symbols of independent Malaysia's success. References to west coast/east coast dichotomies are therefore loaded with meaning, the east connoting a peaceful, pastoral environment of idyllic fishing villages and farms on the one hand, and an area left undeveloped on the other

Table 7.1
Bahasa Malaysia Textbooks Analyzed Tingkatan 1-3

Author	Series Title	Tingkatan 1 (Grade 7)	Tingkatan 2 (Grade 8)	Tingkatan 3 (Grade 9)
Asmah Hj. Omar	Bahasa Malaysia Kini	+	+	+
Hamzah Ibrahim	Asas Bahasa Malaysia Baru	+	+	+
Lutfi Abas	Bahasa Malaysia Baru	+	+	+
Hj. Mokhtar Jh. Dom	Bahasa Malaysia Baru Dewan	+	+	+
Sidang Pengarang	Bahasa Malaysia Kaedah Yunit	+	+	+

Table 7.2
Some Foci of Major Reading Passages by Class Level

Authors	Alter	Hobbs	Howe	Kailasapathy	Koh & Leong	Mustapha & Wijasuriya	Wong, Yeoh Malhi
Tingkatan I (Grade 7)							
Malay	3	6	1	11	4	7	not examined
Chinese	8	3	0	1	11	4	
Indian	1	0	0	2	2	1	
Mixed	3	7	4	3	4	5	
Sabah & Sarawak	1	0	1	0	1	0	
Others*	12	9	13	2	13	6	
Tingkatan II (Grade 8)							
Malay	6	7	4	4	5	4	11
Chinese	5	1	2	1	1	1	0
Indian	2	0	0	2	0	2	0
Mixed	4	11	0	4	2	0	0
Sabah & Sarawak	0	0	0	0	0	0	3

Table 7.2 continued

Others*	5	11	11	6	6	14	20
Tingkatan III (Grade 9)							
Malay	4	7	2	8	2	7	3
Chinese	3	2	1	1	3	2	1
Indian	1	0	0	2	1	1	0
Mixed	2	6	0	5	5	3	0
Sabah & Sarawak	1	0	0	3	0	0	1
Others*	8	13	13	3	5	18	4

Note: * Others refers to passages which deal largely with technical/general knowledge themes: "Journey to the Moon," "Electricity," etc.

with the majority of the population eking out a subsistence living. Although this configuration has changed vastly in the last two decades, textbooks tend to perpetuate the myth of contrasts; consequently, the west coast is seen as a more favorable area to reside. Both Malay and English texts seem to convey the idea that Malaysian life occurs most significantly on the west coast. An intensive reading passage entitled "A Quick Tour of West Malaysia" shows that west coast towns on the peninsula are treated in detail with extremely brief references made to the major east coast towns such as Kota Baru, Kuala Trengganu, and Kuantan.[5] Throughout all the texts analyzed, the east coast is portrayed as an idyllic vacation land where local fishermen and farmers indulge in traditional games such as top-spinning and kite flying. Little attention is paid to the discovery of off-shore oil which has transformed the economic life of the state of Trengganu. Similarly the potential impact of the development of Kuantan port in the state of Pahang is ignored as a suitable topic for discussion.

The issue at hand is more than the need for an accurate reflection of the developmental status of the east coast. One of the major tools of national unity is the New Economic Policy which focuses attention on the eradication of poverty among all races and highlights the need for social restructuring so that race is not identified with occupation.[6] A fundamental bone of contention and ill-feeling between the major ethnic groups stems from economic rivalry. As Malays scrutinized their position in the country's economic and educational sectors after the 1969 riots, they concluded that they were the under-privileged, almostthe dispossessed, in their own land of plenty. Aggressive social policies in both sectors were mounted in the early seventies, safeguarding and promoting the special rights and privileges of the bumiputeras.[7] The strategies proved to be extremely successful and figures within the short span of a decade (1970-1980) revealed that although bumiputeras were under-represented in many categories of economic and educational activity, it was no longer possible to identify race with economic function.[8] It is argued that when economic benefits are seen to be equitably distributed among the ethnic groups, tensions will tend to decrease. Following up this argument, the content of textbooks may be expected to include the new distribution of benefits as represented by life in the west coast, emphasizing the point that the fruits of national development have become accessible to larger numbers and to previously deprived groups, especially Malays. This does little, however, to draw the east coast into the mainstream of Malaysian life.

Comments relating to the portrayal of the east coast of peninsular Malaysia are relevant for ways in which writers depict Sabah and Sarawak, when they do so at all. Education is seen as one of the most important devices in bringing together peninsular Malaysia and the states of Sabah and Sarawak. The focus of educational programmes between 1971 and 1975 was the consolidation of the national education system in order to promote national unity through the implementation, in stages, of Bahasa Malaysia as the main medium of instruction in schools, the closing of the gap in educational opportunities among regions and races, and the eventual integration of the educational system of the East Malaysian states with the national system. The medium of instruction in Sabah and Sarawak, as in the case of the peninsula, used to be English, but membership in the Malaysian alliance meant the acceptance of Bahasa Malaysia as the national language.

With the heterogenous linguistic and socio-cultural background that the two states' ethnic groups represent, the urgent need to identify and successfully utilize instruments of unification was clear to policy-makers. But Malay and English language writers seemed to have ignored the significant role their books would have in helping to draw young Sabahans and Sarawakians into the mainstream of Malaysian consciousness. In the English language texts examined, for example, it was found that only eleven passages out of a total of 476 are based on the two states. Content of these passages is limited to descriptions of natural scenery, rural life, and attractive extracts from folk-lore and legend. Little or no mention is made of the rapid development in Sarawak's oil-rich areas around Miri and Bintulu, and the success of Sabah's timber industry. As in the case of the peninsula's east coast, it is difficult to conceive of pupils developing a sense of belonging or a common identity if their way of life is discounted and inadequately depicted.

Profiles of Ethnic Groups

The textbooks we analyzed project an ethos identifiably Malaysian. However, the majority of texts seem to have interpreted 'Malaysian' as 'Malay' and this is true for both English and Malay texts. Malay language texts and supplementary curriculum materials are heavily dependent on Malay names--names of roads, places in Malaysia, names of people, outstanding personalities, objects such as names of books.

Also, in those English language texts, Malays are most prominently represented, Chinese are second, and there is little reference to Indians, with minimal mention of Sabahans and Sarawakians.

Howe's text (see Table 7.2), for instance, does not include a single passage referring to Indians as a group and includes only one passage of Sabahans and Sarawakians. Of 476 passages, about 63% focus on Malays, 21% on Chinese, 10% on Indians, and 6% on Sabahans and Sarawakians. Except for two of the books, almost all the writers apportion the Malays the majority of passages. Some writers do not include any passages on non-bumiputera groups at all. The largest number of passages by far are on scientific topics and general knowledge. For example, "Journey to the Moon," "Electricity," and so on, indicate that writers are not primarily concerned with issues related to ethnic representations.

Profiles projected of the groups range from those that reinforce stereotypical images held of different ethnic groups to calculated attempts to break the stereotype. Typically, for instance, one reads of Johari, a Malay village boy who looks after a herd of water buffalo; Rahman, a padi planter from a northern state; and Majid, a fisherman from the north-east coast of the country.[9] These are accurately reproduced profiles of Malays in their traditional rural occupations, an image that the New Economic Policy's goals of social restructuring are attempting to change. Chinese and Indians are presented in similarly stereotypical projections. Miss Goh is a hard-working factory employee while Mr. Wong owns a coffee-shop, reinforcing the generally-held perception of the hard-working, enterprising Chinese community. Chandran, the South Indian rubber tapper, however, is locked into the image of the Indian plantation worker who is resigned to his fate. The issue to be considered is the extent to which such stereotypical profiles should be highlighted. Formulating social restructuring policies are not sufficient reason for excluding accurate representations. But more important, perhaps in terms of long-term national objectives, is the offering of alternative options so that birth and membership of a particular ethnic group do not limit an individual's life-chances. The more perceptive writers have a mix of portrayals in typical occupations intermingling with non-stereotypical representations. Ghafar, a Malay from Gopeng, works in a tin mine, the traditional domain of the Chinese, and Kamal, who sells machinery for a firm in Kuala Lumpur, gives the rural Malay image an urban counterpoint. In the same text, the Chinese are not only successful entrepreneurs but also dedicated professionals; Indians however still tend to be confined to rubber and oil-palm plantations.

The portrayal of Sabahans and Sarawakians in both Malay and English language texts must be recorded as probably the weakest feature in these texts. They come through as types rather than individuals resulting in a two-dimensional picture rather than rounded living persons. A typical example is the following:

> . . . The Kelabit himself is a grand chap, often six feet tall and broad in proportion. He shakes hands breast high, not half way down, and lives three thousand feet above sea level, where the climate is cold even in the day time . . . In this world's goods the Kelabit is well off, for he grows more rice than he can eat . . .[10]

A passage entitled "Dayaks in Edinburgh" makes a greater effort to personalize portrayals of two Ibans from Sarawak who are visiting Scotland.

> . . . I clearly remember about that meeting. We had tea in the garden because it was a lovely sunny day. We were astonished to see that this treat was not appreciated by the Dayaks. They were constantly moving their seats around to take advantage of any shade there was. We twitted them on this. They smiled but did not understand why we were amused. Later we knew why. They are forest people, living mostly in the shade of trees. They dislike the open sunlight as it can darken their complexions. Sunlight in a tropical territory is an enemy rather then a friend . . .[11]

This non-Malaysian writer describes the Dayaks, Jawie and Luke, from the outside as curiosities from the East rather than as individuals with personal histories. This attitude probably leads him into the generalizations he makes, losing sight of the two young men as persons. The total effect is one of distance, making it difficult for young Sarawakians to identify with the protagonists or non-Sarawakians to recognize fellow Malaysians.

Inter-Ethnic Interaction

Investigations examining ways in which authors delineate interaction between ethnic groups reveal some damning statistics. Of the total number of 476 English language passages, less than 14% show the various races interacting with each other at work or play (see Table 7.2). The significance of the need for interactive images increases in the face of growing communalism in Malaysia. Educationalists throughout the country admit to helplessness as pupils at all levels cluster together in their ethnic communities both in and out of class. An urgent need exists to tear down negative attitudinal barriers between races. In this area, as Table 7.2 indicates, the writing of a non-Malaysian proves to be more sensitive to the needs for positive interactive models than Malaysians.[12] Approximately one third of the passages in Hobbs' texts at Grades I and II levels are based on the interaction among various races. This contrasts markedly with the majority of writers who tend to pay token service to the notion of ethnic plurality as seen in the following example where the different groups are merely catalogued:

> . . . There are many different kinds of people in Malaysia. There are Malays, Chinese, Indians, Eurasians, Dayaks, Melenaus, Kadazans, Bajaus, Muruts and others. . . . we all live together in peace. We do not have quarrels. We do not fight.[13]

The assertions which follow the catalogue of communities claim that Malaysians live in harmony. Without the force of substantial model situations it is doubtful if such statements have much impact when differences are often aggressively evident in real life.

Interactive situations that present images that children can grow up with have a significant role in communal neighborhoods and mono-ethnic schools. A particularly successful mode of presentation, using a loosely woven story line throughout the text, is found by another non-Malaysian writer.[14] The writer's approach is to establish acquaintance at the outset with three families representing the major Malaysian races and situations. These families are involved throughout the text. In ethnically homogenous school environments, the presence of all races co-existing at different age levels and in a variety of situations is required. It is alarming to note that in one set written specifically for Malay-medium pupils, only eight passages show any level of interactive situations over the three-year series.[15] In terms of linguistic content and pedagogical approach this is the best in the set: the inability to portray Malaysian life in all its complex diversity may possibly be seen as a shortcoming on the part of those responsible for commissioning and selecting textbooks.

The Malay texts completely ignore indigenous Sabahan and Sarawakian names. They contain no references to locations in the two states in relation to other Malaysian groups or regions. Passages that do refer to Sabah or Sarawak tend to be devoted exclusively to them. This is true of English texts as well. The writers appear to see the two states as separate entities, isolated from the eleven states in the peninsula. The formation of the political alliance seems to have had little influence on individual perception. More seriously, by treating Sabah and Sarawak as isolated from the mainstream of Malaysian activities, images created or supported by textbooks effectively perpetuate this view, serving to push notions of integration between the two states and the peninsula further away.

English and Malay language texts most frequently describe Malays and refer to Malays as possessing power and authority. Managers and executives in the texts tend to be Malays, other ethnic groups are depicted in subordinate positions. Where texts produced before 1970 showed European, Chinese, or Indian teachers in science laboratories, the texts published later highlighted Malay teachers. Until recently the proportion of Malays taking science and technology courses has been minimal and the texts clearly attempt to provide role models to motivate Malay youth to enter these fields. By so doing, however, the pendulum of redressal may have swung too far. These portrayals reflect writers', publishers', and Textbook Bureau officials' perceptions of ideal power relationships in Malaysia. Daily life in Malaysia, however, is characterized by more complex, rich, and diverse interactions among groups than those projected by textbooks. While the isolation of groups the texts portray may mirror reality, writers carry the responsibility (or the license) to initiate and develop attitudes and values that contribute positively to the future of Malaysia.

Social Class

Compared with Malay texts, English texts are generally set in a more urban, upper middle class, Western-educated environment. When celebration of birthdays is described, guests arrive by car, the conversation dwells on frilled party frocks, sandwiches are eaten, and the pièce de résistance is a birthday cake and candles.[16] In 'Moving House,' the middle-class Western-educated ethos continues in the description of carpets, plush living room sets, and paintings (one of which is a Picasso).[17] Such life-styles are alien to the majority of Malaysians. Where the rural population distribution far exceeds the urban, as in Malaysia, the texts are insensitive to the many different lifestyles among Malaysians. The texts depict men buying eighteen dollar ties, something beyond the means of most Malaysian men.[18] There is little effort in the texts to balance this picture by showing others who buy local articles of clothing that cost considerably less.

Both Malay and English texts frequently depict Malays in urban areas participating in the modern sector economy in an executive position. While English texts show both Malay and other ethnic groups in urban middle-class settings, the Malay texts are strongest in presenting upward social mobility within the Malay community. Such images are weaker in the discussion of other ethnic and racial groups. This implies that the Malay texts view national unity as being achieved through uplifting the status of the Malay community. The English texts tend to parallel the Malay texts in this regard.

Cross-Cultural Awareness

The official view of Malaysian culture is riddled with contradictions and almost defies any attempt at generalization. The government has set a goal of integrating ethnic groups to counter the reality of their increasing isolation. Official publications make statements such as the following:

> . . . the government through the Ministry of Education with its emphasis on one medium of instruction i.e. Bahasa Malaysia, has brought about socio-cultural solidarity and national unity. The adoption of a common syllabus for all schools with an emphasis on the study of the country's history, people and culture will ensure that school children will perceive history from a Malaysian view point. They become more appreciative of Malaysia's rich history and culture, and the contribution by Malaysians from different groups to its heritage . . .[19]

There is general confusion regarding directions for socio-cultural development, which is reflected in textbook production. In 1984 a document issued unilaterally by the Ministry of Youth, Sport, and Culture asserted that it hoped to "promote socio-cultural assimilation which is the vital ingredient to achieve (sic) national solidarity and nation building."[20] The concept of socio-cultural assimilation clearly contrasts with the widely-accepted tenet of the 1957 Education Act that promised official support for the preservation and growth of the various languages and cultures of Malaysians. Our examination of both Bahasa Malaysia and English textbooks does not match the confident promises made by such official assertions as that quoted above. Historical passages narrate events avoiding explanations or rationales for action and are extremely boring chronological accounts. Passages on information from geography and economics similarly list facts and figures without including explanatory comments which take account of contributions made by the various communities to the building of the nation.

These language textbooks do not seek to integrate Malay ethnic groups. Many textbooks contain readings on abundant religious and cultural festivals and promote them as tangible manifestations of Malaysia's cultural tapestry. Few succeed in conveying little more than a charming quaintness peculiar to each ethnic group but not necessarily integral to Malaysian life. No attempts are made to reinforce the universality of meaning inherent in many religious festivals which can provide important commonalities. Factual presentations of information (some of which are inaccurate) was the common approach taken to portray festivals in the majority of texts. This is the case in 'Malaysian Festivals' that summarizes Hari Raya Puasa (Muslim), Chinese New Year, Deepavali (Hindu), and Christmas celebrations.[21] Such snapshot portrayals represent a better range of cultural activities than do texts in the English Language series mentioned earlier written solely for Malay-medium students.[22] Only Muslim festivals are included (in Books 2 and 3) , implying that Malay students already know, need not know, or will not be interested in the cultural lives of other Malaysian communities. In both English and Malay language texts, there is little attempt to provide, even in the most elementary form, a sense of the need to understand the cultures of fellow Malaysians. Some texts entirely omit this fundamental aspect of life in Malaysia.

What comes through strongly from the texts for the Malay child is the sense of continuity between home and school, individual and Malay society, and present and past. Organic linkages are wrought by a vigorous selection of folk and classical literature as well as history. This sense of belonging is denied to the non-Malay child, given the dearth of content currently relevant as well as the history of that child's people. By ignoring their culture and history, textbooks tacitly assert that the collective lives of Chinese and Indian children began when their parents, grandparents, or forefathers reached Malaysian shores to work in tin mines and on rubber estates. Not only is there insufficient content in the texts which could enhance cross-cultural awareness and understanding, there is also a lack of information for non-Malay pupils that could help them bridge the gap existing between important centers of their lives--the home-community and the school/wider Malaysian society.

There are a few encouraging examples of a balanced approach in the texts, albeit too few. This is exemplified by the delicate balance of language in a Malay text presented below which is not easily translated into English:

> . . . Sungguhpun orang Tionghua menyambut hantu-hantu ini begitu heboh nampaknya, tetapi kebanyakan orang Melayu (misalyna) tidak pula menghuraikan keadaan itu. Mereka tahu ini soal ugama dan soal kepercayaan. Keadaan bising lebih sedikit daripada biasa pun mengapalah![23]
>
> (Although the Chinese welcome/pray to the spirits accompanied by considerable noise, many Malays are not disturbed by it. They know that these are issues concerning religion and faith. If it creates noise that is more than ordinary, what does it matter!)

The passage indicates a light and sensible approach, marked by a poise that would have made a great difference to similar themes throughout the texts. Projected through such statements are values reflective of a willingness to tolerate and, more important, to understand the customs and beliefs of others, a dimension that is lacking in the flat and supposedly value-free narrations that abound in both languages.

Language Texts and "Real" Goals

A former Minister of Education once stated that the task of Malaysia's educational policy was a tremendous one. "Common ideals, common ambitions and common loyalties must be fostered and not enforced and the schools are our most powerful tools for persuasion."[24] The burden of this exploratory study is to examine the powerful tools for peaceful persuasion by looking at one of the primary instruments schools use, textbooks. This analysis has attempted to examine the selection that language textbooks have made from the multi-cultural environment of Malaysian pupils and the extent to which these choices reflect national goals of integration and unity among the various ethnic groups.

This brief report leaves some important questions unanswered. First, what do writers see as their goals? Textual analysis indicates that all wrote in response to syllabus requirements as stipulated by the Textbook Bureau of the Ministry of Education. Obviously, this objective is supported as it is the domain of language teaching and learning that they are primarily concerned with. However, an analysis of content in terms of the presentation of ethnic groups indicates that other messages are being conveyed. These seem to reflect the power and authority structures of the nation, creating a sense of divisiveness rather than unity. When compared with language texts used in schools in the sixties, all the texts examined focus largely on Malaysia rather than Britain as had earlier texts. But this new Malaysian-centric dimension highlighted, firstly, peninsular Malaysia as contrasted with the states of Sabah and Sarawak; and secondly, the predominance of the Malay community, giving a generally unbalanced picture of Malaysia and Malaysians from geographical, historical, economic, and socio-cultural perspectives.

In spite of the skew in favor of one community, why is it that mechanisms applying the criteria of selection of textbooks have made few attempts to correct the balance? A popular explanation is that officials are confused about applying rules in relation to national unity and school texts. Economic policies whose regulatory characteristics, being expressed in quantitative terms, can be more easily implemented and their impact assessed. In the case of national unity, however, no clear framework exists in educational policy, much less in individual subjects, which details particular attitudes, values, and aspects of knowledge that are publicly accepted as contributory to declared goals. Official discussion on the matter, for reasons of political sensitivity, has remained vague. Textbooks reflect the general climate where highlighting the role and heritage of the political elite cannot be objected to: highlighting the contribution and backgrounds of other groups may, on the other hand, prevent a text from being accepted. Omission of such content raises many issues: is there a hidden agenda that precludes their inclusion? Have writers been told to avoid mentioning topics that are even remotely controversial? Do writers feel safer keeping to relatively trivial topics such as "Market Day" and "A Day in Town," and impersonal technical subjects such as "Cells" or "The Discovery of X-Rays"?

The hierarchical structure of decision-making that influences the final outcome emerges. At the top of the pyramid is the Textbook Bureau whose officials are expected to interpret policy into curricular guidelines for publishers. These guidelines are chiefly in terms of syllabus requirements. Publishers demand that texts adhere as closely as possible to the prescribed syllabus and include non-controversial content. Writers enter the ring aware of the rules of the game. In the process one, of the real goals of Malaysian education is relegated to the background.

A Way Forward: Some Policy Implications

Considerable confusion exists among educators, policy makers, practitioners, and the school population regarding the nature and meaning of national unity. Unless some basis for understanding and agreement is reached, it is difficult to see how educational processes can effectively contribute to the growth of inter-ethnic understanding. Calling for broad-based public discussions in the interests of clarification has a certain appeal to rationality: in practical terms, as Malaysian experience has shown, such activities may catalyze volatile communal reactions not easily contained. The agenda for schools, however, can be structured on rational grounds and educational personnel need to recognize their role in the responsible implementation of a sound and desirable social goal. While interpretation of specifics will always be open to variation, professional discussion can hopefully take place which will illuminate fundamental issues which include the following questions. How should authority and superior/subordinate relations be depicted in curriculum materials? What is the profile of interaction that emerges between dominant and minority groups? To what extent do policies isolate and alienate ethnic minorities? Is there a balance between dominant and minority values projected in texts?

Some policy implications emerging from the findings of this study are identified here and they address issues related primarily to textbook policy development, and textbook evaluation and selection activities. They are directed to all involved in textbook production; government officials involved in policy development, officers involved in evaluation and selection, publishers, and writers.

Professional Discussion of Issues Related to the Development of National Unity

1. In-house professional discussions of relevant issues need to be initiated at the ministerial level to enable the production of operational guidelines that will provide practicable directions for action. Representatives of all ethnic groups and geographical regions should be included in these discussions. The outcomes should include a statement on the position and nature of strategies supported by the authorities on issues related to the development of inter-group harmony in schools.

Evaluation of Textbooks

2. Ministry of Education officers responsible for textbook policy development, evaluation, and selection should submit texts in use to careful scrutiny with a view to advising withdrawal of those that are hindering the development of understanding among ethnic groups. Among other activities, they need to develop a checklist of criteria in order to standardize evaluative procedures, to form professional evaluation committees where the various ethnic groups or their interests are represented, and to encourage at school level a textbook evaluation committee that is aware of accepted criteria and procedures of operation. Criteria of selection and evaluation developed by the Textbook Bureau should be conveyed to publishers and textbook writers.

Content-Related Issues

3. Educational personnel and publishers should review the content of textbooks, taking account of their own evaluation exercises and the findings of the study reported here. Considerations such as the following should be included in guidelines given to writers regarding the selection and presentation of content:

(a) that a balanced distribution of content be sought which gives equal weight to Malays, other indigenous <u>bumiputeras</u> groups, and other Malaysian ethnic groups.

(b) that the west coast of Malaysia be seen as <u>one</u> of the regions in the country and not dominate the content of texts.

(c) that developmental changes that have taken place in the various regions be portrayed accurately.

(d) that content and illustration should be representative of the entire spectrum of Malaysian society and not focus on the upper classes.

(e) that attempts to break stereotypical occupational patterns must be applied to all ethnic groups and not left to the judgement of the individual writer.

(f) that writers should portray the various ethnic groups interacting meaningfully at school, at work, and in social situations.

(g) that while diverse points of view are stimulating, textbook writers should be encouraged to emphasize commonalities which cut across all ethnic and social groups.

Finally, we do well to realize that textbooks form only one strand, albeit a crucial one, in the total fabric of national unity initiatives to which Malaysia must pay close attention. Their contribution is effective to the extent that they are seen to exist in consonance with the prevailing ethos in school and society, supported by appropriate institutional structures. While measures suggested may not resolve many of Malaysia's deep-rooted ethnic problems, it is hoped that, if undertaken, textbooks may help to form some images of unity in the minds of children.

NOTES

1. Philip Loh Fook Seng, Seeds of Separation: Educational Policy in Malaya (Kuala Lumpur: Oxford University Press, 1975).

2. Government of the Federation of Malaysia, Second Malaysia Development Plan 1971-1975 (Kuala Lumpur: Government Printers, 1971), p. 1.

3. Hena Mukherjee, Khairiah Ahmed, Lim Hong Kuan, T. Marimuthu, Norani Salleh and Jagdish Raj Sharma, The Malaysian Lower Secondary School Curriculum and National Unity, A Report presented to the Prime Minister's Department, Kuala Lumpur, 1984.

4. The two schedules found to be most relevant were Michael Eraut, Len Goad and George Smith, The Analysis of Curriculum Materials (Brighton: University of Sussex Education Area Occasional Paper 2, 1975) and Robert McCormick for the Course Team Block 7: Analysing Curriculum Materials (Milton Keynes: Open University Press, 1981).

5. D. H. Howe, New Guided English (Kuala Lumpur: Oxford University Press, 1974), p. 38-39.

6. Government of the Federation of Malaysia, 1971.

7. Malays and other indigenous groups are termed the bumiputeras or "Sons of The Soil."

8. Government of the Federation of Malaysia, 1971, p. 23.

9. Hobbs, Key to English Tingkatan 1 (Kuala Lumpur: Longmans, 1975).

10. M. C. Kailasapathy, Bahasa Inggeris Kini (Kuala Lumpur: Federal Publication, 1974), p. 144.

11. Simon Wong, Patrick Yeoh, and Waryam Singh Malhi, New English for Malaysian Secondary Schools Book 3 (Kuala Lumpur: Anthonian, 1974), p. 142.

12. Hobbs, 1975.

13. Howe, 1974, p. 30.

14. Myint Su, Practical English for Remove Classes (Kuala Lumpur, Longmans, 1977). This book is written for the use of Chinese and Tamil medium pupils moving from primary to secondary level in the Malay medium.

15. Nik Faizah Mustapha and Elaine Wijasuriya, Structural Approach to English Book 3 (Kuala Lumpur: Federal Publications, 1975).

16. Mustapha and Wijasuriya, Book Three, p. 44.

17. Mustapha and Wijasuriya, Book Three, p. 74.

18. M. C. Kailasapathy, Bahasa Inggeris Kini I (Kuala Lumpur: Federal Publications, 1976).

19. Aziz Deraman, The Development of Culture, Communication and Education in Malaysia (Kuala Lumpur: Ministry of Culture, Youth and Sports, Malaysia, 1984), pp. 9-10.

20. Ibid, 1984, p. 10.

21. Wong, Yeoh and Malhi, New English Book 3, pp. 4-6.

22. Mustapha and Wijasuriya, Structural Approach to English series.

23. Mokhtar Haji Dom, Bahasa Malaysia Baru Dewan (Kuala Lumpur: Dewan Bahasa dan Pustaka, 1975), p. 41.

24. Mohammed Khir Johari, then Minister for Education, in a speech delivered to Penang Free School on October 17, 1967.

CHAPTER 8

LANGUAGE AND TEXTS IN AFRICA

Dennis Mbuyi

Introduction

This chapter focuses on the content of primary level textbooks in use in English and Swahili in the schools of Kenya and Tanzania. It assesses the extent to which Kenyan and Tanzanian texts reflect government policy. Preoccupation with issues pertaining to educational content is generally grounded within the broader context of opening up curricula to cultural, social, and economic realities of local environments.

There is generally a well established tradition of research that uses textbooks as a way of analyzing curriculum.[1] One of the underlying tenets in this tradition is that school texts are good indicators of "core values" in which the country's leadership wishes to inculcate its younger generations.[2] Within these frameworks, texts are usually taken as reflecting values, key goals, behavior patterns, or social mores that are supposedly congruent with the leadership's ideological orientations. While it is worth noting that textbooks represent only one "element within the school environment," it is nevertheless important to underscore the vital role they do play in the African school environment. Indeed, given the generally impoverished conditions of schooling and the rather heavy emphasis put almost exclusively on a transmission-dominated view of education, children hardly have other options than to learn by rote. Under these conditions, knowledge packaged into "facts" tends to be taken as contained in school textbooks and transmitted by teachers who view these same texts as reflecting the beginning and end of the entire human stock of accumulated "facts."[3]

Another asset of textbooks as a tool of analysis may be found in the fact that they are usually characterized by some uniformity of messages throughout national school systems and their availability is increasingly recognized to be the most consistent and positive "determinant of academic achievement."[4] There are, however, limitations in using textbooks to analyze school knowledge. Such an analysis does not deal with the values that children would internalize as a result of their schooling.[5]

East Africa, in the case of Kenya and Tanzania, affords us the opportunity to examine contrasting national policies. Indeed, official policy statements since the mid-sixties suggest very different conceptions of both social and educational policies in the two countries.[6] In both countries, despite linguistic diversity, Swahili (a lingua franca) has emerged as the national language. English, the former colonial language, has nevertheless retained its influence, although with varying degrees in the two nations. The analysis of texts in these two countries was designed to contrast differing national policy goals. The aim of this chapter is to look at Kenyan and Tanzanian texts and determine the extent to which government policy is translated into the English and Swahili texts in each country.

The selection of texts has been limited to the primary school level chiefly out of a concern for comparability of school structure and types of textual materials between the two countries. But equally important in the choice of this level of schooling is the fact that the primary school, more than any other level, underwent some major reforms in both countries following their formal independence in the 1960s. The texts analyzed here were produced after the major re-evaluations of the colonial school systems by the new leadership in Kenya and Tanzania. The texts were produced by the respective Ministry of Education in each country and were distributed to all primary grades in both countries. The selected texts were carefully matched cross-country for language and grade level. Content analysis of the texts has been done on the basis of seven broad categories broken down into 22 indicators (see Table 8.1).

The initial form of analysis (construction of categories) was derived from a careful examination of planning models and policy in Kenya and Tanzania in the postindependence era. They relate to differences identified in national policy in the two countries. The seven broad categories used to analyze the texts were: (1) Ruralization, (2) Bases for Legitimating Knowledge, (3) Egalitarianism, (4) Africanization, (5) Value of Education, (6) Self-Help, and (7) Work-Emphasis.[7] Kenyan English language and Swahili texts were contrasted with Tanzanian English and Swahili texts to see if either reflected respective government policies. Both quantitative and qualitative methods were used in order to give some depth to the analysis of the texts (including both distribution and frequency of themes as well as the kind of

Table 8.1

Overall Comparative Percentages
From The Four Instructional Contexts

	KENYA		TANZANIA	
	English	Swahili	English	Swahili
Daily Life				
Urban	13.96	14.10	6.32	3.68
Rural	8.11	2.01	16.15	7.25
	22.07	16.11	22.47	10.93
Africanization				
Family	7.97	9.92	2.94	3.37
Ethnic/Tribal	6.83	4.65	1.54	0.10
Nation	6.41	19.53	15.44	23.92
East Africa	2.42	1.86	1.54	1.94
Africa (Continent)	2.42	4.65	5.47	4.39
Europe	1.28	5.27	5.33	9.61
World	5.27	3.87	8.98	5.93
	32.60	49.75	41.24	49.26
Bases for Legitimating Knowledge				
Elders/Community	2.99	3.56	1.68	7.77

Table 8.1 continued

Children	3.13	3.72	2.38	2.96
Books/Schools	8.54	8.83	3.65	3.06
Environment	1.99	2.79	2.10	2.14
Mass Media	4.13	3.10	4.21	1.43
	20.78	22.0	14.02	17.36
Self-Help				
Independence/Responsibility	4.98	2.63	6.46	7.15
Subordination	3.87	0.15	....	....
Collective Efforts	1.13	1.86	4.63	8.79
	9.38	4.64	11.09	15.94
Egalitarianism				
Social Ethic	0.42	0.77	4.35	4.90
Personal Ethic	5.55	3.25	1.12	0.40
	5.97	4.02	5.47	5.30
Value of Education				
Common Good	0.56	0.77	2.52	0.40
Self-Advancement	4.70	1.08	0.42	....
	5.26	1.85	2.94	0.40

Table 8.1 continued

Work Emphasis* (involving modern sector/urban and rural/traditional sector)	3.84	1.55	2.66	0.71
TOTAL	100.0	100.0	100.0	100.0

*Only occupations counted as dominant themes have been included under this category.

treatment accorded these themes). Before discussing the texts, I will briefly outline some of the key differences in Kenyan and Tanzanian policies since the mid-sixties.

Summary of Key Goals of National Policy

Kenya and Tanzania emerged from the same colonial culture and prior to 1967 pursued very similar educational policies within the broad foundations of their colonial legacy. In overall terms of development both countries were faced with similar problems of resources and general constraints of underdevelopment (although Kenya had an economic advantage compared to Tanzania). Starting in 1967, policy-making in both countries diverged sharply.[8] The responsiveness of education to political and economic requirements also tended to vary largely. Tanzania has attempted to adopt strategies and to order priorities aimed at breaking away from capitalist forms of growth. It has also attempted to counter the residual effects of the colonial legacy. By contrast, the leadership in Kenya did not feel the need to search for an alternative.[9] The building of the postcolonial society proceeded based on capitalist models. Accordingly, strategies and order of priorities have been essentially within the inherited colonial model. It is, however, worth noting that policy-making in Kenya, as elsewhere, remains a rather dynamic process and reflects some ambivalence and ambiguity. Following is a listing by country of some significant and known key goals of national policy and values underlying them.

Predominant features of stated policy in Kenya, both social and educational, include emphasis on nationhood and stability, and rapid national growth and efficiency of institutions. High priority has been placed on education. Schools are highly selective and their main focus is on identifying and rewarding talents. Schools are also viewed as the major best "access route" for both the advancement of individuals and society. Kenya has acknowledged importance of rural development and stressed agricultural production and the informal sector of the economy to generate employment in the countryside. The government has also expressed concern about building postcolonial society based upon African traditions.

Tanzania's stated policy is characterized by emphasis on social transformation based upon socialism. Tanzania places greater emphasis on rural development (based upon collective agriculture and communal villages). The government has planned a fundamental re-orientation of education wherein schools are viewed primarily as contributing to societal transformation. The schools are expected to foster a sense of social duty. Rural and peasant environment are emphasized as are cooperative rather than individualistic forms of production.

The analysis of the texts that follows asks whether the texts further national integration, rural development, African traditions, and cooperative behavior. The analysis aims at identifying the extent to which these key goals were translated into school texts from both countries. The underlying assumption in so doing is that idea, ideal, or some other orienting principle that is dominant in a given policy will be reflected in the texts.

National Integration

School texts at the primary level in both Kenya and Tanzania emphasize the importance of national integration. While there are similarities from a quantitative point of view, there are, nonetheless, notable differences on how the texts in both countries discussed nationhood. The Kenyan texts discussed national resources, geographical features, game reserves, and tourist industry in order to underscore their importance to Kenya's economic development. The Kenyan texts paid less attention than did Tanzanian texts to patriotic behavior and loyalty to the nation and government (taken here as embodying the virtues of the nation). The following is a typical example of the way in which Kenyan texts depicted the nation. The excerpt describes the country's wildlife and its contribution to the generation of wealth:[10]

> Many places have great mountains and lakes which attract tourists from other countries, but no country has such wildlife as we have in Africa. In many places that were once rich in wild animals, the people lost this resource through ignorance. Kenya, however, still posesses the richest animal life in the world today. Each year thousands of people from other lands arrive in Nairobi to see this wonder of ours and each year they spend ten to eleven million pounds in Kenya . . . Our animals work for us . . . To protect our resources and use them wisely is to preserve the foundation of the nation.

Mention of symbols of a nation were more limited although the Kenyan texts did include stories such as "Nchi Yetu" (Flag and

Anthem),[11] "Kenya Huru" (independence),[12] and "Baba wa Taifa" (anti-colonial struggle).[13] Kenyan texts reflected a less clear and less consistent image in terms of projecting messages related to national integration than did Tanzanian texts.

Discussion of national integration in the Tanzanian texts, on the other hand, rejected the colonial model (taken to mean a capitalist society stressing individualistic instincts and connected to unjust prevailing social conditions.) They focused on the building of the new society based on a radically different set of values and goals. Equally stressed here were themes on the importance of education in promoting nationalism, a sense of social duty and responsibility, as well as fostering attitudes consonant with social justice. The excerpt below stresses the country's resistance to colonialism:[14]

> After listening to all that, the children came to realize the extent to which our ancestors went through a lot of trouble in order to fight colonialism. In conclusion, the teacher said "in order to remember our heroes, the first day in September is devoted to their memory . . ." These were the weapons that our ancestors used in their struggle against the colonialists. Their goal and conviction to protect our nation were clearly demonstrated because, even with such rudimentary weapons, they gave the Germans a hell of bloody time.

While Tanzanian texts paid a great deal of attention to anti-colonialism as in the excerpt above, most striking in contrast to Kenyan texts, was the concentration of stories on the contribution of farmers to the building of the new nation. The following is typical:[15]

> Kendango was a farmer. He is not particularly clever, and he is certainly not wealthy, he is just an ordinary farmer, and yet he is the kind of man that Tanzania is proud of . . . Among those who left school at the same time with Kendango, some refused to become farmers because they were ashamed to work with their hands. But others . . . knew that farming was Tanzania's most important industry, so they became farmers. And it is the new and educated farmers like Kendango who are gradually building the nation of the future.

Such a focus was completely absent from similar Kenyan materials on national integration. Equally absent from Kenyan texts were stories emphasizing a commitment to government national policy. This type of preoccupation was, on the other hand, clearly reflected in Tanzanian texts in stories such as "Mashujaa wa Azimio" which discussed what was perceived to be a heroic act on the part of a youth who died during a march to support the Arusha Declaration.[16] In this story, commitment to the leadership's political stand was explicitly suggested, even at the heavy cost of self-sacrifice. The text states ". . . this death teaches us youngsters of Tanzania to be ready to die in the name of our nation, because faith without actions is useless."[17]

While the primary texts in both Kenya and Tanzania stressed the importance of national integration, the Tanzanian texts presented a broader range of topics and a richer discussion about the nation than did the Kenyan texts. It was also apparent from the Tanzanian texts, especially through their directing the children toward a clearly defined patriotic education, that the texts supported the leadership's goals than the Kenyan school books did. Patriotically inspired materials in Kenyan texts, as noted above, were rarely reflected. This contrasted sharply to the well acknowledged importance of the whole notion of nation building in Kenya. The background against which policies of national integration have been pursued has roots in the colonial partition of Africa in Berlin in 1885. Much of contemporary Africa reflects boundaries that are but arbitrary lines drawn on the map by agreement among contending colonial nations. Consequently, postcolonial African states are more characterized by those artificial boundaries they have accepted to perpetuate and that are hardly grounded in any historical consciousness of African populations. Under these conditions, one realizes why the theme of national integration has remained constant everywhere on the continent. One also realizes how tremendous the task of nation building is. Generally, it involves fostering new identities, new loyalties, or at best, re-discovering identities that colonialism had either destroyed or falsified. While the significance of national integration has been well articulated in Kenya's policy, one is struck by a lack of a strong corresponding reflection of concerns with patriotic education themes in Kenyan texts. Still the degree of discontinuity here remains minor compared to how other key goals of national policy are reflected in Kenyan texts as we look at rural development and models of society in the sections below.

Green Revolution: Searching for Rural Aspects

In spite of stated policy on rural development, Kenyan texts portray rural life negatively as they often show natural disasters as a consistent part of village life. The texts are full of stories portraying miserable living conditions in the villages, floods, droughts, people starving (if not dying) on the land or at best surviving in harsh environments.[18] The following excerpt from a Kenyan text, describes drought damage, and is typical:[19]

> If it does not rain within the next week, deaths of humans will follow those of the animals . . . The animals that are still alive, with their bones showing clearly through their skins, can be seen moving slowly with their owners between Wajir, Tarbaj and El Wak wells . . . Men and animals move silently and with difficulty, sometimes stumbling in the hot sun. Without a word, the . . . families hold out their water pots to passing Land Rovers or lorries in the hope that they will be given water.

Not only do Kenyan texts portray rural areas negatively, they treat people who live in rural areas similarly. The texts describe rural people caught in the vicious circle of natural disasters, poverty, and ignorance. They imply that rural people lacked the motivation and the intelligence to change conditions in their own environments. Some stories in the Kenyan texts ridicule villagers by presenting them as a diffused collectivity, easily exploited, and whose loss of authority and credibility is shown in the texts to extend even to their own children.[20] The excerpt below is drawn from a story which tells how a group of villagers confronted with a problem (grasshoppers attacking their crops) were not able to come up with a solution on their own. In the meantime, some 'clever' outsider came along and took advantage of their naiveté to sell them a new "miracle insecticide": [21]

> Listen, everybody, I've heard all about the grasshoppers you are complaining of. I've brought you an insecticide. It's special kind of stone and it's cheap, only two shillings for this bag with two pieces and full directions. They are enough to kill all the grasshoppers on your shambas (fields). Nearly everyone bought a bag of the special insecticide . . . While the villagers were busy opening the bags . . . the man quietly disappeared. Inside each bag they found two pieces of stone and a piece of paper with these directions: "To kill grasshoppers with these stones, put a grasshopper on one stone and hit it with the other. It will die immediately."

Kenyan texts also associated farming with miserable lifestyles. In the texts, agriculture was not presented as one of the country's fundamental activities, and least of all, an activity upon which the economy could rely to increase self-employment in the country. The Kenyan texts made no effort to discourage negative attitudes generally associated with manual labor. Messages in the texts contrasted with the leadership's stated views on the significance and critical role of rural development; they also were at variance with the country's agricultural realities. Kenya's agriculture consists of mixed farms and plantations for cash crops such as sisal, tea, coffee. Some agriculture is organized into cooperatives.[22] Despite the existence of such diverse and rich agriculture as compared to Tanzania, Kenyan texts focus on squatter settlements rather than on thriving cooperatives or ranches. The texts dwell on farmers toiling on small and impoverished plots of land. The following typifies such an approach:[23]

> His father was a farmer. He owned 4 hectares of land but year after year he grew crops of maize and beans. He did not fertilize the soil, so he let the land grow poorer and poorer. Each year saw fewer plants growing on his land and often the family did not have enough to eat . . . Jeremy's teacher did not know that he was tired and hungry by the time he reached school . . . They could not afford any lamps, so Jeremy had to do his homework by the light of the dying fire.

While the Kenyan texts abound with depictions of destitute and landless farmers, they sometimes portray farming in more neutral terms. But these neutral images are rare compared to the gloomier ones. The following is an example of a neutral description. The story is about ranching in a Masai rural area and is drawn from a dialogue between two school boys:[24]

> How many animals have you got? . . . I always thought the Masai had hundreds of cattle. Yes, and they used to be thin and bony said Sallash. I remember them. Even when I was young, my parents allowed me to look after ours. But we often had to walk miles to get fresh grass and we could never get them to give enough milk, even when we bought more and more . . . What do you mean you bought more cows to eat the same amount of grass? . . . Yes, people forgot that . . . they forgot to take care of the land. So the cows got thinner and milk poorer . . . We were told ranching would be much

> better here, so we started to keep cattle for meat. Now we've got about two hundred animals so we won't be buying more.

It is, however, important to remember that the excerpt above is one of the very few of its sort to appear in the Kenyan texts analyzed.

School texts at the primary level in Tanzania differ from the Kenyan texts in the way they portray the countryside and rural people and in their effort to orient children toward a life in the village. What is striking in the Tanzanian texts as compared to Kenyan ones, is the complete absence of negative references associated with villagers. The texts consistently stress the vital role of farmers in development. The Tanzanian texts reflect national policy showing the Tanzanian leadership's faith in uplifting the productive capacity and motivation of villagers. Of special interest was the place accorded collective agriculture.[25] The following two excerpts will illustrate how the Tanzanian texts portray country dwellers. The first deals with villagers' participation in the administration of their own affairs and how they have achieved the gradual transformation of conditions of life in the village. Now they are striving for adult education:[26]

> After a few years Manga village had many good things. It had got a good school, a good dispensary, a good TANU office, roads, good houses, water, a big shop, big <u>shambas</u>, gardens, as well as a lorry and many other good things . . . They had brought all these good things to the village, but there was something else they still wanted. This was education for those who had not learned to read and write. The villagers wanted to read Swahili newspapers which they saw in the TANU office. So they decided to meet and talk about this with Mr. Waziri, the TANU chairman.

The second describes the contribution of outside 'professionals' as they use their skills to help villagers in raising productivity. The focus here is on the introduction of new livestock breeds and methods of fighting diseases:[27]

> Mr. Kapufi (a veterinary officer) was very glad to see that the cattle dip was ready. He said that villagers would now be able to dip their cattle every week . . . If you dip your cattle every week, you will be able to kill ticks living on them. After this, there won't be any East Coast fever in your village, . . .

> Every time Mr. Kapufi comes to the village he tells the villagers the way to get better cows and chickens. He says that Jersey cows give more milk than Zebu . . . He advises them to try and get a few Jersey cows . . .

The bulk of the Tanzanian textual materials on rural life abound in depictions, as above, of peasants eager to improve village life, especially through cooperative organization. Nowhere did the texts portray villagers as destitute nor do the texts associate them with miserable lifestyles as did the Kenyan texts. Rather, the texts consistently focus on the need to transform rural mentalities and instill new attitudes by promoting 'authentic' dialogue between villagers and various 'agents' of change (TANU officers or other professionals). Villagers are shown in many stories as having a "voice" in their own affairs and as representing a massive human investment for such public and needed projects as roads, dispensaries, schools, irrigation works, and buses. The Tanzanian texts reflect a massive effort to channel rural development along the lines of mass participation in economic development. Concern with education of rural people in the Tanzanian texts was usually tied to production, as can be seen in this passage about the farmer bwakila:[28]

> Each day Bwakila went to work in his field. After the work, he loved to read newspapers. He read every Swahili newspaper he could manage to find . . . In ukulima wa kisasa he learned things related to agriculture and nature or wildlife . . . He learned also different kinds of fertilizers and their uses.

The following sums up the pervasive attitude of rural life as reflected in the Tanzanian texts. It stresses the promise for employment,[29] for the majority, in the 'traditional' sector as opposed to the 'modern' sector of the economy:[30]

> Land is the source of the existence of the human race. It is in fact the essence of all progress . . . We must come to grips with the fact that land is our inheritance. The uses of land consist mostly in farming. One doesn't involve himself in farming in urban areas, but this is generally done in the countryside. We must realize that there is no work for everyone in cities; therefore we must remain in our villages so that we will be able to use the land for the benefit of the whole

nation. If we do this we won't fail to get the rewards of our investment in the land.

The Kenyan and the Tanzanian texts differ in the way they treat rural life, not only qualitatively, but also quantitatively (see Table 8.1). Tanzanian texts focus on a variety of improvements taking place at the village level. Kenyan texts, on the other hand, choose to stress imperfections of village life. In addition, there is no discernable effort made in the Kenyan texts to orient children toward farming or other related manual activities as is the case in Tanzanian texts. In short, while messages in the Tanzanian texts are consistent with national policy on rural development, they seem inconsistent in the case of Kenya.[31] This same pattern recurs in the way Tanzanian and Kenyan texts portray African traditions and Cooperative forms of production.

Searching for a Model of Society: African Traditions and Cooperative Forms of Development

Before dealing specifically with what kind of society emerges from both the Kenyan and Tanzanian primary school texts, I will touch briefly on the broader socio-economic context in order to clarify the main motivation behind this search for a new society which characterizes many contemporary African states. The nationalist leadership that inherited political power from the colonial regime came rather quickly to the realization that "political independence without economic freedom is but an empty shell."[32] Capitalist forms of growth were the major components of the inherited colonial economic life, in which, free enterprise and the criterion of "profitability" remained vital forces. This is the background against which the development of alternative policies had to be undertaken for those who felt the need to break away from the status quo.

The solutions suggested as alternative economic policies to achieve economic freedom range from indigenization to a search for a model of a new society. In the latter, the option that seems to have appealed to a number of African states, including Kenya and Tanzania, has been African socialism.[33] Regardless of how African socialism is defined, there was "no doubt that the African tradition was seen as holding within itself a main component of socialist development, cooperative production."[34]

Further, central to African socialism is the "Extended Family" which encompasses the conventional Western-type of family and several other kinship groupings.[35] Traditional attitudes to economic life and the notion of African traditions refer to pre-colonial cultures and civilizations in Africa. They do assume a "single body" of cultural beliefs and modes of behavior. A further aspect of African traditions, and closely allied to the search for a model of society, is the importance of the participation of the "ruled" in governmental decision making, through discussion.[36] This would plausibly be expected to be translated into some kind of mass participation in economic development and a promotion of the value of debate to achieve the common good. Traditional socialization patterns also present some relevance insofar as they emphasize conformity to community norms, elders' authority, minimal differentiation within peer-groups, etc.

Kenya and Tanzanzia have actually been constrained in their search for African socialism by prior economic patterns of growth. Both countries emphasize central planning and have applied themselves 'dutifully' at producing development plans at regular intervals. Niether country has succeeded in abolishing capitalist relations of production; the two countries do differ, however, in the kind of society they envision. In what follows, I shall show that the search for an alternative model has been characterized in Kenya by an apparent ambivalence and ambiguity. In Tanzania, on the other hand, the texts reflect a much more "socialized" picture, chiefly via abundant depictions of cooperative forms of production. Under the umbrella of African traditions, the discussion on the search for a new society will be guided by the following categories and indicators (1) family (nuclear versus extended), (2) ethnic/tribal (as contrasted to national integration), (3) elders/community as sources of knowledge, (4) self-help and collective efforts, (5) egalitarianism.

Portrayals of The Family

Are there consistencies between the Kenyan texts and stated policy with regard to building the new society based upon "African socialism"? Images that emerge from the Kenyan texts are generally far from reinforcing any clear pattern. For example, the treatment of themes related to the family favored the nuclear family over the extended family. Many stories feature the nuclear family as the ideal family unit (husband/wife and parents/children). In the story of Alina's "Birthday Present" the whole family numbered three members.[37] In "Adventures on the Lake", the family included just the parents and two children.[38] While the number of family members may increase, the family unit remians confined to nuclear family as the following reading, describing a family at breakfast illustrates.[39]

> The mother is seated on the chair. She is holding a bottle of milk. But she is not looking at the baby. She is looking at the father. What does the father have in his hands? He's got the newspaper. But he is not reading the paper. He is talking to the mother. . .
>
> The little girl is Rehema. She's got four brothers and two sisters.

Most Kenyan textual materials on the family describe the daily activities of family members. The lifestyles portrayed, as in the excerpt above, are taken from the Kenyan urban middle class. Parents and children, as above, are seated around a table, having their breakfast; parents read their morning papers and drive to work in their own cars.[40] The family in the Kenyan texts is a monogamous. Mothers, if they work, are shown doing domestic chores, cultivating small plots around their houses, or engaging in some minor occupations such as pot making.[41] The materials that focus on the extended family in the Kenyan texts are much rarer than those on the nuclear family. Uncles and grandmothers are the relatives most often described in the few stories where the extended family is portrayed. Even in these few instances, the extended family members are introduced and identified as being "outsiders", distinguishing carefully between the two types of families. The story "Stone Soup" is typical:[42]

> What are we having to eat tonight? asked Walter. Soup, said mother, I've got a lot of vegetables and I'm going to make some very nice soup. I wonder whether your uncle Joseph is coming today. I expect he will. He came three times last week, and each time he arrived just as the food was being cooked. The money your father earns is only enough to feed our own family, and the last time Joseph came we all had to have less.

The Kenyan texts underempahsize the role and function of other family relationships outside those of the nuclear family. Rare are there instances where healthy extended family relationships are depicted. The texts seem to imply that extended families are dying out, if they are not already dead. While one might be tempted to read the message as a deliberate effort directed at re-orienting loyalties from the extended to the nuclear-family caused by urban growth, this stands, nonetheless, in sharp contrast to the national policy of Kenya.

Unlike Kenyan texts, Tanzanian texts pay much attention to the extended family. More importantly, the concept of the extended family was/is used in a much broader sense so as to stretch it to include the community at large. This is usually done where the description of the extended family is used to convey the importance of brotherhood in the community.[43] The following excerpt illustrates the way in which the extended family is used to teach about the new sense of solidarity that the leadership in Tanzania fosters. It is drawn from a biographical account of an ordinary citizen called Kazimoto:[44]

> He is an important officer in a big cooperative. You know that in a family of brothers, sisters, uncles, aunts and cousins, one person always helps another by letting him have the things he wants or by telling him anything he needs to know. Well, a cooperative is like something like a big family of farmers or traders in a certain district who work together and help each other in this way. . .

Such allusions to the extended family are totally absent from the Kenyan texts. Even when the extended family is portrayed in conventional terms in the Tanzanian texts, family members are rarely confined to their being just husband, wife, children, uncles, and aunts. Rather, they are portrayed in some other social roles (farmers, party officials, judges, and the like). The following is typical. It depicts various family members as they prepare themselves to attend the funeral of one of theit relatives, Mzee Masulya (who was also a TANU provincial official:[45]

> Mzee Masulya lived in the village of Kisabo in Mwanza district. He had 3 children. All of them males. Malingumu was the eldest and worked in the office of the Second Vice-president in Dar es Salaam. The second son was Mwendapole. He was a judge in Mbeya. Kasubi was the third son. . . and is still living with the parents.

Tanzanian texts, in general, underemphasize family relationships, especially when the family is viewed as a unit of activities. This explains (from a quantitative point of view) the much lower incidence of these materials compared to similar materials in Kenyan texts (see Table 1 for respective proportions in Kenya and Tanzania).

Portrayals of Ethnicity and Tribalism

School texts at the primary level in Kenyan and Tanzania differ greatly in their discussion of ethnicity and tribalism. The incidence of materials that focus on these topics is much greater in Kenyan than in Tanzanian texts (see Table 1). Ethnicity is used to identify and differentiate several self-contained tribal 'units' or enclaves on a variety of levels (culture, language, habitat, food, modes of interaction, beliefs, and education). Most frequently named ethnic groups are the Kikuyu, Luo, Kamba, Masai, Swahili, and the nomadic groups of North Eastern province. The following, which provides a detailed description of traditional education among Gikuyu, is typical:[46]

> Through moving in the forests and jungles with his father the boy learns about a great many wild fruits and flowers, and comes to know those which are poisonous and those which can be eaten. Along with these special duties goes a very important general training. The boy is taught about family, clan and tribal land. . . Care is taken to teach the boy how to be a good observer and number things by observation without counting them, as counting, especially of sheep, goats, cattle or people, is considered as mogiro, one of the things a Gikuyu is not allowed to do, and one which would bring ill-luck to the people or animals counted.

The Kenyan texts abound with descriptions of ethnic or tribal life. Irregardless of whether they describe traditional education, as above, or culinary specialities as in "The Uses of the Coconut" among the coastal Swahili, the portrayals are neutral.[47] In a few instances the texts contain less than glowing descriptions of the Masai and the nomadic peoples.[48]

It is important to point out that the texts ground each ethnic or tribal group in its own cultural enclave, thus presenting a landscape of multiple islands without any structural linkages among them. While this was the case, the texts never refer to ethnic or tribal rivalries. Many readings glorify acts of resistance and defiance to colonial rule on the part of specfic ethnic groups. Typical of these are such stories as "Mambo Ya Kukumbukwa"[49] or "Kenya Huru."[50] These materials also provide the opportunity to broaden the 'tribal enclave' into some kind of awareness of the larger context of the nation-state. Thus two types of messages emerge from the Kenyan texts with respect to tribalism and ethnicity. Readings focusing on "tribal citizenship" are coupled with thost decrying colonization and stressing national integration. One might still argue that co-existence of both messages (on the ethnic enclaves and nation-state) may prove to be a difficult challenge, especially, in the face of the much lesser attention accorded patriotic education in Kenyan texts.[51]

The Tanzanian texts, on the other hand, seem to have avoided this challenge by de-emphasizing altogether images of "ethnic enclave" identities. They focus almost exclusively on messages intended to create nation-state based identity and loyalty. As noted earlier, discussions of ethnicity and tribalism are much rarer in Tanzanian texts than in Kenyan texts. In the few instances where they appear, the stress is on the contribution of various ethnic or tribal cultural heritages to the common Tanzanian culture. Another variation consists in bringing into sharp contrast pre-colonial state of instability and latent conflicts among ethnic groups to the current, post-colonial period characterized by peace and stability in Tanzania. The following excerpt, which describes a wedding ceremony between two young people from previously antagonistic ethnic groups, ends with an elder's speech drawing on the significance symbolized in this marriage:[52]

> Long ago there was trouble and fighting between our tribes... Fortunately, our manners and attitudes have changed for the better. We've learned to respect each other. We've come to realize that although we are from differcnt tribes, we are still one people, and the same race. We are Africans, and we must be proud of it. And I think that all the guests gathered here are grateful to this young man and young woman for reminding us that love is better than war, and the race is greater than the tribe.

Quarrels and conflicts among ethnic groups are, as implied above, things of the past and members of various tribes should live peacefully and work toward a harmonious nation-building. In short, the Tanzanian texts focus on the fight against tribalism in the name of new loyalties and new tasks required by thc post-colonial state. Taken together with the heavy emphasis of Tanzanian materials that focus on "patriotic" education discussed above, messages on ethnicity and tribalism reinforce other messages within the Tanzanian texts.

Legitimate Sources of Knowledge

Both President Kenyatta of Kenya and President Nyerere of Tanzania have written about socialization patterns in East Africa and especially about traditional informal education, both in its content and methodology.[53] Both accounts of pre-colonial education are similar as can be seen by reading the following (by Nyerere):

> They learned by living and doing. In the homes and on the farms they were taught the skills of the society and behavior expected of its members. They learned the kind of grasses which were suitable for which purposes, the work that had to be done on the crops, or the care which had to be given to animals, by joining with their elders in this work. They learned the tribal history, and the tribe's relationship with other tribes and with the spirits, by listening to the stories of their elders. Through these means, and by the custom of sharing to which young people were taught to conform, the values of society were transmitted.[54]

Nyerere has contrasted traditional education to colonial education in much of contemporary Africa. Among the shortcomings of colonial education, he has pointed to overemphasis on book learning and downgrading of other sources of knowledge specifically "traditional knowledge and the wisdom which is often acquired by intelligent men and women as they experience life, even without being able to read."[55]

There is a marked difference in the way Kenyan and Tanzanian texts portrayed elders and community as sources of knowledge. Kenyan texts pay little attention to elders as legitimate sources of knowledge as compared to Tanzanian texts (see Table 1). Elders are portrayed quite extensively in Tanzanian materials and the message remains consistent about their perceived importance as worthwhile sources of knowledge. Indeed, the Tanzanian texts consider elders to be on the same as footing books and schools.[56] The elder as an important source of knowledge is portrayed unambiguously in a variety of contexts in the Tanzanian texts. These included, among others, providing information on a range of topics, answering questions, expressing informed opinions, teaching about the function of certain institutions, or just serving as living 'reference-books' for the community. The following, which describes a detailed lesson on banking given by an elder, is typical:[57]

> If your father didn't save some of his money, what would he do in time of trouble? The wise man always saves some of his money. And that is what banks are for. Banks help people to save. But I can save money by keeping it at home. And let somebody steal it? This is foolish. Remember that you can get your money back from the bank at any time, and sometimes they give you back a little more than you put in. And above all, while your money is in the bank, other people can use it, and this helps the whole country.

The high incidence of Tanzanian materials that focus on elders as legitimate sources of knowledge, when taken together with the relatively low emphasis on books, teachers, schools, could be taken to suggest a deliberate attempt to rehabilitate traditional sources of knowledge in conformity with official stated policy.

Kenyan texts, on the other hand, ignore such 'rehabilitation' efforts. They emphasize the conventional sources, instead. Books and schools and teachers are actually portrayed in many situations where their importance is strongly underscored. Elders are only suggested as sources of knowledge in very narrow contexts which could at best be taken as reflecting some traces of the old traditional socialization pattern. These are related specifically to respect for elders' authority and total obedience to them.[58] These types of portrayals imply "blind" conformism and tend to conflict with such significant values as those, for example, needed to maintain a spirit of initiative, creativity, discovery, spontaneity, and so on.

The same differences in the way Kenyan and Tanzanian texts portray elders as sources of knowledge extend also to how they depict the productive side of traditional attitudes, specifically, as these are related to self-help and collective efforts. The incidence of collective efforts is greater in the Tanzanian materials than in Kenyan (see Table 8.1). The Tanzanian texts' foci are primarily on cooperative forms of living and working under Ujamaa and the benefits derived directly from such forms of organization of production. Images of collective efforts are linked to the peasants' sense of independence and participation. Repeatedly stressed are messages suggesting that success and survival are a direct result of collective endeavors by peasants using local resources as well as local initiatives.[59] The following two excerpts on self-help and collective efforts, respectively, stress both self-reliance as well as communal production through a massive human investment.

The first describes activities at the level of a youth club in rural Zanzania:[60]

> The good harvest is the result of your own efforts, and I understand that you are already planning to increase the area next year and to buy forty chickens too. . . You have shown brotherhood to each other, and to your fellow villagers. And you have shown self-reliance too, because you relied on yourselves instead of relying on others to do things for you.

The second stresses the result achieved from channeling production along the lines of mass participation at the village level: [61]

> . . . Today, Tekimbili is a successful plantation, where tobacco grow in long careful lines, and the people live in small attractive houses, and have radios and piped water.

Ujamaa (cooperative form of living and working communally) was thus portrayed in very positive terms and rural life shown in the texts as continuing to improve steadily, thanks to mass participation in economic development. Ujamaa was also shown as allowing a great measure of awakening villagers and providing channels and institutions to insure their participation in political and economic matters at the local level. In short, Tanzanian efforts at mobilizing rural people (the majority of its population) and giving them a voice in determinig the course of their lives are portrayed in a large number of textual materials. These images contrast sharply with those of collective effort and self-help from similar Kenyan textual materials.

What is striking in the Kenyan texts, as compared to Tanzanian text, is the almost absence of materials that focus on cooperative production. The only traces that could possibly be taken as somewhat related to traditional attitudes on communal labor are portrayed in Harambee-type activities (taken to mean, the capacity or willingness of individuals to contribute in the form of monetary resources to some selected community projects. This is to be contrasted to Ujamaa cooperative side involving both working and living communally). The following, which describes a community effort to collect money for the building of a secondary school, is typical:[62]

> During those two months, people had been collecting money among themselves, that is, merchants, church members, members of other large organizations, and even children were involved. And finally, the

chief chose the last Saturday of the month to be a general collection day for all these contributions whose funds will be used for the construction of two class rooms of secondary school.

The only case deviated from this Harambee-type focus, was to be found in "Siafu" a story that stresses what could at best be taken as images of cooperative forms of working and living.[63] The story focuses on the collective organization and division of labor provided by a community of ants. Overall, the portrayals of collective efforts are scarce in Kenyan texts. The same failure to project strong images on one of the main component of African socialism here is equally apparent in Kenyan texts, with themes related to egalitarianism.

Eqalitarianism

Tanzanian materials that focus egalitarianism consistently aim at teaching the virtues of cooperation, appreciation and respect for others based on "what they are and not on what they have." The texts tend to reflect the leadership's broad program of socialist transformation. They specifically aim at discouraging any kind of social differentiation, or a life based on the privileges of the few. Living and working together is portrayed as significant means to undermine the potential danger of social differentiation and exploitation in the society. Settings in which these themes appear are ones criticizing colonial policies and practices. Colonial settings provide background against which the alternative policies of the Tanzanian leadership can then be portrayed positively. The following, which describes the founding and impact of NUTA [National Union of Tanzanian Workers] and is portrayed as representing a deliberate attempt by Tanzanians to eliminate exploitative social relations, is typical:[64]

> First of all, during the colonial period, there existed only organizations for the rich (capitalists). Their purpose was to search for and realize big profits on the back of natives. Wages paid to natives were too low. These workers came from Mozambique, Rwanda and within this country. . . They had no right, no power and worked like slaves. The colonialists were too powerful and those brothers. . .were exploited.

The Tanzanian texts abound with stories, as above, that discuss the oppressive and exploitative nature of colonialism.[65]

The Tanzanian materials do not just confine themselves to attacking exploitation, individualism, and capitalist exploitative relations, they also talk about alternative policies that stress living together, living like brothers makes it possible to avoid the temptation of individualism" or "It is inappropriate that few people must have a magnificent life while others (the majority) live in distress."[66] Further, the Tanzanian materials portray an already "awakened" and politically "powerful" peasantry trying to make sure that the fruits of its communal labor won't end up by being expropriated by people from outside rural areas. This type of concern is exemplified in "A Cooperative Shop":[67]

> My friend, maybe you don't see things the way I see them. It is true that we made the road. But just look. Whose buses and cars do you see on the road? The three buses belong to people who do not live in our village. Did these people make the road? The cars aren't ours. Whose are they? Unless we do something now our children will be in trouble later. Now I am beginning to understand. I can see the danger. . .

What is striking in the primary school texts in Kenya as contrasted to Tanzania, is the total absence of images that could be taken as suggesting minimal differentiation within peer-groups or within the community at large. Indeed, while social differentiation and striving for personal wealth and status are portrayed negatively in Tanzanian texts, they are, on the other hand, encouraged and largely tolerated in Kenyan texts. Private entrepreneurial activities and other similar concerns intended to create profit are idealized in Kenyan texts. The cleavage between these entrepreneurs, whose concern was profit for themselves, and the majority of the people and their need for improved living conditions is quite visible, as in the following: [68]

> Mr. Musembe was a lucky man. No one in his village had owned a modern mill before. He didn't know much about machinery, but he expected he would make a lot of money. Everyone had to go to him. They couldn't easily go anywhere else, because his was the only modern machine in the village. They complained about the high prices, but Mr. Musembe didn't reduce them. He expected to make a lot of profit.

Other stories where this theme of personal profit is involved even praise individual ingenuity to realize these gains regardless of any moral concern over the means used to achieve the ends and whether or not other people are being hurt in the process.[69] The Kenyan materials that focus on social differentiation also positively depict the rich based exclusively on their wealth and social status.[70] Conversely, the poor are negatively portrayed in Kenyan texts. They are usually associated with second class status and shown to be powerless. Moreover, not only is the "bottom rung" depicted as having major problems to cope within life, they are, in some instances, blamed for their own poverty as in the following:

> The poor man knows not how to eat with the rich man. When they eat fish, he eats the head. Invite a poor man and he rushes in, licking his lips and upsetting the plates. The poor man has no manners. He comes along with the blood of lice in his nails. The face of the poor man is lined from the hunger and thirst in his belly. . .

With such powerful images, Kenyan texts have a long way to go in order to catch up with Tanzanian texts to project coherent messages on the promotion of economic egalitarianism. Kenyan texts, unlike Tanzanian texts, tend to contradict stated policy goals envisioning a socialist society infused with African traditions.

From Macro-level of Policy to Micro-level of Curriculum: Suggesting one Explanation for the Variation.

This chapter has addressed the issue of content of education, specifically, curriculum materials from the point of view of articulation of societal key goals and values into primary school language texts in Kenya and Tanzania. In the case of Tanzania, the leadership's goals and values are translated into practice in texts. The Kenyan texts, on the other hand, are predominantly characterized by large discontinuities between national values and goals, on one hand, and school messages, on the other. In addition, the Kenyan texts evidence a high degree of ambivalence on some of the most significant sets of goals of national policy. This is well illustrated with respect to policies related to both rural development and African traditions. In fact, emphases identified on rural life in Kenyan texts could, at best, be taken as directing children's attention away from rural realities. They usually imply a value-system in which farming and related occupations are taken to be undesirable. This orientation of Kenyan texts contrasts sharply with stated government policy on the importance of rural development.[72] But still more striking is the ambivalence around some of the major components of traditional values in African socialism. Significant stress, at least on policy level, is put on a non-capitalist alternative in the search for a new society, yet, paradoxically enough, what emerges, are strong images that favor opposite tendencies.[73]

This chapter found that there is more harmony between national policy and the content of primary texts in Tanzania than there is in Kenya. The next logical question is surely why is this so? At this point, one can single out the ambivalence and ambiguity that seem to characterize the Kenyan leadership's stand on such fundamental values and goals such as rural development and the model for a new society as a possible way of explaining the noted variation. In practice, Kenya may be depicted as pursuing a capitalist path of development. But this has not prevented the leadership from expressing their 'commitment' to African socialism and African traditions. This apparent lack of clarity on the very nature and orientation of the society they want to build might have created the lack of harmony between the macro-level of policy and micro-level of primary texts in Kenya.[74] By the same token, Tanzania's explicit stand on the type of society it wants exemplifies a well defined policy with direct implications for the articulation of national values and goals.

School Texts Used in This Study

1. Kenya

Kenya Syllabus for Primary Schools (Kiswahili and English). Ministry of Education. Nairobi: Jomo Kenyatta Foundation, 1975, 1977.

Mambo ni Mazuri (F. Dumila, ed.) Nairobi: Jomo Kenyatta Foundation, 1972.

Masomo ya Kiswahili (Book 1) KIE, of Education. Nairobi: Jomo Kenyatta Foundation, 1977 (lst ed. 1971).

Masomo ya Kiswahili (Book 2) CDRC, Ministry of Education. Nairobi: Jomo Kenyatta Foundation, 1977.

Masomo ya Kiswahili (Book 3) KIE, Ministry of Education. Nairobi: Jomo Kenyatta Foundation, 1977 (lst ed. 1968).

Masomo ya Kiswahili (Book 4) KIE, Ministry of Education. Nairobi: Jomo Kenyatta Foundation, 1977 (lst ed. 1969).

Safari (English Course) Children's and Teacher's Books 1. KIE, Ministry of Education. Nairobi: Jomo Kenyatta Foundation, 1977.

Safari (English Course) Children's and Teacher's Books 2. KIE, Ministry of Education. Nairobi: Jomo Kenatta Foundation, 1977.

Safari (English Course) Children' and Teacher's Books 3. KIE, Ministry of Education. Nairobi: Jomo Kenyatta, Foundation, 1977.

Safari (English Course) Children's and Teacher's Books 4. KIE, Ministry of Education. Nairobi: Jomo Kenyatta Foundation, 1977.

Starting to Read. Ministry of Education. Nairobi: Jomo Kenyatta Foundation, 1969.

Wasifuwa Kenyatta. (F. Dumila, ed.) Nairobi: Jomo Kenyatta Foundation, 1971.

2. Tanzania

English for Tanzanian Schools (2 Vol.). Pupil's Book 5. Teacher's Book 5. Ministry of National Education. Dar es Salaam: Longman Tanzania, Ltd.,1973.

English for Tanzanian Schools (2 Vol.). Pupil's Book 6, Teacher's Book 6. Dar es Salaam: Longman Tanzania, Ltd., 1966 and 1967.

English for Tanzanian Schools (2 Vol.). Pupil's Book 7, Teacher's Book 7. Dar es Salaam: Longman Tanzanla, Ltd., 1967 and 1968.

English for Tanzanian Schools (2 Vols.). Pupil's Book 1, Teacher's Book 1. Ministry of National Education. Dar es Salaam: Longman Tanzania, Ltd.,1970.

Tanzania. Wizara ya Elimu ya Taifa. Muhtasari ya Mafundisho ya shule za msingi (Madaras I-VII) Dar es Salaam: Printpack/MTUU, 1976.

Tujifunze lugha Yetu Kitabu cha. 5 Dar es Salamm: Wizara ya Elimu ya Taifa, 1971.

Tujifunze lugha Yetu Kitabu cha. 7 Wizara ya Elimu ya Taifa. Dar es Salaam: Tanzania Publishing House Ltd., 1971.

Tujifunze lugha Yetu Kitabu cha. 8. Wizara ya Elimu ya Taifa. Dar es Salaam: Tanzania Publishing House Ltd., 1974.

Tunjifunze lugha Yetu Kitabu cha. Tisa. Wizara ya Elimu ya Taifa. Dar es Salaam: Printpak/MTUU, 1975.

NOTES

The following abbreviations have been used below:

NCEOP: Kenya, National Committee on Educational Objectives and Policies Report (Gachati's Report)

ETS: English for Tanzanian Schools (Longman Tanzania Ltd.)

SAFARI: The Safari Upper Primary English Course Textbooks (Kenya Institute of Education/Kenyatta Foundation)

TIJIFUNZE: Tujifunze Lugha Yetu (Tanzania Swahili Language Textbooks/Wizara Ya Elimu Ya Taifa)

MASOMO: Masomo Ya Kiswahili (Kenya Swahili Language Textbooks/Kenyatta Foundation)

1. See C. P. Ridley, P. H. B. Godwin and D. J. Doolin, The Making of a Model Citizen in Communist China (Stanford: Hoover Institution Press, 1971); R. W. Wilson, Learning to be Chinese: The Political Socialization of Children in Taiwan (Cambridge, Massachusettes: M.I.T. Press, 1970); J. W. Elder, "The Decolonization of Educational Culture: The Case of India" Comparative Education Review, 15, (no. 2, 1971). pp. 5-23; Roberta Martin, "The Socialization of Children in China and Taiwan: An Analysis of Elementary School Textbooks" in P. G. Altbach, R. E. Arnove, G. P. Kelly, eds., Comparative Education (New York: Macmillan, 1982), pp.137-175.

2. See for example, Robert LeVine, "Political Socialization and Culture Change" in Clifford Geertz, ed., Old Societies and New States (New York: Free Press, 1963), pp. 280-303.

3. Texts become then "the sole determiners of all that is taught . . . they define the curriculum and control the teaching." See, for example, Peter Ladefoged, Ruth Glick, and Clive Criper, Language in Uganda (New York: Oxford University Press, 1968), p. 104.

4. Despite this, they remain (next to trained teachers) the most costly item required for a "minimal standard of education," and their availability is quite inadequate in many developing countries. See for example, Education: Sector Policy Paper (Washington, D.C.: World Bank, 1980); see also, other contributions in this volume.

5. Some studies seem to indicate a discrepancy between official policy and content aspects and suggest the distortions might be caused by affinities and antagonisms of people involved in both designing and teaching the curriculum. And this 'actor factor' taken to determine much of the relationship between policy and transmission. See, for example, G. P. Kelly, "Franco Vietnamese Schools: 1918-1938," Ph.D. dissertation, University of Wisconsin, 1975.

6. See for example, D. Court, "The Education System as a Response to Inequality in Tanzania and Kenya," The Journal of Modern African Studies, 14, no. 4 (1976), pp. 661-690; see also, E. O'Connor, "Contrasts in Educational Development in Kenya and Tanzania," African Affairs (London), 73, no. 290 (1974), pp. 67-84.

7. No reliability checks were carried out in the categorization of textual materials. The coding was checked twice for both Swahili and English Texts.

8. See for example, The Arusha Declaration (Dar es Salaam: Government Printer, 1967) : see also, E. Stabler, "Kenya and Tanzania: Strategies and Realities in Education and Development," African Affairs, 78, no. 310 (1979). pp. 33-56.

9. This is despite official government statements to the contrary that tend to emphasize that Kenya's postcolonial society is based on "African socialism". See for example, African Socialism and Its Application to Planning in Kenya (Nairobi: Government Printer, 1965.)

10. See Safari 4, "Kenya's Resources", pp. 196-198.

11. Masomo 3, pp. 132-136.

12. Masomo 4, PP. 103-108.

13. Ibid., pp. 118-124.

14. Tujifunze 8, "Mashujaa Wapinga Ukoloni", pp. 61-63; see also, ETS 5, "Heroes Day" pp. 126-132.

15. ETS 7, "The Farmer from Standard 7", pp. 82-87.

16. Tujifunze 8, pp. 26-28.

17. Ibid.

18. These gloomy images of rural life in Kenyan texts do, in fact, cut across both English and Swahili languages.

19. Safari 4, "Drought Report", pp. 47-50; see also Safari 2, "A Reward for Courage" pp. 225-228; Masomo 4, "Njaa Kuu", pp. 74-78; Ibid., "Gharika", pp. 63-68.

20. This has mostly involved situations where parents didn't go through a formal education. See for example, "Alividza and the Oranges," pp. 182-188.

21. Ibid., "So Simple," pp. 50-53.

22. See Development Plan 1970-74 (Nairobi: Government Printer, 1969).

23. Safari 2, op. cit.

24. Safari 4, "Ranching", pp. 74-79.

25. This is one of the main components of (Ujamaa) cooperative production and linked to traditional attitudes to economic life.

26. ETS 5, "Adult Education," pp. 24-29.

27. Ibid., "The Veterinary," pp. 2-6.

28. Tujifunze 7, "Magazeti," pp. 92-94.

29. Following the spirit of ESR (education for self-reliance) philosophy, primary schools were reorganized so as to provide a complete education for the majority of the pupils (and take care of primary school leavers.). The reform included dissociation of primary and secondary levels as well as dissociation of primary education from any implied promise of employment in the 'modern' sector of the economy. Rather, schools were to be transformed into communities and provide skills to live in the village.

30. Tujifunze 7, "Mali Ya Asili," pp. 48-51.

31. Kenyan texts abound with stories on urban life which emphasize all sorts of amenities.

32. J. S. Kasambala, statement at opening of All-African Conference on Cooperatives,quoted in B. Davidson, Which Way Africa? (Harmondsworth: Penguin, 1971), p.122.

33. For an interesting discussion about the pattern of thought that has led to the proliferation of African socialism on the continent, see Note No. 32.

34. Ibid., p. 121.

35. Ibid., p. 122.

36. See for example, G. C. Mutiso, Kenya: Politics, Policy and Society (Nairobi: East African Literature Bureau, 1975.)

37. Safari 2, pp. 82-85.

38. Ibid., pp.176-179.

39. Masomo 3, pp. 44-47.

40. The possession of a car is not in itself an attribute of urban middle class.

41. Fathers were portrayed in a wide array of occupations both 'modern' and 'traditional' while ".. mothers were confined mostly

to a narrow pool of 'traditional' and domestic chores. No notable variation by country here.

42. Safari 3, pp. 94-98.

43. The concept of the extended family includes several degrees of kin relationships as opposed to the nuclear family (grandparents, uncles, aunts, cousins, etc.) The extended family is taken to be the foundation and objective of "African socialism," see for example, J. K. Nyerere, 'Ujamaa': The Basis of African Socialism (Dar es Salaam, 1962).

44. ETS 6, "The Success of Kazimoto," pp. 61-65.

45. Tujifunze 7, "Kasubi Afiwa," pp. 27-30.

46. Safari 4, "Facing Mount Kenya," pp. 94-97.

47. See for example, Ibid., "Government Must Supply Water to Masai," p. 107; see also, Ibid., "Drought Report", pp. 47-49.

48. Ibid., pp. 176-177.

49. Masomo 4, pp. 109-114.

50. Ibid., pp. 103-108.

51. It is worth noting that when the findings are organized by linguistic medium, a sharp contrast becomes apparent in Kenyan texts, especially, with respect to national integration, and ethnic/tribal aspects. On national integration, Swahili materials differed greatly from English ones in that the former do in fact stress patriotically inspired materials with colonial themes. English-medium, on the other hand, pays much attention to economic aspects of the nation instead. This raises the issue of text writing process in general in terms of who are the authors of these texts? (class, education, status, region, ethnicity, etc.).

52. ETS 7, "The Stolen Herd," pp. 59-64.

53. See J. K. Nyerere, Freedom and Socialism/Uhuru Na Ujamaa (Dar es Salaam: Oxford University Press, 1968).

54. Ibid.

55. Ibid., p. 277.

56. This seems to be in response to Nyerere's complaint about the general neglect of traditional knowledge". . . the knowledge and wisdom of other old people is despised, and they themselves regarded as being ignorant and of no account . . . Everything we do stresses book learning, and underestimates the value to our society of traditional knowledge." See Note No. 55.

57. ETS 6, "Grandfather Speaks," pp. 91-95.

58. Masomo 4. "Kutii Wakuu," pp. 79-83.

59. This is essentially the philosophy of Ujamaa and self-reliance within the context of "participatory development." Rural people become 'subjects' as well as 'actors' in the transformation of their environment. These images from the Tanzanian texts contrast sharply with similar materials from Kenya where rural people are still depicted as being 'marginalised.'

60. Tujifunze 7, "The Village Youth Club," pp. 138-143.

61. Ibid., "Uforo and the Farming Settlement," pp. 172-177.

62. Masomo 4, pp. 51-56.'

63. Masomo 2, "Siafu", pp. 96-100.

64. Tujifunze 8, "Chama Cha Wafanyakazi, pp. 42-44.

65. See for example, Tujifunze 7 "Siasa Ya Nchi Yetu," pp. 68-71; Ibid., "Mapinduze Ya-Unguja," pp. 121-127; Tujifunze 8 "Mashujaa Wapinga Ukoloni," pp. 61-63.

66. The rejection of any kind of entrepreneurial and related private endeavors aiming at generating personal gains profit is clearly

articulated and messages about it can be seen in "Siasa Ya Nchi Yetu," Ibid., pp. 68-71.

67. ETS 5, "A Cooperative Shop," pp. 74-78.

68. Safari 3, "The House Painter's Assistant," pp. 268-269.

69. See for example, Masomo 2, "Sungura," pp. 62-64.

70. See for example, Masomo 3, "Mchezo Mkali Sana," pp. 50-55.

71. Safarï 4, "The Poor Man," p. 60.

72. Direct reference to Kericho and the Special Rural Development Programme (SRDP). For an interesting discussion on Kericho, see "The Myth of Kericho;" in G. C. Mutiso, op. cit, pp. 132-161.

73. See African Socialism and Its Application to Planning in Kenya, op. cit.

74. Overemphasis of rural images in Tanzanian texts does, paradoxically, raise a basic question on the content of the curriculum itself in Tanzania as well as elsewhere on the continent. This must be summed up in whether the curriculum should be geared to agriculture or other types of industry regardless of current economic realities. In other words, is the future defined in terms of a farming economy and what are the implications in general terms of underdevelopment? And what are the implications for education planners and curriculum experts in particular?

CHAPTER 9

LANGUAGE AND THE CONTENT OF SCHOOL TEXTS: A NIGERIAN CASE

Chuka Eze Okonkwo

This chapter focuses on textbooks in use in Nigeria's schools in the 1970s.[1] It asks whether changes in linguistic medium from English to an African language--in this case Igbo--has aided in indigenization of the content of primary school textbooks. The texts used in this study are, for the most part, language primers in Igbo and in English used in Anambra and Imo State primary schools. Some social studies and mathematics texts were included. The texts, for the most part, were written by school teachers and education officers.

The study asks if there are differences in the texts in terms of the presentation of information about the individual, the family, the village versus the city, nature, arts and culture and political information (including ethnicity and political morality). The focus is on asking whether Igbo language texts necessarily teach anything different from English language texts and, if they do, the substance of those differences. This chapter asks a range of questions about textbook content. Among these are: Are there differences in texts in the interpretation of the past and in the presentation of the present?

What are the differences/similarities in the treatment accorded to Nigeria/Africa and to Europe, as well as to Nigerian/African and European figures and cultural symbols in the texts? Who are named in texts in both languages as important educational, social, political and cultural reformers--Nigerians/Africans or Europeans? What did the texts tell children about themselves as individuals, about the family, customs and traditional institutions, group values, nation, etc?

Content of Texts: Similarities and Differences

Generally, primary texts in both English and Igbo were divided into small units and lessons. Each section was designed to communicate a distinct message which could be about some moral issues, about nature, labor or some other aspects of society. A typical lesson in all primary texts starts with a short story. This is then followed up with some exercises in comprehension and in reading primers grammar. However, in the first three years of school, grammar exercises in the English language texts emphasized those key elements the authors felt were necessary for understanding the language, namely--word order, spelling, pronunciation marks and their uses, capitalization and dictation. Oral and written exercises took the form of completion of sentences with appropriate words, phrases of verb tenses.

All through the entire six years of primary school in the Igbo language texts, and the last three years of primary school in the English language texts, emphasis is on the definition and characteristics of sentences; present and future, for example, and the use of the dictionary. Whereas the Igbo texts focused attention on the writing of letters, compositions, applications and short stories; the English texts focused on problems related to methods, aptitudes, translatability and meaning-sharing, accents, idiomatic and unidiomatic expressions, and so on.

Generally, in the presentation of the material the English texts used proverbs, country/city tales and a few folk tales. The Igbo texts employed proverbs, folktales, folk songs, riddles and tongue twisters. The proverbs used in texts in both languages, were either in the form of a phrase, a full sentence or a short story. Proverbs used in the English texts often reflected European cultural experiences, for example, "Don't throw the baby out with the bath water".[2] The proverbs used in the Igbo texts were reflections of Igbo cultural experiences, for example, "The young man whose father died of a bullet wound in the head sews his caps with steel".[3]

In the English texts, there was the general tendency to tie some of the country/city tales used to some biblical episode or to some popular European literary tale or to some important European historical event. For example, the story of "Bako's Trip Around Nigeria,"[4] and the series of unexpected delays and accidents he encountered on the way, reads very much like the story of the journey of Ulysses/Odysseus back to Ithaca after the Trojan War as told in the Tales of the Greek Heroes. The story entitled "How John and Ayi caught the Gang,"[5] is in effect, a recapitulation of the story of "Ali Baba and the Forty Thieves" as told in the Tales of the Arabian Nights. The story entitled "The Good Samaritan" is tied to a similar story in the Bible.[6] The story about "How John Saved the Train",[7]--a tale of courage, perseverance and determination reads very much like the story Job in the Bible. Moreover, the story entitled "Whose Ruler?"[8] was modeled on Solomon's "Whose Child?" story and the solution effected to this problem was a recast of Solomon's solution to the Biblical story.[9]

In contrast, stories in the Igbo texts tended to be built around Nigerian cultural experiences and largely expressed in the form of proverbs (most of which are not translatable into European languages).[10] To Nigerians these proverbs constitute the language of diplomacy, commerce, oratory, settling disputes between people and among villages, settling the bride price, and the instrument of intelligence testing. It is a common saying in Nigeria "that any man who does not understand proverbs, the money used in paying the dowry of his mother, is as good as money thrown into the sea". One of the primary tests used in this study observed:

> "The importance of Igbo proverbs cannot be over-emphasized. In a language where it is customary for proverbs to be the main medium of discussion on any important subject, it is obvious that a special study ought to be made of their use in texts."[11]

And that:

> "Among the Igbo, the art of conversation is regarded very highly and proverbs are the palm oil with which words are eaten."[12]

The differences between English and Igbo language texts extend beyond the forms in which material is presented. They also involve the use of names for individual characters and the choice of historical figures emulated. The English language texts, for the most part, used English names for characters depicted. These were largely Biblical. The English language texts also chose to extoll famous European explorers, missionaries and administrators (such as Mungo Park, Christopher Columbus, Mary Slessor, Lord Lugard, etc.); and great American Presidents and British Prime Ministers (such as Abraham Lincoln, John F. Kennedy, Winston Churchill, etc.). In contrast, the Igbo language texts used Nigerian/African names and extolled

Nigerians, Igbo and non-Igbo like Nnamdi Azikiwe, Yakubu Gowon, Tafawa Balewa, Obafemi Awolowo, Murtala Mohammed, Aminu Kano, Ahmadu Bello, Mbonu Ojike, Akanu Ibiam, Kwame Nkrumah, Nwalimu Nyerere, etc.

There were differences between Igbo and English language texts that involved more than the form of presentation. Many of these differences were substantive and related to how the texts portrayed the individual, the family, ethnicity, nature, culture and moral behavior. The remainder of this chapter focuses on these differences. They are summarized in Table 9.1.

Presentation of the Individual

Table 9.1 shows that the English language texts place greater emphasis on the individual than do Igbo language texts. Ninety-one readings (or 13.2%) of the English language texts versus 11 readings (or .9%) of the Igbo language texts were devoted to the individual. As Figure 9.1 shows, the texts in each language followed their own distinct cultural patterns. Whereas the English texts identify the development of the individual with the development of the group, the Igbo texts portray the group development alone and see that group development as prior to individual development.

The English texts tended to take a dim view of the Nigerian child. The texts often portrayed him as cheating in his classwork (by asking his friends to do his work for him),[13] or waiting until it is time to do his homework before he realizes that he hasn't got any ink.[14] Some readings presented him as mischievous, mean and dishonest. In one story the child hid away the book his sister had borrowed from her teacher which she needed for her homework.[15] In another story, the child ignored the warning a lorry driver had given him not to touch the clocks, the switches and the steering wheel. He touched them and the result was that he almost got himself and other pupils in the lorry and the inhabitants of a small village killed. In yet another reading, one child lost the money his mother had asked him to use in buyings things for her. And, another child dropped his sandals without knowing when, where and how!

"I must have dropped mine when we began to run."[16] Finally, a short prose section used as a comprehension exercise in one of the texts reads:

Table 9.1
Comparison Table Analyzing the Contents of the English/Igbo Language Texts

English Language Texts				Igbo Language Texts		
Actual No. of Pages Elem. 1-6	Actual No. of Stories/ Readings	Approx. % of Overall English Time Total	CATEGORY: Major Subjects of Interest	Approx. % of Overall Igbo Time Total	Actual No. of Stories/ Readings	Actual No. of Pages Elem 1-6
63	91	13.2	Individual	0.9	11	8
54	65	9.5	Family	12.1	144	107
104	133	19.4	Village/City Ethnicity/pol.	14.7	176	135
88	100	14.6	Information	10.2-	122	93
30	42	6.1	Nature Description	7.5	89	73
22	27	3.9	Arts and Culture	7.0	83	65
241	324	47.0	Moral Themes	48.0	572	460
524	687				1194	939

The actual number of pages do not add up to the overall total number of pages, the actual number of readings do not add up to overall total number of readings, and the percentages do not add up to 100 percent because some lesson themes may have heen listed under more than one category while some others may not have been listed at all if, in any subjective opinion, the lesson's theme did not coincide with any sub-category in any section.

Figure 9.1

English/Igbo Family Relationship

(emphasis is on individualism "I")	English	Family	Igbo	(emphasis is on communalism "we")
	father mother children	children	great grandfather, grandfather father	have their names prefixed by "nnaa" (father).
uncles, aunts, cousins			great grandmother, grandmother mother	have their names prefixed by "nne" (mother).
	grandparents		uncles, aunts, cousins	have their names prefixed by "dede" or "de" "dada" or "da" (not translatable).

> "Taiwo went to the store and bought a packet of salt. Then he ran home. There was a hole in his pocket and the salt was falling through the hole. But Taiwo did not see it. When he got home, there was no salt left in his pocket, and his mother was angry ...."[17]

Not all English language texts presented such negative portraits. Some readings did portray the child as courageous, adventurous, fearless and persevering. For example, one story discussed how David bravely rescued a little girl from a burning hut:

> "David pulled off the shirt that he was wearing and threw it over her to put out the flames on her dress. His arms and hands were badly burned, and pieces of burning grass fell on his back. He picked up the child and carried her through the smoke and out of the hut."[18]

Another reading talked about a child whose dream was to take a trip to the Sahara Desert. He figured that such a trip would be "a real adventure."[19] Yet, another reading tells the story of a child who risked his own life in a dangerous but courageous attempt to save the lives of others after a storm had broken the rail lines and washed away the rail bridge.[20] Still other stories portray the child as hardworking, creative, honest, often very polite and sympathetic towards others' problems, particularly, towards the sick.[21]

Put together, the English texts presented the Nigerian child as a mixed bag. He is bad and he is good. He is at the same time honest but very dishonest, hardworking but very lazy, quarrelsome and yet very appreciative of the good things others do for him; he risked his life to save others and yet he is irresponsible.

The Igbo texts, on the other hand, consistently portrayed the Nigerian child as honest, respectful, helpful, reliable, friendly, and patient, as the following excerpts show:

> "My friend Uzoma is a very honest person. Our teacher loves him. He helps our teacher, obeys and respects him and does whatever the teacher wants him to do."[22]

And,

> "Omenuko was immensely thankful to his master. Omemgboji blessed him saying, 'Let everything go well with you', as you have served me so faithfully, I pray that those who will serve you will be equally faithful to you."[23]

The Igbo texts also portray the Nigerian child as clever, intelligent, kind, obedient, hardworking, good-natured, neat, and very appreciative of the good things others do for him:

> "Ikem is a very clever and intelligent child. He is always very helpful to his mother. He is also very obedient. He works very hard. In fact, he works as hard as adults."[24]

In fact, one of the texts reported that one child refused to travel out to the city during the school vacation despite several invitations from his relatives and in spite of all the attractions. His reason was that the vacation period coincided with the farming season and he wanted to stay at home in the village to help his parents with work in the farm.[25] Some stories in the Igbo language texts associated with the child stressed the importance of self-help, determination, courage, the rewards of kindness and helpfulness, and the dangers of laziness and dishonesty.[26]

Thus, unlike the English texts, the Igbo texts generally painted a positive image of the child and there was consistency in the pattern of presentation. Nevertheless, the fact that the Igbo texts largely placed emphasis on commendable behaviors of the child, does not mean that the animism of the Nigerian society has no imprint of dualism about it. Quite to the contrary, one of the readings categorically stated that:

> "There are good people and bad people, as well as good spirits and bad spirits in the Nigerian society."[27]

However, the emphasis on commendable attitudes and habits comes primarily because the consequences of doing what is not expected of one are so grave that every effort is made, by all involved in the educative process, to keep the child on the right side of the law and the Igbo texts merely reflected this obvious cultural situation. In fact, one of the readings told the story of a young man who committed incest with his mother-in-law. This was an abomination punishable by death, hence, the ancestral gods brought down thunder and lightning which destroyed his entire family.[28]

Presentation of the Family

Table 9.1 shows that the English texts portray the family in 65 readings (or 9.5%), whereas the Igbo texts devote 144 readings (or 12.1%) to the family.

Figure 9.2 shows how the typical Nigerian family is presented in the English texts. It is described as monogamous. Each family has a small number of children: Mr. Bako's family comprises Mr. Bako (who is also presented as the head of the family), Mrs. Bako and their two children (Alade and Biola). In contrast, Figure 9.3 represents the family as portrayed in the Igbo texts. It shows that the traditional Nigerian family is a complex institute. The oldest surviving male member of the extended family is regarded as the head of the family. The family in the English language texts is European and is presented to Nigerian children as their own. The traditional Nigerian family is largely polygamous and usually has many children as the following excerpt from one of the texts confirms:

> "Omenuko has so many wives that no one could count them .... He also has very many sons and daughters. His three brothers also have very many wives and children."[29]

Figure 9.3 shows that there are no such distinctions as cousins, uncles, aunts, nephews, and nieces in traditional Nigerian families. Every member of the immediate and the extended family is referred to simply as either a father, a mother, a brother or a sister. Hence, the texts tell us that in the traditional environment, every African was his brother's keeper.[30] The emphasis in the Igbo texts is cn group solidarity, whereas in the English texts, the emphasis is on individualism.

In general, the English texts present the child's family as poor. The major occupation of the parents is listed as farming (of yams, cassava, and bananas), raising poultry and cattle, fishing, petty trading, lorry driving, pot-making, carpentry, blacksmithing, etc.:

> "Mary and her mother lived in a small house. They had a very small garden. In their garden, there was a goat. They were very poor ...."[31]

Figure 9.2

Presentation of the Nigerian Family in the English Language Texts

Mark

Mary

Ezekiel
(son)

Esther
(Ezekiel's Wife)

Ethel
(Daughter)

John
(Ezekiel's son)

Jane
(Ezekiel's Daugher)

Figure 9.3
Presentation of the Nigerian Family in the Igbo Language Texts

Okonkwo (Husband) 1. Ijeoma 2. Chinyere 3. Ngozi
(Wives)

Aku Okeke - 1. Ugochi Nwoye Igwe Uzoma Uloaku Chinwe Nnenna Ugonna
2. Nkechi
3. Amaka
4. Uloma

Chili Nweke Obodiya

Okpara 1. Olachi
2. Ego Nwafor Ugonma (etc.)
3. Chinelo
4. Obiageli
5. Uju

Eze

Otti Maduka Ebere (etc.)

Nwude Joseph Obi John Issac Okafor

Peter Grace Ruth Stephen - Sophia Ikeji Victor Victoria Ume

Pius Agnes Obioma Ada Joy Charity Okwudili (etc.)

Some other readings show that in spite of all efforts by parents to encourage love, understanding and togetherness within the family, their children hardly love themselves:

> "Biola! Alade!" Mrs. Bako was really angry. If you're going to quarrel every time you talk, then, every time you quarrel you won't be allowed to speak for at least one hour--not even to ask for a drink of water.[32]

In contrast, the Igbo texts portray the Nigerian family as united to the extent that when one person has a problem, it is equally shared by all family members. To teach this aspect of traditional culture, the texts show that the family helps the child develop attitudes, habits, and values of sharing; of love and togetherness; of tolerance, honesty, and truthfulness; of consideration for the feelings of other people; of forgiveness, sympathy and helpfulness; of hard work, obedience, and respect for elders and constituted authority.[33] In addition, parents repeatedly teach their children that there is no problem that is insoluble, but that all that is needed is the will to see what one starts to the end.[34]

Presentation of the Village and the City

Table 9.1 shows that in the English texts, information about the village/city was presented in 133 readings (or 19.4%), whereas the Igbo texts focus on this topic in 176 readings (or 14.7%). The English texts portray the Nigerian village as unplanned non-modern, economically weak and inhabited by poor and illiterate people. Typical is the following:

> Once upon a time, there was a man who lived in a very small village which was generally inhabited by poor people. He had only two goats, four hens and a very small hut. He was poor and he did not know how to read and write English.[35]

The English texts portray Nigerian cities (which represent Western models of growth and modernity) as densely populated and economically strong, with a good number of modern hotels, restaurants, factories, hospitals and schools.[36] In fact, materials dealing with the cities alone were present in 95 readings (or 13.8% of total English time). The cities were generally described as well planned with street lights and a good network of roads. The city dwellers live in tall, fine modern buildings, and are generally presented as full of friendliness, kind, helpful, polite, thoughtful and very appreciative of the good things others do for them. An excerpt from one of the texts reads:

> "One of the things I'll always remember about this holiday, David," said Mrs. Bako, "... is the hospitality and the kindness of the people we've met and stayed with."[37]

Igbo texts present the village 173 times (14.5% of all Igbo texts) and portray life in the typical Nigerian village community as full of cultural activities which follow a rhythmical pattern from the womb to the tomb. The texts present each stage of a person's life in the village as marked by one important cultural performance or another. Thus, at birth, names are given to the child which are a wish and a blessing and that dedicate the new-born baby to the care of the gods, for example, Chukwuka (god is supreme), Okechukwu (god's creation or present from god), Ikechukwu (strength of god), Chioma (luck from god), etc. And, at the times of initiation into adolescence and of death, ceremonies also follow a cultural pattern.[38]

Information about the city in the Igbo texts is presented with three readings (or 0.2% of the total Igbo time). The Igbo language texts describe the city in terms of its artificial and impersonal nature as compared with the naturalness and the togetherness of the village. In one of the texts the city is defined as "an environment where a man does not need to know the name of the person living next door."[39] It is not surprising, therefore, that in spite of its good roads, electricity, pipeborne water, fashionable stores, hotels and restaurants, etc. the Igbo texts show that there is always the desire to return to the quietness of one's village.[40]

Presentation of Political Information/Ethnicity

Political information provided in the English texts (32 readings or 4.7%), centered around the roles of traditional figures like Chiefs, Obas, Ezes, Obis and Emirs. Again, these were presented as mixed bags. Some are kind, very generous and interested in the well-being of their people.[41] Some others are selfish, corrupt, power-drunk and lacked concern about the well-being of their people. In one reading, a Chief gave a piece of farmland to one of his subjects with Western-style strings attached: "You must give me half of everything you grow there."[42] In another reading, the Oba of Benin (one of the oldest traditional stools in Nigeria), took every step necessary including a couple of murders, to safeguard his position: "If Isee does what he says he'll do and kills off some of my warriors, I'll be safer, the Oba thought to himself. So, he gave Isee a cutlass."[43]

In the Igbo texts, on the other hand, political information was provided in 64 readings (or, 5.4%). Unlike the English texts, the Igbo texts show that political leadership in the traditional Nigerian community, is entrusted in the hands of the village head, traditionally the oldest man in the village, who is assisted by the chief priest and the elders. The village head, usually called the Eze, Chief, Obi, Emir or Oba, is portrayed in the texts as a man of high integrity who understands his obligations to his people and loves and protects them. He helps them solve common as well as individual problems, and sees that peace, order and togetherness reign in the village.[44] The village head is also presented as a man full of wisdom, hard-working, diligent, kind, and usually wealthy.[45]

The Igbo language texts defined wealth in traditional African terms and not in terms of having much money and property. Wealth is defined as having many wives, many sons (and daughters), large barns of yams, cows, goats, sheep, large acres of land, etc.[46] If any of these factors is missing, particularly many male children and large acres of land, a man cannot be considered as being rich no matter how much money he has. For example, a reading in one of the texts states:

> Eze has very many wives, but no grown-up sons. This is why he does not consider himself a wealthy man because, in Africa, the wealthy man is the man who has many acres of land, large barns of yams, many wives and many grown-up sons who will look after his family when he dies.[47]

Interwoven with political information are issues related to ethnicity. Texts in English discussed Nigeria's ethnic problems with 68 readings (or 9.9%), while texts in Igbo discussed such issues in 58 readings (or 4.9%). A frequency count of the English texts shows that while Nigeria and Africa are mentioned only 72 times, the different ethnic groups are mentioned 207 times; and Hausa, Igbo and Yoruba (Nigeria's three largest ethnic groups) were mentioned 165 times. Readings on ethnicity in the English texts largely emphasize differences rather than similarities in the languages, customs and traditions -- particularly as they affect trade, housing, dress, and religious practice.[48]

The Igbo language texts focus on those social characteristics which most Nigerian communities share in common. These include -- communal ownership of land; strong feeling of national, tribal lineage, and family solidarity; a strong feeling of continuity with the unborn and the ancestors; polygymy and the bride price as common practices; important rites at birth, puberty, marriage, and death; age-grade political organization; secret societies and work associations; local villages headed by chief priests, the Ezes, Chiefs, Emirs, Obas and elders.[49] The Igbo texts also discuss a number of common elements in Nigerian beliefs. These include the belief that a spiritual force infused such natural objects as rocks, rivers, mountains, trees, animals, and man; the conception of god (Igwe ka ala) as supreme being and creator of the universe and the belief in other gods or powerful spirits immanent in various natural or supernatural entities. The Igbo texts also discuss beliefs in the power of magic to control spirits and the forces of evil and fate enforced through the roles of priests, sorcerers, charms and taboos as well as beliefs that forces of evil cause illness and are largely responsible for untimely deaths. They also describe the use of herbal preparations and the application of psychological and physiological remedies.[50] Literature included traditional animal tales, myths, legends and episodes from the life of the people.[51]

Presentation of Nature

In the English texts, as Table 9.1 shows, the presentation of nature as an area of interest accounts for 42 readings (or 6.1%), whereas similar materials in the Igbo texts account for 89 readings (or 7.5%). However, the descriptions and functions of such elements as the moon, the sun and the stars, sunset and sunrise; the valleys, hills and mountains; streams and rivers, trees, flowers and the seasons of the year as presented in texts in both languages, differ considerably.

For example, while in the English texts the hills and the mountains included the Alps and the Himalayas; the Igbo texts mainly discussed those found within and around Nigeria. Also, in the English texts readings on streams, lakes and rivers included the Thames, the Mississippi and the Seine, whereas the Igbo texts talked about the Niger, the Chad, the Nile, the Imo and the Benue. Moreover, discussions on the seasons of the year in the English texts included the summer, winter, spring, fall/autumn. In fact, one reading in one of the texts is devoted to the description of a snowy winter Christmas day[52] -- a phenomenon foreign to both the teacher and the child. Readings dealing with the seasons of the year in the Igbo texts primarily describe the importance of rainfall and sunshine particularly to the farmer.[53] In addition, while the English texts see in the moon two men with one looking over the other's shoulder, the Igbo texts see a woman (who is notorious for preparing late night suppers) with her baby on her back, a piston in her hands and a mortar in front of her, pounding foofoo (a traditional menu).

Presentation of Art and Culture

Materials dealing with art and culture are presented in the English texts in 27 readings (or 3.9% of total). In the Igbo texts such materials are presented in 83 readings (or 7.0%). The English texts describe the ancient carvings and cowrie shells of Eshu; Igbo and Yoruba traditional masks, the Benin and Ife bronzes, the Olumo rock at Abeokuta (which is presented as serving historical, political and religious functions); the carvings and the famous leather works of Oyo, the blacksmithing of the peoples of Awka and Jebba provinces, the traditional architectural designs of the palaces of the Sultan of Sokoto, the Oba of Benin, the Emir of Kano, the Alafin of Oyo and the Obi of Onitsha; the necklaces, glass and leather works of the people of Bida.[54]

In the Igbo text, readings on art and culture make no distinction as to the ethnic origins of particular works of art. The texts simply state that all over Nigeria, people are involved in such aspects of art as carving, brass, bronze and ivory works; blacksmithing, the designing of different patterns of traditional houses, weaving, mask building and leather works, etc. However, the texts talk about the Argungu festival in the North; the Igue ceremony in Benin, the Ofala festival at Onitsha; the Ikeji festival in Arochukwu, and the New Yam festival in Igboland. The texts further point out that these are largely the same festivals with local labels attached.[55]

Conclusion

> Language is a guide to social reality and conditions all our thinking about social problems and processes. The 'real world' is to a large extent unconsciously built on the language habits of the group ... We see and hear and otherwise experience largely as we do because the language habit of our community predispose certain choices of interpretation.[56]

This chapter shows that while the primary concern of the English texts were to teach English the Igbo texts taught children about themselves, about labor in their community and about their society. The attempt by the English texts to teach culture is fraught with contradictions primarily because many authors of the texts were cultural outsiders (being largely Europeans and their surrogates). They therefore present culture in terms different from Nigerian experiences, beliefs, attitudes and general understanding of traditions. Some of the readings in the texts talked about Nigerian children taking tea, milk, eggs and honey for breakfast. Some other readings even talked about "tea-time", about "having a cup of coffee", and about "bedtime".[57]

The materials in the English texts often present their subjects comparatively, in terms of modern versus non-modern institutions and practices. They sometimes focus on the imperfections of the traditional Nigerian society and practices, or about the excellence of the modern western-oriented Nigerian institutions and practices. Thus, in materials describing the village, the Nigerian way of life was de-emphasized. The village sometimes is depicted as having nothing good to offer the child:

> In the villages, the medical services are poor, the feeding is poor and inadequate, there is little education and much manual labor; therefore, people hardly reach the age of 40 years before they die.[58]

In contrast, the English language texts present Western-style cities as the most desirable places in which to live. Consequently, these texts ignore Nigerian strong emotional ties to the village of birth, as well as to certain rites, rituals and festivals. Finally, the heroes of history in the English language texts are largely Europeans and Americans.

The Igbo texts are generally consistent in what they teach and how they represent Nigerian experiences, attitudes, traditions, and beliefs. These texts present subject matter with a world with which the child was familiar. The images, characters, and illustrations were taken from Igbo experiences and the stories the Igbo child hears as well as the folktales, the folk songs, the proverbs, the festivals, the rites and rituals are all related to occurrences in daily life. The texts describe Igbo ideas of space and time also, and the heroes of history are Africans.

It is pertinent to note that in those areas strongly emphasized in texts in both languages, Table 9.1 shows that more readings were provided in the Igbo texts than in the English texts. This may be the case because the Igbo texts were articulating an environment with which both the child and the authors were familiar and because the authors of the Igbo texts had a wider choice of words (vocabulary) to use with which primary school children were familiar.

If it is the case that the curricular contents of education reflected a people's idea of reality, and that what belongs to reality is given to the people by the language they use,[59] one can then conclude that the obvious differences in what texts teach are due to linguistic medium and that a change from one language to the other as the medium of education necessarily entail a change in the content of education.

Since the content of education given in the Igbo texts through the Igbo language more clearly reflected Igbo influences, feelings, and customs; showed greater signs of real continuity with Igbo traditions and of encouraging indigenous ideas and institutions; and, given the current emphasis on education for self-reliance and social reconstruction, which, in turn, underscores the need for the indigenization of the curriculum, it is imperative that any growth-oriented education in Nigeria, in particular, and the Third World nations in general, can best be achieved through an indigenous medium.[60] Policy-makers and educational planners in the Third World should make sure that future emphasis on educational development recognize the role of indigenous languages in education. In addition, publishers of school texts who show interest in the production of vernacular texts, should be given every amount of encouragement by the government.

NOTES

1. This chapter is based on my thesis. See Chuka Okonkwo, "Language in Education: An African Case". Unpublished Ph.D. dissertation, S.U.N.Y., Buffalo, 1978.

2. F. G. French, The New Oxford English Course, Nigeria (Ibadan: Oxford University Press, 1972), Book 6, p. 60.

3. Chidozie Ogbalu, Ilu Igbo (Ibadan: University Press Limited, 1963), p. 46.

4. F. G. French, The New Oxford English Course, Nigeria (Ibadan: O.U.P., 1969), Book 4, pp. 25-28.

5. Ibid., pp. 65-67.

6. J. C. Gagg, Evans Primary English Course (Ibadan: Evans Brothers Ltd., 1966), Book 6, pp. 68-70.

7. French, Book 4, pp. 35-36.

8. Ibid., pp. 96-98.

9. First Kings, Chapter 3.

10. See Chuka Okonkwo, "Educating the Igbo Child: The Language Question", Alvan Journal of Education, 1, (July, 1981), pp. 35-47.

11. Ogbalu, Ilu Igbo, p. 4.

12. Chinua Achebe, Things Fall Apart (London: Heinemann, 1956), p. 24.

13. F. G. French, The New Oxford English Course, Nigeria (Ibadan: O.U.P., 1969), Book 3, p. 65.

14. French, Book 6, p. 37.

15. French, Book 3, p. 97.

16. F. G. French, The New Oxford English Course, Nigeria (Ibadan: O.U.P., 1970), Book 5, p. 166.

17. French, Book 2, p. 86.

18. French, Book 3, pp. 76-77.

19. French, Book 6, p. 2.

20. F. G. French, The New Oxford English Course, Nigeria (Ibadan: O.U.P., 1969), Book 4, pp. 92-98.

21. French, Book 3, p. 22.

22. Chidozie Ogbalu, Igbo Mbu (Ibadan: U.P.L., 1973), Book 4, pp. 65-66.

23. Pita Nwana, Omenuko (London: Longman, 1932), p. 2.

24. Ogbalu, Book 4.

25. Ibid., p. 63.

26. S.N.C. Obi, Ọkwụ Igbọ (Lagos: Longman, 1975) Book 6, p. 33.

27. T. Nzeako, Nkoli (Lagos: Longman, 1972), p. 56.

28. Ahamba, Okeke Tara Ọse Ọji (London: Longman, 1932), p. 18.

29. Nwana, Ọkẹnụkọ, pp. 22-23.

30. Ibid., pp. 14-18.

31. French, Book 3, p. 16.

32. French, Book 6, pp. 30-31.

33. Nwana, op. cit., pp. 1-18. Also, Nzeako, op. cit., pp. 25-31.

34. D. N. Achara, Elelịa (Lagos: Longman, 1972), pp. 15-19.

35. French, Book 3, p. 14.

36. French, Book 6, p. 3. Also, French, Book 5, pp. 33-39.

37. French, Book 6, p. 46.

38. T. Nzeako, Ọmẹnala Ndị Igbọ (Lagos: Longman, 1972), pp. 25-32.

39. Chidozie Ogbalu, Ọmẹnala Igbọ (Ibadan: UPL, 1975), p. 75.

40. Nwana, op. cit., pp. 58-65.

41. French, Book 2, Lessons 5 and 7.

42. French, Book 6, pp. 110-111.

43. Ibid., p. 165.

44. Ogbalu, Omenala Igbo, pp. 28-30.

45. Nwana, op. cit., p. 48.

46. D. N. Achara, Ala Bingo (London: Longman, 1935), pp. 43-45.

47. S. Ahamba and D. Nwoga, Ogugu Igbo 2 (Lagos: Macmillan, 1975), pp. 36-37.

48. N. P. Iloeje and E. N. Okoro, Beginning Social Studies (Lagos: Macmillan, 1976), Book 6, pp. 54-61.

49. Ogbalu, Omenala Igbo, pp. 42-43.

50. Ibid., p. 82.

51. Ahamba, op. cit., pp. 62-63.

52. J. C. Gagg, Evans Primary English Course (Ibadan: Evans Brothers Ltd., 1966), Book 5, pp. 80-88.

53. Ogbalu, Igbo Mbu, Book 5, p. 13.

54. D. Fadeiye, Ilesanmi Social Studies (Ilesa: Ilesanmi Press, 1980), Book 4, pp. 38-43.

55. Nzeako, Omenala Ndi Igbo, op. cit., pp. 63-66.

56. David G. Mandelbaum, ed., Selected Writings of Edward Sapir (Berkeley: University of California Press, 1949), pp. 160-166.

57. French, Book 6, p. 57.

58. Fadeiye, op. cit., pp. 62-65.

59. Chuka Okonkwo, "Bilingualism in Education: The Nigerian Experience", Prospects, 12 (No. 3 1983) pp. 453-469.

60. Chuka Okonkwo, "Bilingualism and the Nigerian Primary School: Problems Without Prospects", Journal of Research in Curriculum, 4, No. 2 (July, 1986), pp. 31-42.

SCHOOL TEXTS (ENGLISH)

Awoyemi, M., A. Okunade and C. Sakoma. Primary Social Studies (Books 1-6). Lagos: Nelson Pitman Limited, 1982, 1983.

Cairns, J. and J. Munonye. Drills and Practice in English. Aba (Nig.): Pilgrims Press, 1965.

Ekwensi, C. An African Night's Entertainment. Ibadan: University Press, 1962.

Fadeiye, D. Ilesanmi Social Studies (Books 1-6). Ilesa: Ilesanmi Press, 1975.

Floyer, E. Lively English Course (Books 1-3). Ibadan: University Press, 1967.

French, F. G. The New Oxford English Course (Books 1-6). Ibadan: Evans Brothers Limited, 1966.

Gagg, J. C. and J. R. Bunting. Evans Primary English Course (Book 6). London: Evans Brothers Ltd., 1966.

Ihezue, E. Y. I. and O. Onwuegbuna. Social Studies for Primary Schools (Books 1-6). Lagos: FEP International Private Ltd., 1978.

Iloeje, N. P. and E. N. Okoro. Beginning Social Studies (Books 1-6). Lagos: Macmillan, 1976.

Larcombe, H. J. Larcombe's Primary Mathematics. Lagos: Evans Brothers, 1957, 1966.

Onibonoje, B. Onibonoje Primary Social Studies (Books 1-6). Ibadan: Onibonoje Press, 1974, 1982.

SCHOOL TEXTS (IGBO)

Achara, D. N. Ala Bingo. London: Longman, 1935.

Achara, D. N. Elelia. Lagos: Longman, 1972.

Achinivu, K. Akwukwo Nke Mbu. Lagos: Longman, 1964.

Achinivu, K. Akwukwo Nke Ato. Lagos: Longman, 1970.

Ahamba, S. Okeke Tara Ose Oji. London: Longman, 1932.

Ahamba, S. na D. Nwoga. Ogugu Igbo 2. Lagos: Macmillan, 1975.

Ihezue, E. Y. I. Mbido Ogugu Igbo. Enugu: Nwamife Press, 1972.

Iroaganachi, J. O. Oka Mgba. Lagos: Longman, 1973.

Nwana, P. Omenuko. London: Longman, 1932.

Nzeako, T. Nkoli. Lagos: Longman, 1973.

Nzeako, T. Omenala Ndi Igbo. Lagos: Longman, 1972.

Obi, S. N. C. Okwu Igbo (1-6). Lagos: Longman, 1963-1975.

Ogbalu, F. C. Akwukwo Ogugu Igbo Mbu (Books 1-6). Ibadan: UPL, 1965.

Ogbalu, F. C. Mbediogu. Ibadan: UPL, 1963.

Ogbalu, F. C. Omenala Igbo, Ibadan: UPL, 1965.

Ogbalu, F. C. Okowa Okwu. Ibadan: UPL, 1971.

Ogbalu, F. C. Ilu Igbo. Ibadan: UPL, 1973.

Uzoma, R. I. <u>Akwụkwọ Igbo Nkẹ Mbụ</u> (Books 1-6). Lagos: Longman, 1966-1975.

CHAPTER 10

CURRICULUM IN ACTION--MATHEMATICS IN CHINA'S ELEMENTARY SCHOOLS

Julia Kwong

The school curriculum is not just packaged information for students to learn. It has overt and covert contents that reflect the dual role of education as the transmitter of knowledge and social values. The former incorporates the syllabi or knowledge recommended by the ruling authorities aimed mainly at preparing the young to become useful members of the community. It is overt because the training and academic roles of education are openly acknowledged and articulated by the educational authorities, and accepted by members of the society. The covert curriculum includes, besides the written texts, the organization and activities of the schools aimed mainly at imparting social values to students to facilitate their acceptance of the status-quo. This function of the curriculum is not as obvious as the former. Moreover, the inculcation of values is usually deemed distasteful in a capitalist society committed to pluralistic and liberal ideology. Hence this role is rarely highlighted, and sometimes not even recognized by the educators involved.

The curriculum, however, is much too complex to be captured by these categories alone. There is not only the dual role of the curriculum but also its dual structure--static and dynamic aspects--a dimension that has been alluded to but seldom analysed within this context. Both the static and dynamic structures transmit overt and covert curricula. The former includes the textbooks, the school rules, and regulations; the latter encompasses the interpersonal interactions occurring within the schools geared to communicating the messages in the curriculum to the students. Just as overt and covert curricula are interwined and difficult to disentangle in realilty, the dichotomy of the curriculum into its static and dynamic aspects, while adding to analytical clarity, is also artificial.

These two structures are closely interrelated, reinforcing each other, circumscribing each others' effectiveness, and ideally dedicated towards the same ends. For example, the instructional and non-instructional activities organized by the schools are oriented around the messages and contents of the textbooks and defined by established school rules and regulations. On the other hand, some of the activities of the schools represent the school regulations in action and are a measure of their effectiveness. Likewise, the messages of the printed texts are made meaningful to the students through the instruction of the teachers and other activities sponsored by the schools.

Textbooks constitute a major component of the curriululm. They reflect the dominant culture and reinforce values of the ruling group. If this is so, and if the activities in the schools are so carefully oriented around the messages in the texts, how can we explain the many instances in which youth reject this dominant culture? Willis and others have viewed such occurrences as a form of student resistance and a way whereby schools can become a locus of change.[1] The content of the curriculum is irrelevant to the students' world. The problem, in short, lies in the incongruities between the static aspect of the curriculum and the students' social background. Such an interpretation, however convincing, overlooks the dynamic aspect of curriculum. It is too idealistic to assume a perfect fit between the hegemonic ideology and those of the teachers, or to assume that the schools are completely effective in transmitting their pedagogy. The latter point is obvious and I shall not elaborate. If the teachers should choose to reject the ideology transmitted in the textbooks, they will be in a better position to do so than the students because of their more powerful role in the schools. The students may engage in passive resistance or create their own rival culture using their limited resources to reach a small circle of peers. The teachers can use their position of advantage in the classroom to spread their ideas, organize counter activities and reach out to a larger audience. Even if they do not do it consciously, their lack of enthusiasm will be reflected in their teaching style, and their reticence will not escape the young.

Thus, the curriculum in practice may not always transmit the messages of the ruling group. There may be a disjuncture between the curriculum content and the curriculum in action. This chapter is a case study of how this may occur; it focusses on the elementary mathematics curriculum in China between 1968 and 1985. Two sets of texts are used in the analysis. The first set, published in the late sixties and early seventies, consists of four elementary texts used in Inner Mongolia and another used in Beijing. The style and content of the texts published in Inner Mongolia and Beijing are similar. There is no reason to believe that they deviate to any great extent from others used across the country at the time. The second set, published mainly in 1983, is comprised of seven second semester primary mathematics texts used across the nation in the early eighties. These texts constitute the core of of the mathematics curriculum in China during this period.[2] I shall first analyze the academic (overt) and cultural (covert) content of these two sets of textbooks. To more fully appreciate its function, I also look at its dynamic aspects, namely, how mathematics were taught in the classroom and supported by other related activities in the schools.

Historical Background

The curriculum in China's schools can be fully appreciated only against the political and socioeconomic development of that country. To emphasize the importance of the social context is not to opt for the correspondence theory between education and its economic base, namely, that education is a superstructural reflection of the economy. Even Bowles and Gintis, the proponents of this theory, recognized in a later article the inherent autonomy of the educational system, and the contradictions in the socioeconomic structure and culture of the society, which permeate and generate contradictions in the educational system.[3] Providing a brief history of China's sociopolitical background gives the backdrop for readers to better understand changes in the curriculum in that country and to appreciate the specificities of the nature of the curriculum in a socialist society.

While China remained communist between 1968-1985, in 1976 she experienced a change in the composition and the ideology of the ruling group. The present official Chinese position labels 1966 to 1976 the ten years of the Cultural Revolution. These ten years marked the political domination of the Gang of Four and the thoughts of Mao Zedong. This faction of the hegemonic group was against rapid industrialization achieved through foreign capital investment assistance or the importation of foreign technology. To preserve national independence, they were ready to accept a slower growth rate based on the country's existing technological level and abundant labor power. Their priority was egalitarianism: the abolition of rank and social class, the disparities between rural and urban areas, and inland and coastal regions. Whether they succeeded in so doing is not the question here, but education during this period was faced with the onerous task of providing human resources for this type of economic development. According to Mao, there was to be a close integration of theory and practice, mental and manual labor. The young graduates were to be equipped with knowledge and skills required for the nation's economic needs and imbued with a sense of mission, ready to sacrifice personal ambition for the good of the country.

After two turbulent years of student unrest, some form of political order was restored in 1968 and the ruling group prepared a new set of textbooks for the newly re-opened schools. The government did not introduce a nationwide curriculum but argued for decentralization and participatory democracy, as well as accommodation to local interests. Committees made up of trusted teachers were commissioned to develop the curriculum in their localities. They consulted workers and peasants and drafted the school texts. The government might not have been directly involved in the preparation of the curriculum, but the oppressive political climate immediately following the Cultural Revolution (1966-1968) and the close surveillance exercised by party faithfuls at the local level more than compensated for the lack of government intervention in textbook writing. The end result was the same: curricula might vary across the country, but they all conformed to the ruling ideology and this explains the similarities in the texts published in Beijing and Inner Mongolia used in this analysis.

The Gang of Four fell from power in late 1976, and this radical change in the political situation was accompanied by an equally dramatic change in the curriculum, which ironically highlighted only more clearly its stabilizing function. In the academic term after the Gang of Four was removed from office, the more controversial sections of school texts praising them were eliminated. At the same time, the government entrusted groups of experts in the different disciplines to draft new sets of textbooks that reflected more closely their viewpoints, which could be used across the nation. By 1980, a new set of textbooks became available. Unlike curriculum development in capitalist countries, which is mediated by the involvement of publishing companies and considerations of the market place, this direct state participationin curriculum planning ensured a much clearer reflection of the state's political, economic, and cultural demands in school texts.[4]

The dominant faction under Deng Xiaoping came to power in 1976, and by 1978 they were politically entrenched. They had a different view of the country's future and its developmental strategies. China remained socialist, but unlike their predecessors, they measured the country's achievements not according to the conditions prior to the communist takeover, but by comparing China with the West. China was behind and had to catch up with the industrially advanced countries. They were willing to abandon the isolationist policy and cooperate with Western capitalist nations. They welcomed foreign aid, investment, and technology. They aruged that this was in keeping with the orthodox

Marxism which held that communism would take root only in countries with advanced means of production. China had not reached that stage and therefore had to develop her productive forces. Equality had to be sacrificed for rapid development and inequality tolerated for a time. Increased prosperity, in their opinion, would in the end wipe out inequities. The educational system had to be modified to fit this new model of development. Just as it would be acceptable for a few to prosper ahead of others, it was also permissible for the educational system to focus on the training of a few instead of the mass. Education became very competitive. Instead of producing human resources adapted to local and often simple if not backward means of production, the transmission of advanced science and technology and the inculcation of a dedication to the pursuit of knowledge were the schools' new priorities. The schools became equipped with a strong academic orientation. This and its more elitist character, while departures from the 1976 educational philosophy, were more in tune with the traditional conception of education, which, as we shall see, had an important effect on the curriculum.

The Academic Content of the Mathematics Curriculum

Bourdieu argued that the inclusion of some forms of knowledge and not others in the school curriculum was in a way arbitrary.[5] The hegemonic class defined certain knowledge as legitimate in school not simply because of its pragmatic function, but because they themselves monopolized it, and thereby made attainment of high status contingent on the mastery of that body of knowledge. This analysis might be applicable to the elitist French educational system he analysed; the same cannot be said for the inclusion of mathematics, or really arithmetic, in the elementary schools we are looking at. The possession of basic arithmetic skills as taught at the elementary level is crucial to the individual's functioning in society. In fact, so fundamental are these skills that there is little difference in the content of the mathematical knowledge in the curricula despite the very different views of the model society in the periods before and after 1976.

The level of arithmetic skills to be mastered by the elementary school students in China in the two periods, 1968-76 and 1976-85, was more sophisticated that those currently required in the West. Chinese students were expected to learn addition, subtraction, multiplication and division, simple statistics, concepts as decimals, integers, averaging, and the use of the abacus. The materials to be mastered before and after 1976 were the same, but the emphasis assigned to the different concepts and the demands on the students were different. The abacus serve as calculators in China, and because of its practical utility and the educators' emphasis on the integration of theory and practice, learning to use the abacus figured much more importantly in the curriculum before 1976. In contrast, later students were expected to master many of the other concepts earlier than those attending schools prior to 1976. They learned multiplication in grade two, whereas their predecessors in the early seventies mastered it only in grade three. In addition, there were more assignments and exercises accompanying the introduction of each new concept and skill. The number of concepts in the texts issued after 1976 did not increase dramatically but the average length of texts almost doubled. The grade one mathematics primer published in 1969 was only forty-nine pages in contrast with the ninety-six page text used at a similar level in the later period. All these changes reflected the strong emphasis on academic learning in the second period to prepare students for scientific pursuits that the new ruling group deemed so important to development.

The pre-1976 mathematics texts drew a close link between mathematics and its application. The students would soon be joining the labor force and the majority would be engaged in agriculture. The learning of statistics and the use of the abacus provided them with skills essential to become accountants or to take up other clerical positions in production teams. Exercises in the texts helped them in bookkeeping, showed them how to keep inventories, and register workpoints. As a fitting end to a group of exercises of this nature, students were asked "to carry out social investigations in the factories, farms and enterprises and to apply the knowledge they learned in these texts to solve real problems."[6] The post-1976 texts, as mentioned earlier, were more concerned with academic training. Here, there was also a general mathematics problem that marked off the end of a set of exercises. Instead of asking students to apply their skill to the real world, it asked them to "develop a problem that has to use the equations 100+50, 100-50" clearly illustrating a scholastic emphasis.[7]

The Cultural Content of the Mathematics Curriculum

Contrary to the stereotypical image that mathematics, like other science subjects, is value-free and apolitical, the following section will show that mathematics, in China at least, is far from being neutral. The cultural and social messages were embodied not only in the mathematical concepts but also in the medium carrying the mathematical knowledge. They were interwoven in the texts and not amenable to manifest content analysis; quantitative content analysis will only denude it of its richness and overlook it subtleties.

Communism was the ruling ideology in the two periods and was emphasized. In the first period, communist ideology permeated the texts. Students were not told that it was the ruling ideology or that it was good, but that Mao embodied communism. They were asked to calculate the number of Mao's works that the world loved so much to read or the number of visitors who adored him and toured his former residence.[8] The post-1976 texts did not deify Mao. They did ask students to calculate the years that elapsed since the Chinese Communist Party was formed in 1921 and to give the number of years since the birth of the People's Republic of China in 1949.[9] These later texts were not as 'political' as those of the earlier era. Unlike the mathematics textbooks before 1976, they did not carry pictures of Mao Zedong, his quotations, or quotations of Lin Biao, Mao's appointed successor before he fell from grace. But even in these post-1976 texts, class divisions were distinct with the landlords and capitalists portrayed as political pariahs in Chinese society. A grade one text used in the 1980s asked students to evaluate capitalist exploitation; students were to count the number of child laborers left after thirteen died of fatigue and fifteen died of illness.[10]

The mathematics texts in both periods convey a sense of national pride. In the pre-1976 texts, students were told that the 6,700 meters long Yangtze Bridge at Nanjing was designed and built by Chinese with no foreign help.[11] The texts published after 1976 also impressed upon the students the grandeur of the accomplishment, asking them to estimate the miles of railroad tracks and highways on the bridge.[12] Furthermore, both sets of texts told the students the importance of raising agricultural and industrial outputs. They had to tally economic production statistics. Agriculture was the basis of the Chinese economy and many examples in the two sets of texts came from agriculture. One example from the first period read:[13]

> In 1971, the average food crop production of Daizhai Brigade was 1096 catties per mou, what is the yield on a piece of land of 95 mou?

Similar examples could easily be found in the post-1976 texts, one problem read:[14]

> The commune members harvested 3350 catties of cucumbers. The yield for tomatoes was three times that of cucumbers and

> 260 catties more than that of the eggplants. How large is the eggplant harvest?

The implication was clear: economic development was very important to the country's well-being and the young were to work hard towards this end.

As Marshal MacLuhan pointed out, the medium is the message.[15] The mathematical problems not only let children practice their mathematical skills but also drilled into them acceptable values. Unlike the languages texts in which students were told who to emulate and what was good or bad, such information and points of views conveyed in the mathematics texts were presented as a given-natural elements in the social order where people operated. To tell them outright what to do might invite resentment, debates, criticisms, or resistance, but a message subtly conveyed and repeated often enough acquired a veneer of truth and would likely be internalized. Communism, nationalism, and improving the country's economy were to be integral elements of the national character.

This cultural role of the mathematics texts becomes even more evident when we recognize that these messages accompanying the teaching of the mathematics were modified to meet the different political and social demands in the two periods. The mathematical problems sets of the pre-1976 period liberally drew illustrations from the social contexts of the time nurturing the readers' interest in social and political issues. References were made to the workers-peasants-soldiers committee in charge of the schools, the students' long march (travelling across the country) during the Cultural Revolution, the wallposters, the criticism meetings, the distribution of Mao's red books, the military training in schools, and the economic progress made. A typical example would read:[16]

> The proletariat revolutionary faction in the Red Flag Printing Company was filled with the proletariat love of Chairman Mao. As part of their contribution to the national day celebration, they enthusiastically printed pictures of Chairman Mao. They printed 4392 copies in the morning and 5608 in the afternoon. How many could they produce in one day?

Another problem read:[17]

> Revolutionary teachers and students of the Long March Primary School attended the criticism meeting of the renegade,

> traitor Liu Shaoqi and his agent in Inner Mongolia, the 'contemporary emperor' Ulanfu to expose their crimes. 254 from the first platoon attended. In the second platoon, 340 took part, and 308 came from the third. How many came from the three platoons altogether?

Some of these mathematical problem sets also referred to the enemies and friends of China. The United States was portrayed as rife with worker and racial unrest, and in foreign policy, it was described as the aggressor in Vietnam, Cambodia, and Laos.[18] On one occasion, students were asked to calculate the number of American airplanes damaged and destroyed by the "patriotic army and people of Laos"; on another occasion they were to tally the number of demonstrators in three of the twenty cities protesting against the Johnson Administration in 1966.[19]

Thus, one gets a relatively clear picture of the official stand on certain issues and glimpses of the social, political, and economic situation from examining these problems, as well as the attitudes students were expected to share. The workers-peasants-soldiers revolutionary committee was the decision-making group within the schools, and by implication the classes/groups they represented were superior to other social categories, including the intellectuals. Attending criticism meetings and writing wallposters were portrayed as normal activities, implying that students could rebel against traditional authorities in schools, namely, the intellectuals. Young people were working alongside the peasants and the workers in the texts, thus psychologically preparing the students for what was likely in store for them in the future. The country's agricultural and industrial output had risen since 1949, it had also increased since the Cultural Revolution; of course, the communist government and the current leaders were to be given the credit. Projects were accomplished ahead of schedule through the joint efforts of the people; collective effort was therefore good.

Given the positions held in these texts, it was not surprising that they were revised when Deng Xiaoping and his faction came to power in 1976. As Anyon pointed out, it is important not only to look at what is included in the textbooks, but also what they exclude.[20] Deng's group wanted political stability and not the turmoil of the Cultural Revolution. Activities such as counting the number of wallposters and criticism meetings were dropped in the new texts as these might encourage student rebelliousness. References to the workers-peasants-soldiers revolutionary committees were also eliminated because the intellectuals and not the working class were the new elite. Negative portrayal of the United States disappeared because these examples would not justify the new policy of cooperation with that country. Instead of totalling attendance at criticism meetings or the miles covered in their long marches, the children calculated the number of black and white rabbits, yellow and white chrysanthemums, and the balls each group would get.[21] There were still references to student participation in labor, but the nature of work dedscribed was vastly different. Textbooks between 1968 and 1976 described students resettling in the rural areas, reclaiming wasteland for agriculture, harvesting wheat and other crops, and irrigating and fertilizing the land. In the new texts, examples of student participation in labor declined, and when they occurred, students were cutting grass, planting trees along the road, or engaged in other light duties in the schoolyard.[22] The pre-1976 texts gave glimpses of the society, but examples in the later ones focussed more on the immediate and sheltered environment of the children and provided readers little information about the adult world. Social and political tensions marked both periods. In the earlier period students were told simply who the winners and the losers were, but in the post-1976 period students were cordoned off from these realities. Studying hard was their major role at this stage of life; political and social involvement was not encouraged.

The mathematics texts in the pre-1976 period emphasized the importance of production with hardly any reference to the marketplace. The majority of the problems were put in settings such as this:[23]

> The iron maidens of Daizhai were courageous in their thinking and action. They used scientific methods in farming methods and produced 6500 catties of corn from 5 experimental fields. What was the average yield per farm?

Another predominant theme was drawn from transportation. This is one illustration:[24]

> The People's Liberation Army planned to help the Support the Military Commune to transport 836 tons of food. They had already transported 18 truckloads averaging 2 tons each and they intended to finish their job in four more rounds. If each truck held 4 tons, how many trucks would they need?

The marketplace was condemned. One interesting problem asked students to calculate the "'extraordinary amount of profit'" made by a socialist imperialist country that bought 7.7 million barrels of Iraqui oil at three dollars each and then sold it to West Germany at eight dollars a barrel.[25] One could draw no other conclusion from this except that the government wished to draw attention to the danger of China being exploited by participating in world trade. When references were made to the internal market, the sales items referred almost invariably to Mao Zedong's pictures and works, or political publications like The Red Sun Lightened the Path of Daizhai.[26] In contrast, messages that discouraged foreign trade were dropped from the post-1976 texts, and in the examples of the internal market, they referred to the sale of consumer goods, such as televisions, radios, washing machines, and food items. Some of these read:[27]

> A store ordered 75 catties of fruit candies, but 8 times as many milk candies. How many catties of milk candies did the store order?
>
> A television set cost $396, it's a $18 more than the price of 2 washing machines. What is the cost of a washing machine?
>
> A department store had 20 packages of towels delivered. In each package, there were 20 towels each selling for $3. How much is the total shipment worth?

The texts no longer condemned profit making and they demonstrated greater tolerance of consumerism and the marketplace. It was no longer for students to enjoy consumer items.

Transmitting the Mathematics Curriculum in the Classroom

Studies have shown that students often resist the values and rules of the schools, devise their own pastimes, and develop their own lived culture distinct from and often opposed to that of the official one.[28] My limited observations suggest that counter-cultures also exist in China's schools. However, my concern here is not so much to evaluate school authorities' success in making students conform to the academic and cultural demands of the curricula, but how the schools transmit them.

A large number of school teachers in China were trained in the pre-communist era with ideas different from, if not opposed to, the hegemonic ones. By 1968, older teachers brought up under the pre-communist political system retired and were replaced by new teachers. However, many remained and held onto their views, and their ideas were shared by the new teachers who were their former students. Some teachers were not committed to communism, and others were alienated by the egalitarian and pragmatic orientation in the educational philosophy of the late sixties and early seventies. As pointed out earlier, when the teachers in the West do not agree with the school authorities, they may use the sanctuary of the classroom to spread their ideas. In China, few teachers would openly defy the system; however, even in this tightly regimented society, pedagogues still enjoyed relative autonomy in the classroom and could subvert and hegemonic ideology embodied in the textbooks if they chose to.

Despite the Chinese government's recognition of the important role of education in transmitting knowledge and inculcating values to the young, teachers generally perceive themselves as pedagogues of a certain discipline. They believe the task of shaping students' character, especially their political outlooks, was the responsibility of teachers, of politics, or of party secretaries. They saw the transmission of knowledge as their major role and the officially defined curriculum as the centerpiece around which they organized their instructional activities. Except for the brief recess or lunch period, the children spent most of their time in school listening to teachers' lectures or engaged in activities organized by them. Theoretically, these activities were supposed to reinforce or facilitate the children's mastery of the knowledge and skills, if not the values, conveyed in the texts.

McNeil has pointed out that sometimes the transmission of knowledge may be compromised in enforcing discipline in the classroom.[29] Discipline in China's schools, compared with the West, has never been a major problem, and students' activities are highly regimented making diversions to enforce classroom order rare. Even in the early seventies when the educational system was supposedly more democratic, foreign visitors, like Kessen, were struck by its strict discipline and the predominant role of the teachers.[30] The occasional visitors' presence might have affected the students' behavior, but even those who taught in China confirmed that such good behavior was the norm. The classroom then was very orderly with the monitor announcing the entry of the teacher and all the students standing up to greet him/her. Students raised their hands if the instructor wanted class response. They would only stand up and speak when called upon to do so. The teachers could devote almost exclusive attention to the teaching of the textbooks.

In carrying out this work, the teachers restricted their lectures to course materials, presenting the knowledge from the textbooks clearly and systematically, deviating from their contents only during political campaigns or to make special announcements from the school administration. This behavior continued throughout the two periods. The motivations for this strict adherence to the texts were, however, not entirely the same. In the late 1960s and early 1970s, intellectuals were criticized for spreading bourgeois ideology. Many were reluctant to teach because a careless remark might land them in trouble. Since the outlook of some of the teachers and those presented in the texts were not entirely indentical, what better way to avoid controversies and protect themselves than to follow strictly what was prescribed by the school authorities, namely, the textbooks. The political pressure on the teachers eased in the late seventies and their status rose, but so did the pressure to prepare students for examinations. Students were tested on a number of subjects, including mathematics, before they could enter high schools, and competition was keen. Teachers felt compelled to cover the complete syllabus giving students additional exercises and training them to solve mathematical problems as fast and as accurately as possible. Not a minute could be wasted in the classroom. Despite all the criticism of this didactic method, lecturing from the text was still seen as the most efficient way to convey maximum information within the limited time period.

Besides lectures, giving students drills was the predominant and acceptable form of pedagogy within the Chinese schools. During my four visits to China in the early 1980s, I visited numerous classes and sat through demonstrations when teachers almost invariably applied these techniques. Multiplication was learned through memorizing the multiplication table, repeating "one times one equals one," etc. The mastery of the abacus was acquired in the same manner. Students repeated, "Five down one equals four," and so on, with each dictum accompanied by the appropriate movement of the fingers on the sliding balls of the abacus until these concepts were internalized and the movement almost automatic. Mental calculation was learned through repetitions with the teacher reading off the numbers and the students giving the answer in unison or individually, and they seemed to do it willingly and enthusiastically.

Lectures, drills, and memorizing were not the teachers' inventions. These practices were very much part of the Chinese academic tradition. The present formal educational system was a Western import introduced only in the nineteenth century. Traditionally, education was largely a prerogative of the rich who could afford private tutors, and the civil service examination, the national examination that evaluated Chinese intellectuals and from which government officials were selected, measured to a large extent the persons' ability to memorize and regurgitate the classics. The civil service examination was abolished in 1905, but one could not have expected the practices and values endorsed by this system that had been operating for centuries to be completely eradicated in a short time.[31] Drills and memorization continued to be popular among the intelligentsia, and therefore encouraged in the schools. Besides, intellectuals had always been respected in Chinese society, and even though the communist leaders distrusted them, they were still looked up to by the people. This was another reason for the perpetuation of the lecture system in the classrooms. Lecturing as a social arrangement rested on an unequal relationship between the instructor and the audience, and its continuance rested on the former commanding high status and respect. The superior status of the intellectuals at the elementary school level was embodied in the teachers and assured by the expertise they offered the students.

Governments could legislate formal changes but found it hard to execute them because their implementation depended upon the commitment and preparedness at the grassroots level. It would be even more difficult to enforce changes in the informal structure. In curriculum changes, the government could introduce new textbooks (formal and static aspects of the curriculum) but could not be sure if the teachers would welcome them, nor could they legislate how these were to be taught (dynamic aspect). Mao might advocate a more open and democratic classroom climate, but even he could only encourage and not legislate it. Teachers schooled in a particular pedagogical tradition would be reluctant and, even if they were willing, would find it difficult to adapt to a new one. They would do things as they used to. Despite the official endorsement of a more flexible teaching style, many teachers conducted classes in the old way. Even the authors of the textbooks in the late sixties did not completely escape the grip of tradition. The exercises in these books still recommended drills and rote learning. As a result, in spite of the dramatic contrasts between the covert curricula in the two periods, continuity characterized the interaction pattern between the teachers and the students in the classrooms, and indeed since the establishment of the People's Republic.

Such traditional pedagogical methods might be consistent with the curriculum of the latter period when mathematics was seen as skills to be acquired and demonstrated at examinations with great accuracy and speed. But these teaching techniques conflicted with the educational philosophy of the earlier period, which as more akin to the Freirian pedagogy of what Young would call curriculum as praxis whereby the learner is an active participant in the discovery and application or knowledge.[32] Lectures and drills required a hierarchical, if not an authoritarian, relationship between the students and the teachers for these techniques to function smoothly in the classroom. Such a hierarchical relationship contrasted sharply with the messages in the texts that encouraged students to be critical of, among other things, the authorities. The pedagogical techniques used turned students into passive recipients of knowledge and mitigated their chances of becoming active participants. The lectures and drills converted the curriculum as praxis into curriculum as facts whereby learning became the mastery of pieces of information to be memorized, thus defeating what the educational philosophy of the late sixties and early seventies hoped to accomplish. Furthermore, as mentioned before, some teachers educated in the pre-liberation period were against the values emphasized in the late sixties and early seventies textbooks. Even if they did not openly articulate their objections, their reticience concerning these positions could not have completely escaped the students. These conflicting messages and the incompatibility between curriculum content on the one hand, and the teachers' attitudes and teaching methods on the other, no doubt contributed to the failure of the educational system in the early seventies to meet the targeted goals of the ruling group. Its failure to fully implement the curriculum as praxis, however, did not mean that it succeeded in transmitting the curriculum as facts. The materials in the textbooks were not arranged or edited for the latter purpose. Supportive structures designed to encourage students to achieve academically, such as the emphasis on examinations, were absent. As a result, students did not get good solid training in basic subjects, like mathematics, and its failure to do so was a major criticism of the educational system of that period.

Supportive Structures Outside the Classroom

The government in the late sixties and early seventies, realizing that its educational philosophy ran counter to academic traditions and would not be acceptable to the majority of teachers, took remedial measures. It put pressure on the teachers to conform to the new educational norms by using rules and regulations within the jurisdiction of the school administration to create a favorable environment for the implementation of the new policies, and organized activities to reinforce the messages to be conveyed to the students. To discourage excessive preoccupation with academic pursuits, the schools honored students who did not do well in examinations because of their commitment to production. The glorification of Zhang Tiehsheng in 1971 was an example. Campaigns were launched to criticize capitalist education with its emphasis on achievement, and teachers who encouraged academic performance were branded as bourgeois. To eliminate students' anxiety in examination, its importance was downplayed and promotion to the next higher level was made automatic. To develop their political consciousness and involvement, the government organized political movements in the schools. The late sixties and early seventies witnessed a series of such campaigns, from the Cultural Revolution, to a Criticize Lin Biao-Confucius Campaign, a Criticism of Teachers' Authority Campaign, a Criticize Water Margin (a novel) Campaign, and others. To encourage children to appreciate manual labor and the working class, workers and peasants were brought in to lecture on production skills and to talk about their 'bitter past' (their suffering prior to the communist takeover) to bring out the accomplishments of the communist government. Arrangements were made for the young to work in the factories and farms for about two to three months each academic year and those who excelled in such activities were rewarded. All these mandated activities, independent from and outside the teachers jurisdiction, were designed to create a social climate consistent with the messages carried in the textbooks--a love of labor and communism, and probably also to forestall and counteract any conflicting messages teachers might pass on to their students.

Such activities encouraged in the early seventies were deemed extra-curricular, unnecessary, or harmful diversions in the second period, which devoted exclusive attention to academic training. School administrators impressed on the students the need to do well in their examinations. The young were discouraged from taking part in activities other than academic ones. A predominant amount of extra-curricular activities consisted of taking part in interschool competition in mathematics and other academic subjects and extra-curricular activities offered in the youth palaces were in the arts, giving students who demonstrated their talent training in calligraphy, painting, music, dancing, and sometimes even in academic subjects. These measures to impress on the students the importance of academic achievement were perhaps unnecessary. This academic emphasis in the curriculum was in tune with most teachers' outlooks. Instructors of the graduating class, and sometimes even in the lower grades, gave students extra lessons after class and on weekends to bettger prepare them for the public examination, and attendance was made compulsory. Here the overt and covert curricula embodied in the textbooks and the activities organized by the teachers in the classroom were congruent, and students got the message loud and clear--doing well in school was most important.

Conclusion

The analysis of the mathematics textbooks between 1968 and 1985 shows that the curriculum is meant to be a stabilizing element in society, a form of social control transmitting certain messages, prescribing and proscribing allowable behavior for the young, meting out punishment to the deviants and rewards to the conformers. The organization of the curriculum in China, as elsewhere, was not left to chance; perhaps much more so than in capitalist countries, the ruling group closely dictated and shaped its contents. Even mathematics was not immune from such manipulation. With each change of political leadership, the overt content of the curriculum was modified and the covert messages embedded in the problems were changed.

Furthermore, the analysis points to a way whereby the curriculum can defeat its own purposes, not achieving the ends it is supposed to accomplish. In general, mathematics teachers abdicated their responsibilities in socializing the young into accepting the dominant ideology. They focussed instead on teaching mathematics. In the late sixties and early seventies, teachers disagreed with the curriculum's pragmatic orientation and cultural messages. Despite the government's attempts to intervene, and even though teachers did not speak out openly against the values condoned in the curriculum, they subverted (more likely subconsciously and unconsciously) the messages and rendered ineffective the transmission process through their pedagogical style, making the teaching of the overt and perhaps even the covert curriculum ineffective. In the late seventies and early eighties when the teachers endorsed the philosophy and applied the appropriate teaching style, the tension and contradictions in the curriculum-in-action were reduced and academic quality improved as planned. The teachers' potential to successfully implement or subvert the curriculum is indeed great, and points to the importance of examining this crucial but often overlooked dynamic aspect of the curriculum--how the messages are transmitted by the teachers.

*I am grateful to Professor K. Osborne and the two editors for their comments on an earlier draft.

Notes

1. Paul Willis, Learning to Labor (Westmead: Saxon House, 1977); Henry A. Giroux, Theory and Resistance in Education: A Pedagogy for the Opposition (South Hadley: Bergin and Garvey, 1983); Peter McLaren, Schooling as a Ritual Performance (London: Routledge and Kegan Paul, 1986).

2. Mathematics (Inner Mongolia: Mongolia Education Committee of the Revolutionary Committee of Inner Mongolia, 1969), Volume 3, 4; Mathematics (Inner Mongolia: Mongolia Education Committee of the

Revolutionary Committee of Inner Mongolia, 1970), Volume 5; Mathematics (Mongolia: Mongolia Publishing Company, 1975), Volume 5; Mathematics (Beijing: People's Publishing Company, 1975), Volume 7; Mathematics (Tienjin: People's Publishing Company, 1983), Volume 2; Mathematics (Beijing, Tsinghua Publishing Company, 1983), Volume 4, 6, 8, 10, 12.

3. Samuel Bowles and Herbert Gintis, Schooling in Capitalist Society (New York, Basic Books, 1976); "Capitalist and Education in the United States," in Michael Young and Geoff Whitty, Society, State and Schooling (Brighton, Sussex: Falmer Press, 1977).

4. Francis Fitzgerald, "Onward and Upward with the Arts: Rewriting American History," The New Yorker, (1979), February: 47-77; March: 41-91; April: 48-106.

5. Pierre Bourdieu and Jean Claude Passeron, Reproduction in Education, Society and Culture (Beverly Hills: Sage, 1977).

6. Mathematics, (1975), Vol. 7, p. 108.

7. Mathematics, (1983), Vol. 4, p. 63.

8. Mathematics, (1969), Vol. 4, p. 5.

9. Mathematics, (1983), Vol. 6, p. 86.

10. Mathematics, (1983), Vol. 2, p. 42.

11. Mathematics, (1969), Vol. 4, p. 34; Mathematics, (1970), Vol. 5, p. 20.

12. Mathematics, (1983), Vol. 4, p. 98.

13. Mathematics, (1976), Vol. 5, p. 30.

14. Mathematics, (1983), Vol. 6, p. 70.

15. Marshall McLuhan, Kathryn Hutchon, Eric McLuhan, Media, Messages and Language: The World As Your Classroom (Skokie, Illinois: National Textbook Co. 1980).

16. Mathematics, (1969), Vol. 4, p. 4.

17. Ibid., p. 7.

18. Mathematics, (1970), Vol. 5, p. 16, 48.

19. Ibid., p. 24; Mathematics, (1969), Vol. 2, p. 34.

20. Jean Anyon, "Ideology and United States History Textbooks," Harvard Education Review, 49 (1979): 361-386.

21. Mathematics, (1983), Vol. 2, pp. 17-18.

22. Mathematics, (1983), Vol. 4, p. 33.

23. Mathematics, (1970), Vol. 5, p. 20.

24. Mathematics, (1970), Vol. 5, p. 44.

25. Mathematics, (1975), Vol. 7, p. 104.

26. Mathematics, (1969), Vol. 4, p. 34; Mathematics, (1970), Vol. 5, p. 20.

27. Mathematics, (1983), Vol. 6, p. 35, 51, 60.

28. Henry A. Giroux, op. cit.; Peter McLaren, op. cit.

29. Linda M. McNeil, "Defensive Teaching and Classroom Control" in Michael W. Apple and Lois Weis, Ideology and Practice in Schooling (Philadelphia: Temple University Press, 1983); pp. 114-142.

30. William Kessen, Childhood in China (New Haven: Yale University Press, 1976).

31. Ping-ti Ho, The Ladder of Success in Imperial China (New York: Columbia University Press, 1962).

32. Paulo Freire, Pedagogy of the Oppressed (New York: Continuum Books, 1983); Michael Young and Geoff Whitty, op. cit.

CHAPTER 11

TEXTBOOKS IN REVOLUTIONARY IRAN

M. Mobin Shorish

Iran is a multiethnic society differentiated by language, religion, and other factors that distinguish its ethnic boundaries. The majority of Iranians belong to the *12 Imami Shi'i* school of thought in Islam. Shi'ism as a school of thought has been around since early Islam. But it was only at the beginning of the sixteenth century that it became the state religion in Iran. However, Islam as a general system was never implemented in the country.

This chapter is about the effect of the 1979 Islamic Revolution on Iran's educational system. The revolutionaries in Iran are rearranging many of that country's institutions, including the contents of the curricula, in order to implement the Islamic ideals and values that were articulated at the dawn of Islam 15 centuries ago.

The chapter has two aims: [1] to profile the ideal Islamic person in the context of the aspirations of the Iranian revolutionaries as expressed in the pages of the school textbooks and [2] to speculate on the degree of congruity between values taught in the schools and other government sponsored media and those disseminated through other socializing agencies of Iran not controlled by the government. It is assumed that the existence of congruities [or incongruities] between the socializing agencies of a society has a great deal to do with the effectiveness of the socialization processes in the development of its citizenry.

This chapter also appears in the Comparative Education Review, 32 (February, 1988], pp. 58-75. Reprinted with the permission of the Review.

Method

The research is based on the analysis of significant themes in a sample of the textbooks published in the Islamic Republic of Iran [IRI] during the 1984 and 1985 academic years. The textbooks used for this purpose were Farsi language texts for grades 1-5 of *Dabistan* [primary cycle]: Islamic culture and religious education texts for grades 2-5, teachings of the sacred religions and ethics for the religious minorities in texts for grades 2-5, texts for the second year of the guidance cycle. and, finally. Islamic perception texts for *Dabiristan* [years 1-3 of the senior high school].[1]

These four categories of texts on the Farsi language, on Islamic culture and theology, on theology [for the children of national minorities], and on the Islamic worldview are very much interrelated and have common themes outlining the ideal citizen that the IRI wants to develop. They have one single focus: the developnment of a thoroughly committed individual to one God. These texts are persistent in this aim and are also consistent pedagogically, starting with themes that are concrete and simple in the first or second grade, expanding on these themes as the child grows older, and, finally, ending them at more complex and abstract levels in one of the Islamic perception series (*Binish Islami*] in high school. Themes are repeated partially in each grade and text and overlap each other continuously from one category to another and from text to text.

The inculcation of the themes continues in the texts in a more formal and specific manner, to reinforce what has already been suggested in more general terms informally in the family and in the mosque and in other places of socialization not controlled by the government. This process, it is hoped by the leadership of Iran, will create a program for the Islamization of the Iranian people. The texts selected are written to reflect the views of the revolutionaries on the development of the "Islamic Person" (see below). They are filled with the political symbols and great personalities of Islam and the present Iranian leadership, in contrast to the secularism and nationalism whose political symbols inundated textbooks under the late shah.

Because of the newness of their contents in the context of the Iranian education, these texts have a uniqueness not present in other Iranian textbooks. For example, the textbooks dealing with the sciences have remained almost unchanged since before the revolution. The history textbooks have all been purged of the materials dealing with former regimes, replacing those with materials dealing with Islam and the lslamic Revolution in Iran. There is nothing new in this technique. It has been used in all of the previous revolutions. It is a simple method of substituting various former political symbols with new ones reflecting the new order in the country. Other texts such as the series on social sciences *[Ta'Limat Ijtima'i]* are essentially social studies texts describing the structure and the functions of various governmental agencies and organizations. Therefore, the rest of this article is devoted to an analysis of some of the major themes running through these 16 textooks.

As in most societies, the textbooks in the Iranian schools are looked upon by this regime as a major means of introducing the ideals of the revolution to the Iranian children. These texts echo the authorities' belief that Islam is the answer to the unbridled secularism, corruption, and oppression that troubled Iranian society for centuries prior to the revolution. The revolution is the process of resocializing the Iranians to Islamic ideals, establishing, according to the present regime, a far better alternative not only to Iran's immediate past but also to capitalism and socialism as general social systems. Through the texts [and other media at the disposal of the government], the values desired by the revolutionaries are inculcated into the schools. These same values are reinforced by other socializing agencies of the country. In other words, since Islam is the religion of most Iranians as well as *the* revolutionary program of the government, one seldom finds inconsistencies between the official revolutionary values of the government [values the texts and other media are asked to communicate] and values taught by other agencies, such as the home and places of worship and work.

The revolution in Iran, as will be seen, is very different in many respects from other revolutions. There are also many factors that differentiate the IRI from, the rest of the so-called Muslim world. But the IRI shares with most of that world the sense of importance that the Iranian revolutionaries attach to textbooks and to other aspects of the curricula.

Analysis

The Iranians are very clear about the aims of education, and their expectations are very high that books, such as those discussed here [along with other supports that IRI is building], will eventually lead to the creation of the Islamic person. This person is variously defined by scholars but is the following: God-fearing [*muttaqi*], learned ['*alim*], and brave *[Shuja']*. [These, incidentally, are also the criteria for election of a person to the leadership of the Muslim community, the *Ummah*.] What follows are parts of prefaces to the second and third years of primary school textbooks called *Farhang Islami wa Ta'Limat Dini* [Islamic culture and religious education], which clearly describe the aims of education in the IRI:

> The purpose of this book and teaching is not to memorize and answer things correctly. The essential aims are to develop the spirit and life and to complete the lives of children... The aim is the internalization of correct religious beliefs.. The aim is to develop from the children of today men and women who are worthy [*sha'istah*], committed [*muta'ahid*], constructive [*durustkar*], goodwilled [*khayrkhah*], kind [*mihraban*], highly chivalrous [*balandhimmat*], and God-loving [khudadust]. [With these qualities] and with a heart of faith [*iman*] they will stand up to spread the life giving ideology [*a'in hayatbakhsh*] of Islam and the Islamic Revolution, help to prosper the great Islamic country, rush to help the oppressed and struggle against the arrrogant [*mustakbirin*], and help to move the helpless and the weak of the world.[2]

In the preface to the text for the third grade, a very important sentence is added. It reads, "Thanks to Allah that with the help, kindness, and great leadership of *Imam* Khomeini and the efforts of the Muslim *Ummah*, the Islamic Revolution was successful, the Cultural Revolution started, and *Imam's* message was received that *training and purification is prior to education [tarbiyyat wa tazkiyyah muqaddam bar ta'Lilm ast]*" [emphasis added]. This is a very important statement that constitutes a major theme in the Islamic pedagogy. In Islam, training and commitment have always come before everything else that a person does, regardless of the stage of economic development of the society. *Tarbiyyat* is more than training. It is the acquisition of desirable attitudes and characteristics in addition to what is understood in the Western pedagogy by the word "training." A similar concept to that of *tazkiyyah* is the concept of *adab*, the process by which one frees oneself from wrong and evil thoughts and actions through orderliness and discipline. *Ta'lim* is the process by which one gets knowledge [*'ilm*] and information [*ma'lumat*] through such media as books and teachers.

All four, *adab* [*tazkiyyah*--purification, discipline] *tarbiyyah* [training, fostering, nourishing], *ta'lim* [indirect learning through teaching, studying, and exposure to mass media], and *ma'rafah* [gnostic learning,direct learning through communication with God, who is the source of all knowledge, according to the Islamic teachings] together constitute Islamic education. In this process of education the role of the textbook and the teacher is crucial. None of the four processes can take place without the guidance from members of the family, community, and the *teacher*, in its broadest sense including those in the position of leading, such as *Imam* Khomeini or a *Murshid*, as in the *sufi turuq*, the mystical orders in Islam.

The Farsi text for the first year of primary school starts with the teaching of writing and reading of the alphabet and introduces various phonemes, the vowels, and the vowel points. Still using some of the more important vowel points to assist in the correct reading of the text, children are introduced to the concept of God through very simple sentences such as the following: "God has created the Sun and the Earth. God has created the Moon and the stars. God has created plants and the animals. God has created us... O, Compassionate God that created everything, we will always worship you."[3]

The next topic introduced is the concept of prophethood and Muhammed the messenger of God and teacher to mankind. This is followed by the concept of the Qur'an as the word of God and the Holy Book of the Muslims, followed by some words of 'Ali, the son-in-law of the Prophet and the most important person after Muhammed in the Shi'i [the school of thought followed by the majority of Iranians] Islamic hierarchy. Then there is a rather long discussion on the importance and the place of the teacher in Iranian society. The following is a sample:

> The day when we came to school for the first time we did not know how to read or write. From the first day our very kind teacher guided us. Teacher taught us to read and write. Teacher taught us to keep our paper and books clean. Teacher taught us to be kind to our friends. Teacher taught us to keep ourselves always clean so that we do not get ill. Teacher taught us to be respectful to our parents. Teacher taught us to be kind to our brothers and sisters. Teacher taught us to be friendly with others and try to help them. We are grateful to our teacher who taught us reading and writing. We are grateful to our teacher who, like a kind father or mother, taught us to do good things.[4]

As can be expected, the two major themes of all Iranian texts are religion and patriotism.[5] But religion and patriotism cannot be separated from each other. In all of the IRI textbooks under study,the unity [*wahdat*] of citizenship [*millat*], homeland [*watan*], religion [*din*], and government [*dawlat*] in Islam is emphasized through anecdotes, poetry, and Islamic events and notables.[6] The unity of these four concepts is fundamental to the understanding of the Islamic perception of the world. Positive activities on behalf of each and all are acts of worship of one God who is the source of all knowledge and the creator of all beings. "Love of one's homeland is an act of faith" is a Muslim saying. One's homeland is analogous to a bowl that contains citizenship, religion, and the government. Hence, the inseparability of the religion and the government--of the church and state in Islam. This complex theme of unity [*wahdat*] is taken up again and again in the texts. It is a theme that not only runs through these texts but also constitutes the most important theme in Islamic epistemologies of the sciences, the arts, and architecture. This theme is explained in the following, "Iran: My Homeland," for third graders:

> O, Iran, O beautiful home, I love you. I love the laughter of your children, the voices of your youth, and the battle cries of your men. O, my beautiful home. Your clean earth which is red with the blood of the martyrs is sacred to me. I kiss the red tulips which have grown from the graves of the martyrs. O, Iran, my beautiful land. I look at your mountains to remind myself of the courage and honor of your children. Your wide meadows and broad valleys are manifestations to me of your independence and freedom. The sounds of your restless rivers for me are a reminder of the cry in unison of *Allahu Akbar* [God is great] by those who are free. O, Iran, my lovely home. O, Land of purity and bravery. O, Land of the people who love Liberty. O, Country of Islam and Faith! I respect you. I will strive for your development. With great and unblemished faith I love your people. I will hasten to help them, and with anger and hate I will destroy your enemies.[7]

The concept of unity is also used to teach the unity of mankind and the unity of the Islamic *Ummah* [the Islamic Community]. Through this concept others, such as sympathy, empathy, compassion, and solidarity with the oppressed, are taught to the Iranian children, using these textbooks. One example of this is cited here in a story whose themes of solidarity and compassion are repeated [in most texts either directly or by implication] with numerous variations:

A Teenager from Palestine

When I saw him he was alone, leaning against the tent stick. He was a teenager from the Palestinian people in diaspora. He had a sad face and, with eyes full of anger, was looking at the ground. I moved forward and sat next to him. He did not notice my getting closer, as if his heart was elsewhere. I made *salam* [greetings] to him. He became aware of me and answered softly and returned to his deep thoughts. A long silence followed. Finally I had to break the silence and said, "Brother I see that you are sad and uncomfortable. Your discomfort has made me uncomfortable also. Tell me your secret. Maybe I could reduce the heavy burden of sadness that you are carrying." He turned his face toward me and said,"Have you ever heard of such a thing, where a person is driven away from his home and others come and occupy his house, and if the owner opens his mouth in protest the occupiers reply to him with bullets? Have you ever heard that refugees living in their desert tents are being massacred by machine guns? Has it ever happened to you that with roar of the bombers the classroom fell on your head? Have you ever heard that they have flattened hospitals with defenseless wounded inside them? Have you ever heard of a doll becoming the cause of death of a child? On our heads all kinds of bombs rain every day. There are even bombs that look like dolls. If a child picks up one of these it explodes in his hands and kills him. My brother, if you have not heard of these or have not seen them, I have seen and heard them. They have driven us Palestinians from our homes and houses and they have taken over our homes in a cowardly manner. The Israeli butchers have burned even our refugee tents. They have flattened classrooms on the heads of our children and teenagers. With their savage attacks they have destroyed the hospitals. They have burned the babies with their butterfly bombs. My brother, these are the sufferings which have pressed my heart, and melt the heart of any human being who loves liberty. I want someone to fight beside me for the salvation of my homeland and the liberation of brave Muslim people. You, O my brother, how can you help me in my efforts?"[8]

Similarly, children are asked in these textbooks to model themselves after the Prophet and his children and descendants and other Muslim and non-Muslim notables at all times. Children are also asked to emulate scholars like Ibn Sina [Avicenna, A. H. 370-428/A.D. 980-1037] the American inventors Wilbur and Orville Wright, and, of course, their parents and teachers.[9]

The concept of Iran as a nation comes next. It is described as a multinational country with a great many beautiful places. This is followed by a poem glorifying Islam and those who died for it in Iran during the Islamic Revolution and the expulsion of the shah.[10]

The Farsi language texts for the other years are similar except that concepts become more complicated as the child grows older. The texts for later years discuss the world of work and the world around the children and emphasize the importance of many days associated with peoples' uprisings against the shah and the victory of the Islamic Revolution.

The two books of *Farhangi Islami wa Ta'Limat Dini* [Islamic culture and religious teaching] for the second and third year of *Dabistan* [primary school] are similar in content except that the teaching of the Qur'an [in Arabic] starts in the second part of the third-year book. These textbooks, as the title implies, emphasize the ethical and the religious aspects more than do the Farsi language books discussed above. By means of stories and historical events and persons, the texts make points about generosity, faithfulness, self-sacrifice, and sharing, in addition to the topics in the Farsi language texts mentioned above. Most of the contents of the *Farhangi Islami wa Ta'Limat Dini* textbooks for the Muslim children of Iran are similar to those for the children of the non-Muslim religious minorities: the Jews, the Christians, and the Zoroastrians.

It is not clear how many countries have sponsored textbooks for religious minorities. Iran has created, over the past few years, a series of texts for Jews, Christians, and people following the Zoroastrian faith. These books, which are titled *Ta'limat Adyan Ilahi wa Akhlaq Wizha'i Aggaliyyatha'i Mazhabi* henceforth, TAIAWAM [Teaching of the sacred religions and ethics for the religious minorities], are produced by the Ministry of Education after consultations, meetings, and workshops with the teachers and religious leaders of each faith. The rationale for the production of religious texts for minorities was stated as follows by a high official of the Ministry of Education: "The major problem which this country has had, has been with those people who do not believe in anything. This has been a problem with many of the so-called Muslims as well as many among this country's religious minorities. A system of beliefs such as those held by the Christians, the Jews, the Muslims, and the Zoroastrians gives all of us a sense of purpose and the sharing of some convictions. It is much harder for us to get along with someone who is nothing. The most important aim of these books is the creation in children of a system of beliefs based on the existence of a supreme Creator, God."[11] The following are some of thc topics discussed in these textbooks: In the praise of God; how to know God through His creations, including the children themselves, animals, and plants; God loves those who do good works and frowns upon those who do evil; who is a religious person, God's prophets, and the good God.[12]

The TAIAWAM text for the third year of primary school starts with the usual praise of God and explains that no work will be without any result. The text illustrates this by using the concept of echo. The children are told that they will see the "echo" or the result of their work in the next world. Other topics covered are the reality of the Day of Judgment through a dialogue between a child and his mother, the concept of prophethood, and the prophets as teachers of humanity. The text praises the prophets of God mentioned in the Qur'an such as Jesus, as well as some of those mentioned in the Old Testament.[13] The texts in these and other passages try to teach children the commonalities which exist between these faiths and Islam. For example, the text for the fourth year of Primary school starts with praise of God and a discussion that He is the source of all the creation. By using the senses and motor functions of the body, it teaches biology as well as the existence of God. By means of several other examples, the book attempts to teach the child conservation, describing the evils of excessive exploitation of nature and the destruction of the environment. The only way to remain free is to fear only God and to have confidence in yourselves, the text tells the children. One way to be free and to have confidence is to follow the examples of the prophets.[14] Through all of the IRI textbooks, including the TAIAWAM texts under study here, the idea of the unity of God and the concept of prophethood is emphasized. The teaching of these two concepts finds reinforcement in other socializing agencies of the country. For the Muslim children of Iran, these concepts instill the unity of all Muslims and, by extension, of all peoples of the earth. It affirms the IRI's government as the vicegerent of God on earth just as the Prophets were Allah's representatives.

The TAIAWAM textbook for the fifth year of the primary school discusses the sciences [*'ulum*] through which God can be known. It starts with the working of the human body; the greenness in the leaves and the grass; digestive, circulatory, and respiratory systems; the usefulness of work; the usefulness of life; the cells, arteries, and veins--

all these prove the existence of God, according to this text. They are all signs of God. We know the existence of God through His signs in the same manner that we know of the existence of intellect and mind through such signs as writing, drawing, and calculating. God is not matter; God is like mind and intellect.[15]

The final text to be analyzed is one used for the religious minorities of Iran in the second year of the middle school, or the second year of what is called in Iran the guidance cycle [*Dawrah'i Rahnama'ii Tahsili*], ordinarily for children who are 12 years old. This book begins with a discussion of how further to know God the Creator. After the usual Praise of God in very beautiful poetry, it asks the students to look at the orderly nature of things around them and then asks them to look within themselves. The text explains the concept of theology as a viable form of discourse and discusses how to find the right path to God. The text then goes into several discussions about the justice of God. The second part deals with the Day of Judgment, eternal life, the resurrection, and the assessment of one's deeds in front of God. The third part discusses the prophets, their characterisics, and the criteria of prophethood, the need of humanity for prophets and the importance of God's unity [*Wahdat]*, and the agenda of the prophets.[16]

It is very interesting to note that all three religious minorities [the Jews, the Christians, and the Zoroastrians] use the same texts for their religious education in the IRI schools. Apparently the topics chosen for inclusion in these books are not those on which there is disagreement among these religions. The texts for the religious education of the minorities are, in general, very similar to those used for the same purpose by the Muslim students in Iran. To be sure, there are some very important differences. For example, Islam differs fundamentally from each of the above-mentioned religions with respect to the general purpose of the Muslims' life and their mission. But all four religions share values that are so general as to constitute a common denominator for all in the minds of the children. The purpose is not to solicit conversion from one religion to another. Rather, it is concern with irreligiousness [which to the IRI authorities is a synonym for irresponsibility] that has been a major factor in the production of texts for religious minorities and has promoted extensive coverage of religious themes in all of the IRI textbooks, especially those texts under study here.[17]

Following is the gist of the materials from the textbook *Binish Islami: Nabuwwat, wa Qur'an wa Mi'ad* [Islamic perception: prophethood, the Qur'an, and the Resurrection][18] for the second year of general secondary school.

It is sometines difficult for some Muslims and non-Muslims to believe that there is very little in a good Muslim's everyday behavior that is not potentially political. The Iranian Muslims believe that once an individual has realized the existence of Allah he can be nothing else but political. Muslims are political men and women as long as there remains a single oppressed person on the face of the earth. There are a great many statements in the Qur'an and the *Ahadith* [singular: *hadith*, Muhammed's sayings and tradition] on this particular topic. All one has to do is to read the Qur'an, these textbooks say, and also to listen carefully to one's own daily prayers, as in the case of "A Letter from Father."[19]

There are many parts of the Qur'an that declare Allah's isolation from oppression, *Ummah's* obligation both to help the poor and the dispossessed and to isolate itself from the *mustakbirin* [the arrogant] and from the *dhalimin* [the oppressors]. All a Muslim's activities in this area are looked on as his or her duty. These activities are forms of struggle [*jihad*] against evil.

However, this textbook declares that the best examples of the *jihad* [struggle] of the Muslims for the just distribution of power and wealth have been given throughout human history by the prophets of Allah. The messages of the prophets on this and on other topics are universal, it says. They are not limited to a specific group. When Allah commanded Musa [Moses] to go to the *Fir'aun* [Pharoah], this showed the world that the duty of the Muslim is to try to correct evil regardless of the material and power position of the wrongdoer. The textbook quotes the following from the Qur'an:" [O, Musa] go to the *Fir'aun* [Pharoah] who has rebelled. Then tell [him] do you want to be cleansed of your defects and I guide you to your Lord so you can become humbled in front of His greatness."[20]

This is a universal message not confined to one ruler but common to all rulers who do not deviate from Allah's commandments. It would also be non-Islamic if the prophets were worried only about one group. The message of the Qur'an is clear in its emphasis on people regardless of ethnicity and even of religion. The textbook brings in other *ayat* [singular: *ayah* ; plural: *ayat* ; verses from the Qur'an] to document the above point. Here the operating word is *annas*, the people.

All these *ayat* are concerned with all human beings and declare to all the good tidings of the Allah's *rahmah* [mercy] in the person of His messenger, the *rasul* and also an invitation to the *annas*, the people, to the *wahdat* [unity] of their creator and the fact that they have all been created from one person [*Bani Adam*--Adam's children]. In the school of prophethood, according to this high school text, there is only one way to fight against *shirk* [giving Allah a partner], *kufr* [hiding the truth],and oppression. That is for all to find out how to satisfy Allah and how to be on the side of Allah. Muslims and non-Muslims suffer, according to this text, whenever oppression and arrogance increase in the world.[21]

The prophets were consistent [according to the series of texts titled *Binish Islami* for the high school students of Iran] in their *jihad* [struggle] against oppression and arrogance. Their consistency and perseverance has often brought them allies from the very quarters against which the prophets were making *jihad*. There are many examples of these occurrences in the Qur'an: the story of Mu'min al-Fir'aun; the story of Asiyah, Fir'aun's wife; the story of *suhara* [the magicians] of Fir'aun.[22] These stories and a great many statements in the Qur'an testify to the feasibility of creating a revolt among the oppressors' own group to fight against them and in support of justice. It is very difficult to find any statement in the Iranian textbooks that is not anchored in the Qur'an, *Ahadith*, other prophets' traditions and the traditions and the behaviors of the *imams*. These three, the Qur'an, the tradition of the prophets [including Muhammed's], and the *imams*, constitute the sources of authority [that flows from Allah only] in the Iranian Shi'i Islamic theology. Hence, the importance of *Imam* Khomeini [and others in the religious leadership of Iran], as religious and political leaders of the Iranians, cannot be overestimated.

Allah's school for prophets is a far more powerful university than any that can be imagined, according to these Iranian texts discussed above. This revolution is called *tawbeh*, or repentance. This is one of the many unique features of the school of the prophets. Neither capitalism, which preaches to man that he is of the first and foremost importance, nor the school that advocates class struggle and violence of one group against the other has ever been able to create a revolution in men and women against themselves. Similarly, capitalism and socialism, are unable to provide the mechanism through which man is able to control himself from within. To control oneself is the training [*tarbiyyah, adab, tazkiyyah*] that one gets in the school of the prophets. To fight against *dhulm* [oppression] and to seek justice are two of the many aims of the school of the prophets. To protect the rights of the oppressed is in its curriculum. It should be pointed out that not all Muslims are oppressed, nor are all non-Muslims oppressors. But in general throughout history, the majority of those who have followed the prophets have been the oppressed, *mustadh'afin*, and those who have fought against the prophets have belonged to the group of the *mustakbirin*, the arrogant.

Now we know that one of the aims of the school of the prophets was to instill justice and to invite all of humanity to join this struggle for Allah's way. But does this mean that the school advocates détente between *dhulm* [oppression] and freedom, between ignorance and knowledge, between *shirk* [giving God partners] and *whadat* [unity of God]? Not so. This Islamic school [Muslims believe that all the prophets, some of whom are mentioned in the Old Testament, and Jesus, were in this school] strives for the creation of a just society conposed of men and women who are veterans of revolutions against the oppressors and *mustakbirin* [the arrogant] and who are also veterans of revolution within themselves--the *tawbeh* [the repentance].

So it is a revolution for social justice and against oppression, discrimination, racism, colonialism, and imperialism, on the one hand, and a revolution against self-ignorance and *waswas* [mischief] that reside within individuals, on the other. The school is as much for intellectual freedom as it is for social justice. One without the other cannot really be achieved in a manner that satisfies the stated goals of the school of the prophets. This school is Islam that, at the time that it declared the intellectual and psychological commitment of the individual [*iman*] to Allah, also declared *jihad* [struggle] against the social injustices of the larger human community.

When the prophet of Islam sent messages to his contemporary rulers announcing his *risalat* [prophethood],he was pointing to the following: "O, People of the book come toward one word and one truth which is the same for all of us [with this there is no particular favor toward us nor toward you] and that is to worship the singular Allah and making nothing His partner." This *ayah* then moves from the level of the individual's invitation to *tawhid* [unity of God] to the level of the problem of the social *tawhid* when it continues: "That we erect not from among ourselves, lords and patrons other than God."[23] Only Allah is our *rabb* [the Lord]. We should not become separated from the *wahdat* [unity] of Allah as the Lord, to participate in social relationships where some people act like gods [*arbab*] and others like slaves. Let us reject all those social relationships, this textbook urges the children, that result in creating persons competing with God, and organizations that rival His relationship with the people. These are revolutionary statements that this textbook and others make to the Iranian children.

The message continues when the text again quotes from the Qur'an: "What is the matter with you? Why are you not fighting for Allah's sake and for the sake of the oppressed and for the men and women and children who say, 'O, Allah, take us out of the city of the oppressors and grant us with your mercy and kindness someone to be a leader and a helper to us.'"[24] Again, in this *ayah* there is a clear *tahrik* [incitement] to *jihad* [struggle] for Allah's sake and for the amelioration of the lot of the oppressed.

Comments and Conclusions

As the above discussion of a sample of the Iranian textbooks shows, there is great emphasis put on the concepts of prophethood, teaching, *walayat* [governance], *imamat* [leadership], God's vicegerency, the Prophet's family, and the *imams* [the 12 rightful heirs to Prophet Muhammed, according to the Shi'i Muslims who constitute the majority of the population of the IRI]. These concepts are very much related to each other, and, as presented in the textbooks, there is continuity and legitimization from Allah to His representatives on earth in the persons of the prophets and the *imams,* including those in the political/religious leadership of Iran. The emphasis on these concepts is essential to an understanding of the Shi'i Muslims' worldview. The emphasis on these concepts in all the socializing agencies controlled by the governnent is, in part, because

> in the religious vocabulary of traditional Islam what men lack and most desperately need is guidance--not salvation or redemption--but guidance. There is no more basic concept in the Islamic order of things than the notion of guidance, for it is this which can supply the need that poses the fundamental dilemma. Men require to be told how to live, to be given directions about what is right and proper and what is wrong and detestable. If this information is supplied in a form that makes it accessible and so that men can understand it, then Muslims have every confidence in their ability to do what is asked.[25]

The idea of continuity and indispensability of leadership by teachers and of texbooks as guides for the realization of the new Islamic society then becomes clear. Investment in the production of books and the training of teachers [which include the IRI leadership] for the guidance of Muslims then becomes logical. The idea of the teacher [leader, the *imam*] is absolutely central to the concept of guidance. For all practical purposes, guidance is the process that constitutes the sum total of all the activities that fall under the rubric of Islamic education discussed above. Its institutionalization from the beginning of Islamic history in one form or another, inculcated into children not only their goal and their mission but also their dependency on a leader to guide them, futher demonstrating to them the inseparability of the leadership in Iran from Allah and His Way, the *Shari'ah.*

The task of the guide is sometimes perceived differently by different Muslim scholars. Some see the guide as a teacher, while others see the guide as both a teacher and mediator between the individual [or the community] and God. This is clearly a very controversial topic for the Muslim scholars who, on the one hand, see no need for any kind of a medium between man and his omnipresent God but who, on the other, cannot deny the importance that people attach to prophets and others in position to be God's representative on earth [such as the *imams* and other saints].

These schoolbooks, along with the Friday prayers [when millions of Iranian Muslims gather to pray and to listen to the sermons that are delivered by men who are both the religious and the political leaders of the country], demonstrate the religious character of the government and the strong congruency that exists among the textooks, the sermons of the Friday Prayers, and the decrees and laws issued by the government. The support of the Iranians for the government cannot readily be separated from their support of God, judged by the Friday gatherings and the contents of the textooks. The legitimacy of the Iranian leadership [which was never in question because of the regular elections and the people's support by acclamation] cannot be questioned now on religious grounds. A Muslim who disobeys the leadership is breaking the law of the land and the law of God. Any act of disobedience is a sin. The Muslims are commanded to obey Allah, His Messenger, and those with authority to rule among them.[26] Also, it is obligatory for a Muslim to overthrow the govenment if it is disobeying the laws of God. These relations between citizens, their government, and Allah are very clear in the textbooks and the Friday sermons of the rulers, as well as in the offcial religious documents of the Muslims, the Qu'ran and the *Ahadith* [the Prophet's sayings and tradition]. However,in practice men are more likely to obey their government than to overthrow even those governments which have been clearly rebellious to Allah.

It is very difficult to find any government enjoying this type of legitimacy and protection. Unlike most other governments, the Iranian regime does not favor one specific socializing agency over others. Islam, which the regime claims to represent, permeates all of these agencies. However,the school is the socializing agency most accessible to the government because of its formalness and impersonality. It is in schools that the government's programs can be presented in a much more systematic manner than in places of worship, work, or in the family.[27]

The IRI, unlike most other revolutionary governments, does not feel threatened by other socializing agencies such as the family, peer groups, and places of work and worship. In Iran these are mutually reinforcing institutions. The differences among them, which the texts try to minimize, are more at the level of value inculcation than at the level of value conflict. The government, however, feels threatened by groups and individuals who do not subscribe to its policies and programs and the manner in which these are implemented. It is clear, after years of secularization of the Iranian society, that the number of these individuals and groups can be substantial.

The IRI tries, through the texts and other media, to instill Islam [which forbids nationalism of any kind] but apparently it has been unable to remove the feeling of nationalism from the average Iranian and from some of those in the leadership itself. This demonstrates again the strong hold that modern and ancient nationalism has on some Iranians. As long as Islam is perceived by the Iranians [and others] as a form of Iranian nationalism, the revolution will not only fail to grow beyond Iran but it will also act as a divisive factor in further fragmenting this multiethnic society. The textbooks, for example, do not address the particular needs of the Sunni Muslim citizens of Iran who constitute more than 10-20 percent of the population. The textbooks essentially give the Shi'i Iranian version of the history of Islam. The Sunnis disagree about the facts as represented in these texts and about the degree of emphasis put on various events and personalities.[28] Another major problem of IRI involves the concept of *marja'* [literally, a place to return to, a place to go to for spiritual guidance and prayer]. Different Shi'i Iranians who are devout Muslims have a different *ayatullah* [literally, the sign of God, a very important religiopolitical leader] as his or her *marja'*. Not all of them look on *Imam* Khomeini as their *marja'*. Some even have as their *marja'* an *ayatullah* who may not even be an Iranian and who may live in a country other than Iran. This Shi'i internationalism is, ironically, problematical for the IRI, which asks for the loyalty of everybody including the other Shi'i Muslims, and non-Shi'i Muslims. The problems become even more exasperating when the IRI Constitution defines,in purely Shi'i *and* Iranian terms, the character of the Islamic State. Until these problems are solved, the Islamic state will not only remain provincial but will also have difficulty rooting itself thoroughly in Iranian soil.[29]

How to differentiate between what is Iranian, what is Shi'i Iranian, and what is Islam as perceived by each of the multitudes of Muslims with their own particular cultural reservoir and ethnic boundaries, has been for centuries a monumental task not only for the revolutionaries of Iran but also for other Muslim scholars. The clarification of the concepts and ideals, and the agreement on how these are to be formulated into policies, plans, and programs, to be implemented for the realization of the genuine Islamic state and society, will take a very long time. [Paradoxically, it is nationalism and the cultural hegemony of the West that will hasten the processes of Islamization of many of the countries in the Muslim world.]

In the short run, however, it is the leadership that can bring the destruction on itself by straying from the straight path, according to these textbooks. That is when people feel that Allah has withdrawn His support from the leadership. People are asked by the texts to see whether the deeds of the leaders do not match their Friday sermons and their other utterances. Students are encouraged to detect the lack of congruity between the values instilled through the textbooks and those instilled through the government's actions. In the event of any inconsistency people are asked in these textbooks [as in the Qur'an] to rebel against the government and to try to overthrow it.

More specifically, the following topics are emphasized in the textbooks and other socializing agents and agencies in and outside the schools in the IRI: personal virtues and attitudes, social relationships, family, peers, parents, interpersonal relationships, village life, role models, education and study, cleanliness, reward and punishment, patriotism, solidarity, self-sacrifice, religion and worship.

At present, the Iranian textbooks enjoy great support for their contents in all the socializing agencies of this Islamic community, support seldom matched in any other society. The Iranian texts simply discuss materials that for centuries have constituted the building blocks of the normative structure of Islam and the Iranian Muslims. The Islamic Revolution is trying to remove some of the imported anomalies as well as the ancient Iranian nationalism. Unlike those in most developing countries, the Iranian textbooks are free of extraneous materials and therefore draw support from the environment. There are few items, it seems, that can keep a child from becoming what he is expected to be--a Muslim citizen of Iran who has the obligation to rid the world of oppression and injustice for the sake of Allah.

In the textbooks under examination there is never any mention of pre-Islamic Iran, which was admired very much in the prerevolution books. One cannot, of course, deny pre-Islamic Iran [which is dealt with in the textbooks for history], but for the present what matters to the Iranian revolutionaries and to most other Iranian intellectuals is that their history is indistinguishable from the history of Islam.[30] Both the Soviet Union and the United States are portrayed in these textbooks as exploiters of the poor and the oppressed of the world. However, children are encouraged to learn from the good aspects of all societies but not to succumb to their artificiality and dazzle. In short, Iranian texts discourage the development of personalities that have been known in Iran as *gharbzade*, those who have swallowed what comes out of the West, hook, and line, and sinker. Iranian children are taught to look at Islam as a general system that is superior to both capitalism and socialism.

Summary

The government of Iran has embarked on a program to realize the enthronement of justice in the country and the world. This starts with the process of Islamization of the Iranian people. The process is nowhere more formalized and systematized than in the four categories of textbooks, those dealing with the Farsi [Persian] language, with Islamic culture and theology, with theology for the non-Muslim national minorities [not in order to convert them to Islam but to make them aware of the virtues of religiosity], and with the texts articulating the Islamic worldview [*Binish Islami*]. These textbooks are interrelated. They reinforce what has been already outlined to the children--in the family, the mosque, and in other socializing agencies such as the print and electronic media--prior to their coming to school.

It seems that the revolutionaries so far have been able greatly to increase the congruity between the values instilled through various socializing agencies of the country. Nevertheless, the regime in Iran faces opposition to the implementation of its prograns from those outside and inside the country, who follow non-Islamic ideologies such as nationalism, socialism, and capitalism. The textbooks alert the children to avoid these ideological pitfalls. The textbooks teach rebellion against the oppressors and repentance for one's own shortcomings as a duty of a Muslim. They also teach as sinful disobedience to legitimate authority. Consequently, the leadership of this theodemocracy of Iran interprets all opposition to itself as heretical, and has declared *jihad* against some of them, such as the Iraqi government, including the Shi'i Iraqis in its service.

Similar to the children of previous, revolutions, Iranian school children are taught that commitment is superior to competency. In previous revolutions. commitment to revolutionary ideals was necessary in order to meet the requirements imposed by men. In Iran, however, such a belief is essential to one's being a good Muslim and to keeping Allah satisfied. Allah's satisfaction through guidance and education, the textbooks and other media, is the hallmark of one's achievement in this world and leads to rewards in the hereafter.

NOTES

1. For Farsi language texts for Islamic culture and religious education, grades 2-5, see Jamhuri Islami Iran, Wazarat Amuzish wa Parwarish (Islamic Republic of Iran, Ministry of Education, and Training [hereafter cited as JII-WAP]], *Farhang Islami wa Ta'limat Dini* (Tehran: JII-WAP, 1364/1985. For teachings of the sacred religions and ethics for the religious minorities in grades 2-5, see JII-WAP, *Ta'limat Adyani Ilahi was Akhlag Wizha'i Aqqalliyyatha'i Mazhabi* (Tehran: JII-WAP, 1363/1984. For the second year of the guidance cycle, see JII-WAP, *Dawra'i Rahnama'ii Tahsili* (Tehran: JII-WAP, 1364/1985). For the Islamic perception texts for years 1-3 of the senior high school, see JII-WAP, *Binish Islami* (Tehran: JII-WAP, 1364/1985).

2. JII-WAP, *Farhang Islami wa Ta'limat Dini, Sal Dawwum Dabistan* (Islamic culture and religious education, third year of elementary cycle) (Tehran: JII-WAP, 1364/1985), preface. This and all subsequent translations are the author's.

3. JII-WAP, *Farsi, Sal Awwal Dabistan* (Farsi, the first years of primary school) (Tehran: JII-WAP, 1364/1985), p. 88.

4. Ibid., p. 92. This theme is repeated also in all other Farsi Texts for *Dabistan* students.

5. JII-WAP, "A Letter from Father," in *Farsi, Sal Sawwum Dabistan* (primary school) (Tehran: JII-WAP, 1364/1985), pp. 121-24, drives home forcefully the inseparability of religion, homeland, citizenship, and the government. All four themes are emphasizd in all texts under review. Religious studies per se (the study of Qur'an and of religion and ethics) range from 3 hours per week for grades 1, 2, and 9-12, to 5 hours for grades 3-8. See JII-WAP, *Education System of the Islamic Republic of Iran* (Tehran: JII-WAP, 1984), app. 1, tables 1-6.

6. M. Mobin Shorish, "The Impact of the Kemalist 'Revolution' on Afganistan," *Journal of South Asian and Middle Eastern Studies* 7, no. 3 (Spring 1984): 34-55.

7. JII-WAP, *Farsi, Sal Sawwum Dabistan*, pp. 101-2.

8. Ibid., pp. 106-9.

9. Ibid., pp. 29, 62, 63, 86-88, 163, 180.

10. Ibid., pp. 168-70.

11. Author's interview with Dr. Haddad Adil, Deputy Minister of Education, August 24, 1985.

12. JII-WAP, *TAIAWAM, Sal Dawwum Dabistan* (Tehran: JII-WAP, 1363/1984), p. 1-36.

13. JII-WAP, *TAIAWAM, Sal Sawwum Dabistan* (Tehran: JII-WAP, 1363/1984), pp. 1-32

14. JII-WAP, *TAIAWAM, Sal Chaharum Dabistan* (Tehran: JII-WAP, 1363/1984), pp. 25-36.

15. JII-WAP, *TAIAWAM, Sal Panjum Dabistan* (Tehran: JII-WAP, 1364/1985), pp. 1-30.

16. JII-WAP, *TAIAWAM, Sal Dawwum Dawrah'i Rahnama'ii Tahsili* (Tehran: JII-WAP, 1364/1985), pp. 2-59.

17. Roger M. Savory and Dionisius A. Agious, eds., *Logos Islamikos: Studia Isamica in Honorem Georgii Wickens,* Papers in Medieval Studies, no. 6 (Toronto: Pontifical Institute of Medieval Studies, 1984). These religious minority students are enrolled in the state schools. They also have their own religious schools in which they are inclucated with particulars of their different faiths and customs. These schools, similar to others throughout the world, are not always immune from the wrath of nationalism.

18. JII-WAP, *Binish Islami: Nabuwujat, wa Qur'an wa Mi'ad sal Duwwum Dabiristan* (The Islamic perceptions: prophethood, the Qur'an, and the resurrection) (Tehran: JII-WAP, 1363/1985). In this series, the text for the first year of Dabiristan details and documents (from the Qur'an and other sources) lessons of theology (Khudashinasi, pp. 1-122) and ethics (*Ikhlaq*, pp. 123-160). The text for the third year explains to the students concepts of leadership (*Imamat*, pp. 2-99), rulership and governance (*Walayat*, pp. 100-131), and laws and orders (*Ahkam*, pp. 132-200). All these texts were published in 1364/1985.

19. See n. 5 above.

20. The Qur'an, 79:17-19.

21. Ibid., 34:28; 7:158; 4:1.

22. Ibid., 23:25-48; 66:11; 7:113-26; and 20:61-73.

23. Ibid., 3:64.

24. Ibid., 4:75.

25. Charles J. Adams, "Islam and Christianity: The Opposition of Similarities," in Savory and Agius, eds., p. 300.

26. The Qur'an, 4:59.

27. Many Iranian and non-Iranian Muslims complain, however, about the "politicization" by the regime of all formal gatherings, including the congregational prayers and the classroom. In these gatherings, the following is said aloud in unison by the participants: "Death to America. Death to the Soviets. Death to Israel, Death to Saddam Husayn. Oh, God, oh, God until the Mahdi [the reappearance of the 12th *Imam*] Revolution protect Kohmeini. Deduct from our lives and add it to his life."

28. See, e.g., JII-WAP, *Tarikh; Sal Dawwum Dawra'i Rahnama'ii Tahsili, Marhala'i Dawwum Ta'limat 'Umumi* (Tehran: JII-WAP, 1364/1985), esp. pp. 21-27. For a Sunni version of the events, see Syed Abu al-Ala Maududi, *Khalafat wa Malukiyyat* (Lahore: Islamic Publication, 1966); Muhammad Hamidullah, *Muslim Conduct of State* (Lahore: Ashraf, 1961); and Abdulrahman Abdulkadir Kurdi, *The*

Islamic State: A Study Based on the Islamic Holy Constitution (London: Mansell, 1984).

29. See JII-WAP, *Ta'limat Ijtima'i, Sal Dawwum, Dawrah'i Rahnama'ii Tahsili* (Tehran: JII-WAP, 1364/1985).

30. Ahmad Birashk, "Guftagu: Ustad Akbar Danasirisht wa Riyaziyyat az Biruni," *Kayhan Farhangi* 5 (Mardadmah, 1364/1985): 3-14.

BIBLIOGRAPHY

Prepared by Philip G. Altbach

Books

Farrell, Joseph P. and Stephen B. Heyneman eds. Textbooks in the Third World: Economic and Educational Choices. Washington, D.C.: The World Bank, 1988.

Heyneman, Stephen P. Textbooks and Achievement: What We Know. Washington, D.C.: The World Bank, 1978.

Liu, Alan P. Book Publishing in Communist China. Cambridge, Mass.: Center for International Studies, Massachusetts Institute of Technology, 1965.

Loveridge, A. J., et. al. Preparing Textbook Manuscripts: A Guide for Authors in Developing Countries. Paris: Unesco, 1970.

National Book Trust, India. Educational Publishing in Developing Countries. New Delhi: National Book Trust, 1980.

Neumann, Peter H. Publishing for Schools: Textbooks and the Less Developed Countries. Washington, D.C.: The World Bank, 1980.

Nischol, K. Women and Girls as Portrayed in Hindi Textbooks. New Delhi: National Council of Educational Research and Training, 1976.

Nomani, Rashid. Textbooks for Secular India. New Delhi: Sampradayikta Virodhi Committee, 1970.

Pearce, Douglas. Textbooks Production in Developing Countries: Some Problems of Preparation, Production and Distribution. Paris: Unesco, 1982.

Rastogi, K. G. Preparation and Evaluation of Textbooks in Mother Tongue: Principles and Procedures. New Delhi: National Council of Educational Research and Training, 1976.

Searle, B. General Operational Review of Textbooks. Washington, D.C.: Education and Training Department, The World Bank, 1985.

Articles

Aliwowo, A. A. "Textbooks and Materials for Africa" International Social Science Journal 31 (No. 1, 1979) pp. 10-20.

Altbach, Philip G. "Key Issues in Textbook Provision in the Third World" Prospects 13 (No. 3, 1983): 315-325.

Altbach, Philip G. and S. Gopinathan. "Textbooks in the Third World: Challenge and Response," in P. Altbach, A. Arboleda and S. Gopinathan, eds., Publishing in the Third World (Portsmouth, N.H.: Heineman, 1985), pp. 13-24.

Aprieto, Pacifico N. "The Philippine Textbook Project" Prospects 13 (No. 3, 1983): 351-360.

Bantug, V. P. "Elements of Propangandistic Bias in Philippine History Textbooks used in Philippine Schools during the American Era and the Era of the Philippine Republic." Unpublished Ph.D. Dissertation, New York University, 1976.

Brams, Patricia. "Reading Between the Lines: Societal Norms in Sierra Leonan Readers." International Review of Education 26 (no. 4, 1980) pp. 483-500.

Elguea, Javier, A. "Scientific Revolutions, Paradigms and Textbooks in Development Theories," International Journal of Educational Development 5 (No. 2, 1985), pp. 77-81.

Gopinathan, S. "The Role of Textbooks in Asian Education," Prospects, 13, (No. 3 1983), pp. 343-350.

Haq, E. "Sociology of Curriculum: The Role of School Textbooks in Nation Building," Indian Educational Review, 11 (January, 1976), pp. 1-16.

Heyneman, Stephen P. and Dean T. Jamison. "Student Learning in Uganda: Textbook Availability and Other Factors," Comparative Education Review 24 (No. 3, 1980), pp. 206-220.

Heyneman, Stephen P. and Dean T. Jamison. "Textbooks in the Phillipines: Evaluation of the Pedagogical Impact of a Nationwide Investment," Educational Evaluation and Policy Analysis, 6 (Summer, 1984), pp. 139-150.

Jamison, D. T., B. Searle, K. Galda and S. Heyneman. "Improving Elementary Mathematics Education in Nicaragua: An Experimental Study of the Impact of Textbooks and Radio on Achievement," Journal of Educational Psychology 73 (No. 4, 1981), pp. 556-567.

Kalia, Narendra Nath. "Women and Sexism: Language of Indian School of Textbooks," Economic and Political Weekly, 21 (May 3, 1986), pp. 794-797.

Kumar, Krishna. "Textbooks and Educational Culture," Economic and Political Weekly, 21 (July 26, 1986), pp. 1309-1311.

Kumar, Krishna. "The Textbook as Curriculum," Bulletin of the Indian Institute of Education, No. 2 (1981), pp. 75-84.

Lockheed, Marlaine, E., Stephen C. Vail and Bruce Fuller. "How Text Affect Achievement in Developing Countries: Evidence from Thailand," Educational Evaluation and Policy Analysis 8 (Winter, 1986), pp. 379-392.

Lorimer, James. "Canadian Textbooks and the American 'Knowledge' Industry," This Magazine is About Schools, 5 (Summer, 1971), pp. 47-63.

Pearce, Douglas. "Textbook Production in Developing Countries," Prospects, 13, (No. 3 1983), pp. 327-342.

Quek, Vivian. "The Textbook Writer and the Publishers," Singapore Book World, 5, (1974), pp. 14-16.

Singh, Amrik. "Educational Publishing and Textbooks," in O. P. Ghai and Narendar Kumar, eds., International Publishing Today: Problems and Prospects, (New Delhi: The Bookmans Club, 1984), pp. 96-106.

Yadunandan, K. C. "Nepal: For Better Planning of Textbook Production," Prospects, 13 (No. 3 1983), pp. 361-372.

Wagner, Susan. "Textbooks in Third World Education: The World Bank's Changing Role," Publishers Weekly, 215, (March 26, 1979), pp. 41-43.

CONTRIBUTORS

KHAIRIAH AHMAD is on the staff of the Faculty of Education, University of Malaya, Kuala Lumpur, Malaysia.

PHILIP G. ALTBACH is Professor and Director of the Comparative Education Center, State University of New York at Buffalo. He is editor of the Comparative Education Review. His most recent book is The Knowledge Context: Comparative Perspectives on the Distribution on Knowledge (SUNY Press).

KAREN BIRIAMAH is Assistant Professor of Education at Central Florida University, Orlando.

JOSEPH P. FARRELL is Professor of Adult Education at the Ontario Institute for Studies in Education, Toronto, Canada. He has been a consultant to the World Bank.

S. GOPINATHAN is Head of the Department of Comparative Studies, Institute of Education, Singapore. He has written widely on book publishing in the Third World.

STEPHEN P. HEYNEMAN is Director of the Economic Development Institute at the World Bank, Washington, D.C. and was coordinator for the Bank's textbook development seminar.

GAIL P. KELLY is Professor of comparative education and Chair of the Department of Educational Organization, Administration and Policy at SUNY-Buffalo. She has served as president of the Comparative and International Education Society.

KRISHNA KUMAR is Professor in the Department of Education, University of Delhi, India.

JULIA KWONG is Associate Professor in the Department of Sociology, University of Manitoba, Canada.

DENNIS MBUYI has been a Lecturer in the Faculty of Education, University of Calabar, Nigeria.

HENA MUKHERJEE is Education Officer at the Commonwealth Secretariat, London, England. She is also an Associate Professor at the University of Malaya

CHUKA EZE OKONKWO is Head of the Department of Foundations of Education, Alvan Ikoku College of Education, Owerri, Nigeria.

M. MOBIN SHORISH is Associate Professor of Economics of Education, University of Illinois-Urbana.

INDEX